Navigating the Return-to-Work Experience for New Parents

Parenthood can be one of the most fulfilling, altering, and challenging life events. This book is set within the background of the reality of many parents' return-to-work experience, the task of re-engaging with work and maintaining a job or a career, and the difficulties that parenthood poses for balancing the demands of a new family with the demands of work. It helps us understand this reality, give voice to new parents, and offer relief in the knowledge that we know a lot about these challenges and, most importantly, how we can start to address them.

The book brings together a number of internationally recognized experts from research, practice, and policy to explore the issues and offer evidence-based solutions around return-to-work after having children. It takes a balanced approach to theory and practice to cover topics such as equality, stereotypes, work-family conflict, training and development, and workplace culture, among others, whilst integrating research and policy, and illustrating learnings with case studies from parents and examples from countries that lead the way.

It will appeal to parents, researchers, and employers in any sector or economy across the world. Ultimately, it will help to develop ways for new parents to re-engage with work successfully while maintaining their work-family well-being.

Maria Karanika-Murray is an Associate Professor in Occupational Health Psychology at the Department of Psychology, Nottingham Trent University. In her work she brings together different methodologies, disciplines, and stakeholders with the aim to understand the context and develop ways to support work-related health and well-being.

Sir Cary Cooper, CBE, is the 50th Anniversary Professor of Organizational Psychology and Health at ALLIANCE Manchester Business School of the University of Manchester, President of the Chartered Institute of Personnel and Development (HR professional body), Immediate Past President of the British Academy of Management, and President of the Institute of Welfare.

"What a fascinating book! As both a researcher and campaigner in this area, I welcome the way that the authors have pulled together a terrific mix of contributors from research, practice and policy, to tackle the issues faced by both mothers and fathers in returning to work after childbirth. We have so much to learn from the countries represented here."

Sue Vinnicombe, CBE, Professor of Women
and Leadership, Cranfield University, UK

Navigating the Return-to-Work Experience for New Parents

Maintaining Work-Family Well-Being

Edited by Maria Karanika-Murray and Cary Cooper

Routledge
Taylor & Francis Group

LONDON AND NEW YORK

First published 2020
by Routledge
2 Park Square, Milton Park, Abingdon, Oxon OX14 4RN

and by Routledge
52 Vanderbilt Avenue, New York, NY 10017

Routledge is an imprint of the Taylor & Francis Group, an informa business

British Library Cataloguing-in-Publication Data
A catalogue record for this book is available from the British Library

Library of Congress Cataloging-in-Publication Data
A catalog record for this book has been requested

ISBN: 978-0-367-22299-4 (hbk)
ISBN: 978-0-367-22301-4 (pbk)
ISBN: 978-0-429-27433-6 (ebk)

Typeset in Baskerville
by Apex CoVantage, LLC

Printed and bound by CPI Group (UK) Ltd, Croydon, CR0 4YY

To my dad – Maria

To all my former PhD students – Cary

Contents

Contributors

Justine Alter is a psychologist and co-director of Transitioning Well. She specializes in providing support to navigate life transitions at work. Justine has a master's degree in organisational psychology and more than 18 years of coaching, solution-focused counseling and consulting. Driven by her passion to assist working parents and the need to provide support for managing work-life integration, Justine co-founded Transitioning Well in 2011.

Erica L. Bettac is a doctoral student in the industrial/organizational psychology program at Washington State University Vancouver, USA. A member of the Coalition for Healthy and Equitable Workplaces Lab, she examines the work/non-work interface, work- and health-related outcomes, and the interaction of these constructs cross-nationally and, most recently, among self-employed individuals.

Danielle Boyer is a researcher in the Family branch of Social Security (CNAF), Paris, France. She created and has overall responsibility for the Early Childhood National Observatory (ONAPE). Her studies focus on the work-life balance and more particularly on the place of fathers. She is currently leading a research program on early childhood professionals. Recent publications include: Boyer D. (coord.), L'accueil du jeune enfant, Observatoire national de la petite enfance, 2019, Cnaf. A paraitre Nov 2019; and Boyer D., Crépin A., 2017, Baromètre d'accueil du jeune enfant 2017, Stabilité du recours et des souhaits d'accueil, L'e-ssentiel, n° 179.

Adrienne Burgess is head of research and joint CEO of the Fatherhood Institute. Adrienne's *Fatherhood Reclaimed: The Making of the Modern Father* (1998) set a new agenda on fatherhood in the UK and internationally. Adrienne was recently (2018) Special Advisor to the UK Government's Women and Equalities Committee and co-authored the influential Nuffield Foundation–funded *Cash or Carry? Fathers Work and Care in the UK*.

Sarah J. Cotton is an organizational psychologist and co-director of Transitioning Well. She specializes in best-practice strategies to navigate life transitions at work. With a PhD in work-stress and more than 18 years of coaching, training, and consulting, Sarah has a comprehensive background. Committed to reducing the costs of work-life conflict, Sarah co-founded Transitioning Well in 2011.

Jeremy Davies is head of communications at the Fatherhood Institute. Jeremy is one of the UK's leading advocates for father-inclusive policy and practice. As well as providing communications support to the Fatherhood Institute's Nuffield Foundation–funded *Contemporary Fathers in the UK* programme, he is co-investigator for Lancaster University's ESRC-funded Gender Diversification in Early Years Education study and consulted on Manchester Business School's *Making Room for Dad* project (2017–18).

Sarah Dawkins is a clinical psychologist and Senior Lecturer (Management) at the Tasmanian School of Business and Economics, University of Tasmania, and co-director of Pracademia. Her primary research interests focus on the development of positive psychological resources for enhanced performance and well-being in work-teams and individual employees. She is also involved in research investigating the interface between work and family.

Hans van Dijk is Assistant Professor at the Department of Organization Studies, Tilburg University, Tilburg, the Netherlands. His research focuses on how differences among individuals in organizations shape dynamics in groups and organizations and affect social inequality as well as performance. He also examines how refugee inclusion at work can be facilitated and has a number of pet projects that focus on improving the publication system.

Jamie L. Gloor is a post-doctoral research fellow in business administration at the University of Zurich, where she also earned her PhD after working as a research associate in social psychology at Yale University. She studies leadership and humor under the broad umbrella interests of gender/diversity and social relations.

Marc Grau-Grau is a research fellow at the Women and Public Policy Program at Harvard Kennedy School and a researcher and coordinator of the Joaquim Molins Figueras Child Care and Family Policies Chair at the Universitat Internacional de Catalunya. Marc has a PhD in social policy from the University of Edinburgh.

Sara De Hauw is an HR advisor for academic personnel at Ghent University, Belgium. She obtained a PhD on work-home balance at the KU Leuven. Afterwards, she worked as post-doc at Vlerick Business School and as an assistant professor at the Open Universiteit. Her research focuses on work-home balance, well-being, and careers.

Alina S. Hernandez Bark is Assistant Professor of Social Psychology at Goethe University Frankfurt in Germany. In her research and teaching, she focuses on two main topics: (a) gender and diversity in organizations and (b) leadership. Further, she supports organizations on those topics as an invited expert.

Nina M. Junker is Assistant Professor of Social Psychology at Goethe University Frankfurt, Germany. She earned her PhD in psychology at Goethe University Frankfurt. Her research interests include the social identity approach, the work-family interface, and burnout. In particular, she is interested in the positive side of managing work and family roles and in possibilities to increase such positive effects.

Gayle Kaufman is the Nancy and Erwin Maddrey Professor of Sociology and Gender & Sexuality Studies at Davidson College. She is the author of *Superdads: How Fathers Balance Work and Family in the 21st Century* and the forthcoming *Fixing Parental Leave: The Six Month Solution*.

Lindsey M. Lavaysse is a doctoral candidate at Washington State University Vancouver. Her research focuses on threats to occupational health and safety among vulnerable populations (e.g., pregnant, minority, intersectional) as well as outcomes of economic stress (e.g., job insecurity), and how stereotypes and prejudice jeopardize workers' health and safety.

Angela Martin is Professor at the Menzies Institute for Medical Research, University of Tasmania, and co-director of Pracademia. Angela has extensive expertise as an academic researcher and educator in the area of employee mental health and well-being and the work-family interface. She is currently focussed on knowledge translation and promotion of evidence-informed practice.

Claude Martin is Research Professor at CNRS (National Center for Scientific Research), University of Rennes (Arènes UMR 6051) and chair CNAF on "Childhood, Well-Being and Parenting" at the EHESP School of Public Health. He teaches social policies and welfare state systems in different universities in Paris and Rennes. He is a member of the boards of different academic journals (*Social Policy and Administration*, *International Journal of Care and Caring*, *Sociologie*, *Lien social et Politiques*; *Revue de politiques sociales et familiales*). His main fields of research are in childcare, family, parenting, and long-term care policies. He has published extensively on these issues, including: Le Bihan B., Martin C., Knijn T., (Eds), 2013. *Work and Care under Pressure. Care Arrangements across Europe*, Amsterdam & Chicago University Press; and Martin C, Palier B. (eds), 2008. *Reforming Bismarckian Welfare Systems*, Oxford, Blackwell.

Inés Martínez-Corts is Associate Professor at the University of Seville. She studied psychology and obtained her master's degree in human resource management and her PhD in social psychology (cum laude and award for the Best Doctoral Dissertation, 2003) at the University of Seville (Spain). Currently, she is an associate professor of work and organizational psychology.

Loes Meeussen is a FWO postdoctoral researcher at the Center for Social and Cultural Psychology at KU Leuven, Leuven, Belgium. Her research focuses on two challenges: First, organizations and societies need to rethink gender norms driving under-participation of women at work and men at home to create equality and better work-life balance, and second, cultural diversity challenges schools and organizations to create equal opportunities and pursue the added value of diversity.

Vanessa A. Miles is a master of organizational psychology candidate, Macquarie University. She is an HR and culture change consultant, specializing in coaching leaders and their people through transitions in their jobs, careers, and personal lives. With more than 15 years' experience in high-performance organizations, including Bain & Company and Partners in Performance, Vanessa has comprehensive experience across the employee life cycle.

J. Pablo Moreno-Beltrán is Researcher at the University of Seville. He studied psychology and is finishing a master's degree in human resource management at the University of Seville (Spain). He has also been working in the social psychology department as a researcher.

Helen Pluut is Assistant Professor at Leiden University, the Netherlands. She holds a doctorate in organizational behavior from Tilburg University, where she also obtained her bachelor's and master's degrees. Her research examines areas related to organizational behavior, such as employee well-being, work-family interface, social support, and group dynamics.

Tahira M. Probst is Professor of Psychology at the Department of Psychology, Washington State University Vancouver, USA. Her research focuses on economic stress and job insecurity, with a particular emphasis on understanding multilevel characteristics of these phenomena. She is currently editor-in-chief of *Stress & Health* and sits on five additional editorial boards.

Hans-Joachim Wolfram is Associate Professor in Work Psychology, Kingston University, UK. He received his PhD from the University of Leipzig, Germany. His main research interests include employee well-being, gender in the workplace, and social psychology perspectives within organizational settings (e.g., stereotyping).

Joanna B. Yarker is Senior Lecturer at the Department of Organizational Psychology, Birkbeck, University of London, UK. She earned her PhD in applied psychology at the University of Nottingham, UK. She works at the interface of research and practice, where she is director of Affinity Health at Work, a consultancy specializing in workplace health and well-being. Her research interests span the field of health at work, with a particular interest in helping employees and employers navigate the return-to-work journey through integrated interventions that promote individual-, group-, manager-, and organizational-level action.

Julia Yates is Senior Lecturer in the Department of Psychology at the City, University of London, where she runs the MSc program in organizational psychology. Her research interests are in career coaching, the career paths of women, and career decision-making.

Foreword

Work and family are two of life's most important experiences that shape overall well-being for individuals; the interrelationship between the two is a major factor in creating workplace culture and its impact on individuals. This can either be positive – where work-life or work-family balance is the norm and careers continue to flourish in a productive and inclusive culture – or negative – where stress, bias, and the inability to combine work and family responsibilities weighs heavily on individuals and careers. The issue is multifaceted, complex, and very fundamental to today's society. This book is therefore incredibly timely and presents, for the first time, a wide variety of research, practices, and views on the topic. Sir Cary Cooper is one of the leading experts in this field and as a (grand) parent himself cares deeply about it, as does his co-editor and also a parent, Maria Karanika-Murray.

I know firsthand the vital difference supportive work makes to motherhood. As a middle manager and divorced single mother in the throes of a custody suit, I was hugely relieved when my employer allowed me to be late for a key management meeting because I needed to take my daughter to school. I extended flexible working rights to my team, and we were recognized globally for our results and productivity. Equally, I was a senior executive when another employer made my travel schedule so demanding and relentless that it meant I would only see my daughter every other weekend. No amount of money or status could offset the emotional stress I experienced feeling torn between my career and my child. My choice was easy. I quit. That was some twenty years ago when discussions on this topic were in their infancy.

The situation today, although acknowledged and talked about more widely, is still problematic. Family-caring responsibilities lie overwhelmingly with the mother – and the situation is far from ideal. According to the website Mumsnet. com two thirds of women claim they suffer career setbacks upon their return, and anecdotal evidence is, alas, still rife with stories of discrimination or poor reintegration of women when they return from maternity leave. Stigma surrounding flexible working arrangements, gender bias, assuming returners won't want a demanding role, as well as lack of access to senior leader sponsors at out-of-hours events are all obstacles that stand in the way of mothers' progress. The result is that there are still far too few women in senior management and leadership roles across many sectors, and the gender pay gap is alive and well in most countries, driven in part by the impact of stalled careers and salary progression. Known as the "motherhood penalty," the Institute for Fiscal Studies in the UK reckons it is responsible for up to half of the gender pay gap. This leads many to say that combining work and family is an inherently fraught proposition. Thankfully, the book offers a comprehensive review of these barriers and explores solutions from both a policy and employer level.

But the real prize comes when we move to the point where parenting is regarded as just another life-stage for both men and women – and the ways of working truly reflect this. Equal participation of fathers (still pitifully low in most countries), agile working practices that offer truly stigma-free flexible working (easier said than done), and successful returners programmes are some of the good practices this book explores more fully. Training programmes and vital changes to workplace culture, behaviours, and biases are also fully explored. Policy, too, plays a vital role as women's participation in the workforce is rightly linked to the availability and cost of childcare. Indeed, this is one of the biggest challenges facing the US and the UK, whereas many countries in Europe offer a model that is well ahead.

Whilst much of the book focuses on the role of employers and policy-makers, parents also rely heavily on support networks outside work in social circles and settings, both real time and online (such as the aforementioned Mumsnet), and their impact is also considered. Of course, families come in many shapes and sizes, and the book acknowledges that combinations outside the "nuclear family" face different challenges.

Solving the parenthood trap and turning it into a parenthood triumph is a huge opportunity for individuals, employers, and societies. The benefits of enabling work and family balance are well documented – they lead to big jumps in well-being, workplace productivity, and happiness. This book is designed to offer real, evidence-based, and comprehensive insights and practices from a cross-section of global leaders in the field. It is a much-needed book. My hope is that even if the parents, employers, and policy-makers who read it now don't fully benefit from all its insights, their children will!

Ann Francke
CEO, Chartered Management Institute
Author, Create a Gender-Balanced Workplace

Foreword

The discussion around parents' return-to-work is grounded in broader societal and economic debates related to equality in opportunities, treatment, and outcomes between women and men in the world of work. Return-to-work measures are more broadly and holistically perceived as essential to support individuals through the increasing labour market transitions over the life course, especially those related to unpaid care work (ILO, 2019a, p. 11; ILO, 2018). These debates are deeply ingrained in cultural norms on gender roles and expectations, rendering them difficult to align to the changing reality of parents' experiences and a world of work in rapid evolution. A notable mismatch emerges when we place practice and policy against the reality of working parents. In the end, outdated practice can perpetuate overt and covert inequality. This mismatch is most obvious when we look at the persistent work-related gender gaps, which have not seen any meaningful improvements over the past twenty years (ILO, 2019b). Between 2005 and 2015, the "motherhood employment penalty" increased by 38 per cent. Fathers' experiences also show that the main barriers to work-life balance for them relate to traditional gender views and the masculine identity together with unsupportive organizational cultures (Stovell et al., 2017). If practice was aligned with the social justice principles and international labour rights put forward by the funders of the International Labour Organization, 100 years ago, including maternity protection, equal remuneration between women and men for work of equal value, and the principle of the eight-hour day (ILO Constitution, 1919), then cases of discrimination, unfair dismissal, and harassment would be rare. As the chapters in this volume show, the problem is complex and multifaceted, and the range of existing solutions has yet to fully capture this complexity.

We have seen commitment to action by policy-makers, women leaders, and influential figures in business. In June 2019, the International Labour Conference adopted the *ILO Centenary Declaration for the Future of Work*, which commits to "a world of work free from violence and harassment" and calls for "achieving gender equality at work through a transformative agenda . . . which . . . enables a more balanced sharing of family responsibilities; provides scope for achieving better work-life balance by enabling workers and employers to agree on solutions, including on working time, that consider their respective needs and benefits" and "promotes investment in the care economy" (ILO, 2019c).

Another positive recent development in the EU is the introduction of the Directive on Work-Life Balance for Parents and Carers (Directive EU, 2019/1158). This new directive sets higher minimum standards for existing rights, is designed to be more inclusive, and aims to "help working parents and carers by not obliging them to make a choice between their family lives and their professional careers" (www.eubusiness.com/news-eu/work-life-balance.19en). It is based on considerations of gender equality, supporting those with caring responsibilities, and increasing women's representation in the workforce. By setting higher minimum standards, the directive is designed to create more convergence between EU Member States, notwithstanding broad variation among EU Member States in the legal and policy measures related to parental leave and in the generosity in pay and duration of leave (OECD, 2019; ILO, 2014). In addition, as the ILO report on legislation and practice related to maternity and paternity at work highlights, between 1994 and 2013 "there was notable progress in improving payment levels and a gradual shift away from reliance on employers to provide maternity leave benefits" (ILO, 2014, p. 27). But the economic crisis and austerity measures in many countries have hit much of this progress, and the reality states that more needs to be done (Ortiz & Cummins, 2019).

The complexity of work and family life necessitates that different partners and actors work together: parents, employers, trade unions, and governments. The ILO's "5R Framework for Decent Care Work" calls for *recognizing*, *reducing*, and *redistributing* unpaid care work; *rewarding* paid care work by promoting more and decent work for care workers; and guaranteeing care workers' *representation*, social dialogue, and collective bargaining. The role of the fifth R on *representation* in enabling a democratic space for transformative care policies to be shaped, implemented, and evaluated is fundamental (ILO, 2018). This partnership has to involve both employers and public bodies and focus on developing a supportive culture that permeates all good intentions.

Specifically, in addition to the adequacy and effectiveness of national laws, policies, and guidance, parents' experiences of return-to-work also rely on initiative and commitment from the employers, such that the role of a responsible and supportive employer cannot be overestimated. With work organizations mirroring society, action at the workplace can be powerful in promoting opportunities and addressing the transition and adjustment to work (e.g., the introduction of flexible working policies and practices; Brynin, 2017; Hegewisch, 2009). The ILO has documented a range of good practice cases by proactive employers supporting workers with maternity protection, parental leave, and childcare and a range of workplace programmes (ILO, 2010; ILO, forthcoming). But workplace and public policies ought to be aligned with each other to be efficient. For example, the ILO reports that "workplace initiatives can supplement but cannot substitute for public policies aimed to improve the availability, quality and affordability of childcare services and facilities. State-funded or subsidized childcare plays a key role in enabling parents, and especially women, to engage in paid work after childbirth, by reducing their unpaid care work. In addition, it also contributes to job creation in the social care sector, which in turn replaces some of the unpaid care and household work mostly performed by women and girls and thus expands their income-earning options" (ILO, 2014). The benefits of aligning workplace and public policy are tremendous. Investments in government policy can yield economic outcomes such as, for example, in the link between investment in childcare and productivity of the workforce (e.g., ILO, 2018). Investing in care work matters for gender equality at work and a brighter future of work. The ILO estimates that investing in the care economy to achieve the Sustainable Development Goals could generate 269 million additional jobs, of which 120 million would be in education, health, and social work, compared with 2015 levels. This will require doubling the current total public and private expenditures on care service provision by 2030 (ILO, 2018).

Because at the centre of any action are attitudes and beliefs around family roles and norms, governments, employers, and workers all have a role in challenging and transforming culture. Culture is built on enacted ingrained attitudes and beliefs, in society and the workplace. A "culture where traditional gender roles prevail" (House of Commons, 2018, p. 32) can undermine efforts to support the well-being of families. In the UK, for example, "in 2013, almost 70 per cent of fathers reported having to return to work while their baby was still on the neonatal unit" (House of Commons, 2018). But the UK is only just one example. Despite generous maternity leave provision, there is a large disparity in leave allowance, in terms of time and in the pay, that mothers and fathers are entitled to (ILO, 2014). Attendance management policies often conflict with parental leave (e.g., www.theguardian.com/technology/2019/jul/09/tesla-workers-terminated-claim-maternity-sick-leave), whilst the uptake of paternity leave or shared parental leave, where this exists, is patchy across European countries (Eurofound, 2019). Therefore, successful action is about the state, employers, working parents, and their representatives working together. Removing workplace hurdles and changing societal attitudes to allow parents to exercise their rights falls on the shoulders of both governments and employers. For example, a range of countries has introduced legislation to allow employees to adjust their work schedules (Eurofound, 2017), but practice is slow and there is also a need for stronger enforcement mechanisms (Hegewisch, 2009). As the Women and Equalities Committee notes, "the Government must ensure that the design of its policies is bold enough to overcome these cultural barriers, and that those policies go hand-in-hand with action to change the culture" (House of Commons, 2018, p. 32).

"The world of work begins at home" (ILO, 2019a, p. 11), and "the way in which we organize work and labour markets plays a major role in determining the degree of equality our societies achieve" (ILO, 2019a, p. 18). Developing good jobs, a positive culture, and supportive national policies are extremely important, so we start by understanding parents' return-to-work experiences. The context for this book is the workplace, working parents and families, and those who look after them in an employer or policy-making capacity, with wide-ranging learnings and implications. This book is a welcome resource with actionable support in a lively needed debate on parenting and the world of work.

Laura Addati
Policy Specialist, Women's Economic Empowerment
International Labour Organization
ILO Office for the United Nations

References

Brynin, M. (2017). *The gender pay gap*. Manchester: Equality and Human Rights Commission. Retrieved from www.equalityhumanrights.com/sites/default/files/research-report-109-the-gender-pay-gap.pdf

Directive (EU) 2019/1158 of the European Parliament and of the Council of 20 June 2019 on work-life balance for parents and carers and repealing Council Directive 2010/18/EU. Retrieved from https://eur-lex.europa.eu/legal-content/EN/TXT/?qid=1565821 942318&uri=CELEX:32019L1158

Eurofound. (2017). *Working time patterns for sustainable work*. Luxembourg: Publications Office of the European Union.

Eurofound. (2019). *Parental and paternity leave: Uptake by fathers*. Luxembourg: Publications Office of the European Union.

Hegewisch, A. (2009). *Flexible working policies: A comparative review*. Manchester: Equality and Human Rights Commission. Retrieved from www.equalityhumanrights.com/en/publication-download/research-report-16-flexible-working-policies-comparative-review

House of Commons. (2018). *Fathers and the workplace*. United Kingdom House of Commons Women and Equalities Committee. First Report of Session 2017–19. Retrieved from https://publications.parliament.uk/pa/cm201719/cmselect/cmwomeq/358/358.pdf

International Labour Organisation. (1919). *The constitution of the International Labour Organisation*. Retrieved from www.loc.gov/law/help/us-treaties/bevans/m-ust000002-0241.pdf

International Labour Organisation. (2010). *Workplace solutions for childcare*. Retrieved from https://www.ilo.org/wcmsp5/groups/public/---dgreports/---dcomm/---publ/documents/publication/wcms_110397.pdf

International Labour Organisation. (2014). *Maternity and paternity at work: Law and practice across the world*. Retrieved from https://www.ilo.org/wcmsp5/groups/public/---dgreports/---dcomm/---publ/documents/publication/wcms_242615.pdf

International Labour Organisation. (2018). *Care work and care jobs for the future of decent work*. Retrieved from https://www.ilo.org/wcmsp5/groups/public/---dgreports/---dcomm/---publ/documents/publication/wcms_633135.pdf

International Labour Organisation. (2019a). *Work for a brighter future*. Global Commission on the Future of Work. Retrieved from https://www.ilo.org/wcmsp5/groups/public/---dgreports/---cabinet/documents/publication/wcms_662410.pdf

International Labour Organisation. (2019b). *A quantum leap for gender equality: For a better future of work for all*. Retrieved from https://www.ilo.org/wcmsp5/groups/public/---dgreports/---dcomm/---publ/documents/publication/wcms_674831.pdf

International Labour Organisation. (2019c). *ILO centenary declaration for the future of work*. Retrieved from https://www.ilo.org/wcmsp5/groups/public/@ed_norm/@relconf/documents/meetingdocument/wcms_711674.pdf

International Labour Organisation, EU and UN Women. (forthcoming). *Empowering women at work: What works in the workplace.*

Organisation for Economic Co-operation and Development. (2019). *OECD family database: PF2.1. Parental leave systems.* Retrieved from www.oecd.org/els/soc/PF2_1_Parental_leave_systems.pdf

Ortiz, I., & Cummins, M. (2019). *Austerity: The new normal.* A joint report by: Initiative for Policy Dialogue (IPD), International Confederation of Trade Unions (ITUC), Public Services International (PSI), European Network on Debt and Development (EURO-DAD), and The Bretton Woods Project (BWP). Retrieved from www.ituc-csi.org/IMG/pdf/austerity_the_new_normal_ortiz_cummins.pdf

Stovell, C., Collinson, D., Gatrell, C., & Radcliffe, L. (2017). Rethinking work-life balance and wellbeing: The perspectives of fathers. In C. L. Cooper and M. P. Lester (Eds.), *The Routledge Companion to Wellbeing at Work* (pp. 221–234). London: Routledge.

1 Introduction

Understanding the return-to-work experience for parents: what is and what could be

Maria Karanika-Murray and Cary Cooper

Parenthood is one of the most fulfilling but also challenging and life-altering events. It brings not only new responsibilities in a parent's expanded family domain but also asks for adjustments to other life domains, work and leisure, often with a request to edit personal or work-related roles and goals against this new reality. This entails a process of negotiating needs and resources to meet new demands. The impact of a potentially unsuccessful negotiation can range from mental ill-health (for both mother [www.who.int/mental_health/maternal-child/maternal_mental_health/en/] and fathers [Ruffell, Smith, & Wittkowski, 2019]) to economic precariousness for the working family (NCE, 2017). This impact may differ for women vs. men or for new vs. current parents, as some parents' lives may change more dramatically while others may have a more robust or richer repository of resources. For the parents, return-to-work is a negotiation process that includes both an initial transition and ongoing adjustment. But this process is set within a powerful broader context that involves employers, families, societies, agencies, and governments, and that can define the success of parents' return-to-work.

Thus, we offer a collective work that is set within the background of the reality for parents returning to work after starting a new family or after growth of the family with new children, the task of re-engaging with work and maintaining one's career, and the difficulties that parenthood poses for balancing the daily demands of a family with those of work. This book aims to acknowledge and illuminate this reality, give voice to parents, offer strength in the knowledge that we know a lot about these challenges, and – most importantly – start to craft effective and sustainable solutions for all those involved.

Parenthood as a transition process and a focus on work-family well-being

Parenthood involves a renegotiation of life domains and an ongoing transition process. Major changes in life circumstances, goals, and resources mean that many parents decide not to return to work after starting a family. A belief that parents are more or less forced to make a choice between work and family presents the two domains as mutually exclusive. The language used in the field of work-life or work-family 'balance' is limiting, as implies competition between different domains of life. It focuses responsibility on the individual and, as Lewis and Beauregard (2018) have noted, work-life balance has been viewed "as a matter of individual choice and responsibility with regard to establishing priorities and organizing schedules", neglecting, as a result, broader "structural, cultural, and practical constraints on individuals' agency" (Lewis & Beauregard, 2018, p. 720). It also presents this balance as a state that can be achieved temporarily rather than as a sustainable longer-term aim.

In perspective, achieving balance among life domains is a longer process of accommodation with changing needs, responsibilities, and resources for individuals and families though the life course. Rather than viewing work and family as competing life domains, the focus should be on how the two can work synergistically and how work fulfilment and family well-being can be achieved in tandem. Viewing a parent's transition back to work as a process acknowledges the interdependence rather than separation among life domains. It also denotes that employers and other agents also have responsibility for supporting individuals through this process. As Phyllis Moen argues, a shift of focus from 'work-life balance' to 'life-course fit' can help to resolve this conflict (and bring a more realistic perspective) by acknowledging that different domains are complementing rather than conflicting and irreconcilable.[1] Here, fit is achieved through this process of adjusting to a new reality. Another way to broaden the focus from "work-family balance" is to talk about "work-family well-being", thus turning the 'balancing act' into a positive goal and placing the focus on the family unit (i.e. how the parents in that unit negotiate their individual roles) and encouraging us to look at the whole system in addition to its components.

In summary, we view the return-to-work experience as a process of (re)adjustment, often major and lengthy, the success of which depends on a range of multiple factors within the individual, the family unit, employment, and society.

Why do we need to pay attention?

There are two types of arguments, beyond the principles of fairness and equality, why we should attend to the return-to-work process and develop ways to support parents in the workplace.

Starting with the obvious, there is a case for increasing the employment rates, participation, and economic activity of women. One of the main reasons for the lower involvement of women in the workforce is the conflict with the role as carers, which in the short and the long term is reflected in a gender pay gap as high as 22% (International Labour Organisation, 2019). For example, the UK Office for National Statistics (ONS) reports that "1.81 million women were economically inactive because they were looking after family or home" compared with approximately 0.3 million men (ONS, UK Labour Market bulletin, Table INAC01, in: House of Commons Briefing Paper No. CBP06838, March 2019), whilst the European Statistics Office (Eurostat) reports that the rates of inactivity in labour marker terms for adult women range between 9% in Slovenia and 33% in Italy.[2] Family commitments are also reflected in the growing gender pay gap across age groups, which ranges between 9% and 20%, with an average of 16% in Europe,[3] with negligible or negative differences for those in their 20s or 30s widening considerably for those in their 40s. When these numbers reflect the pay gap between mothers and non-mothers, they describe the motherhood wage penalty. In the UK, "one reason for these age differences is that factors affecting women's employment and earnings opportunities become more evident when women are in their 30s and 40s. For example, time spent out of the labour market to care for children or elderly relatives could affect future earnings when a person returns to work. Similarly, the need to balance work with family commitments and the availability of flexible working practices may restrict individuals' employment options" (House of Commons Briefing Paper No. CBP06838, March 2019). The situation is the same across European countries[4] and worldwide (e.g., World Economic Forum, 2018). Although the law enforces non-discrimination, life-related and contextual factors mandate differences in opportunities. Plugging the gender employment gap makes good economic, moral, and even practical sense. In the UK, for example, PricewaterhouseCoopers (PwC) has estimated that "addressing the career break penalty for female professionals can deliver significant economic benefits" at the scale of £1.1billion in earnings and £1.7billion in additional economic output annually (PwC, 2016).

As well-documented as the economic benefits are the social and health benefits. We are witnessing substantial changes in attitudes in relation to gender roles and norms, expectations of parenthood, and the role of women in family, work, and social life, at least in higher-income counties. Although the return-to-work decision is heavily gendered (Burgess & Davies, this volume) and non-traditional roles bring new challenges (Barker et al., 2012), there is evidence for a growing number of fathers deciding to stay at home to look after their family.[5] This has a considerable impact on parents' mental health and the well-being of families. For example, mothers report less stress, increased health benefits, and higher earnings; fathers observe reduced early mortality; whilst for the children the benefits include lower risk of developmental problems and better school and social adjustment (Brenning, Soenens, Mabbe, & Vansteenkiste, 2019; Håkansson, Axmon, & Eek, 2016; The Fatherhood Institute, 2014). Positive changes are taking place worldwide in employment support and policy relating to parenting (ILO, 2014). The Nordic countries are leading the way with excellent examples of how equality in provision for parental and childcare support can support family well-being. However, the rate of progress varies broadly across the world when it comes to equality between the genders (as reflected in cultural customs and norms – e.g., only recently, in 2019, were women in the Kingdom of Saudi Arabia allowed to travel independently).[6] Misconceptions about parental leave are still common (e.g., beliefs that maternity leave is 'a walk in the park'), and there is a long way before non-traditional gender/parent roles are widely accepted (e.g., negative stereotypes that stay-at-home dads experience).[7] The state of play in the workplace often contradicts our shared values of family and equality. A case in point here is the lack of or resistance to adequate investment in childcare, even in some developed countries.[8] Action can be slow, especially when it comes to changing ingrained or institutionalized practices.

Most encouraging are notable examples from individuals who are swimming upstream and trying to normalize an integrated family and work life. Role models of mother politicians who have taken their babies to parliament include New Zealand Prime Minister Jacinda Ardern, UK leader of the Liberal Democrats party Jo Swinson, Australian parliament Senator Larissa Waters, Swedish MEP Jytte Guteland, Spanish MP Carolina Bescansa, and former MEP Licia Ronzulli.[9] These parents are setting an example for changing traditional norms and ineffective policy. What changes do we want to see in the workplace and how can parents returning to work be supported to re-adjust to their new lives, demands, and life circumstances? The arguments for supporting parents' return-to-work are persuasive. Feasible and effective solutions can also be complex, as this volume evidences, but the wide-ranging benefits for families, society, and the economy are also sizeable for our and for future generations.

Outline of this volume

Life experience often offers the backdrop and stimuli for debate and an impetus for change. When we had the idea for this book, Maria was nearing the end of her second maternity leave and preparing for her return-to-work and Cary had become a grandfather for the seventh time. At that time, there was a lively discussion in the Media about equality in the workplace, parents' rights, breastfeeding at work, and equal pay, reflecting public concerns at the time. We wanted to be part of this discussion. Parents returning to work are an neglected group, perhaps because they are also often a transitory group or because other prominent concerns such as gender equality and work-family balance absorb the limelight. Nevertheless, parents returning to work personify many of the public debates, changes, and challenges in society and in the workplace.

The book takes a balanced approach to theory and practice to cover topics such as stereotypes, work-family conflict, career development, human resource management, career development and training, leadership, and workplace culture, among other topics. It integrates research and policy, with case studies from parents and examples from countries that lead the way. Clearly, there is a need for employment, economics, and public policy to come together to address these major issues for working parents, employers, and society. At least, this is the consensus. But in reality, the answer to the question "how do we put these ideas and good intentions into practice" is complicated, and improving policy is a lengthy process. In the meantime, it is possible to explore, in practical terms, what new parents and employers can do to re-engage with work successfully and maintain the well-being of individuals, their families, and their workplaces. We do not claim to have covered all the issues or provided all the answers, but we offer this collective work as a positive step forward.

This edited volume brings aboard a group of internationally esteemed scholars, practitioners, and policy-influencers to explore the issues and offer evidence-based solutions around return-to-work for new parents. We asked the contributing authors to discuss the relevant literature and provide a practical perspective on their topic. We asked them to consider parents, employers, and policy-makers as the target audiences and to consider issues relating to context and culture, as relevant. To combine different foci was a big request, but the resulting volume is rich in knowledge and informative for practice, with illustrative examples and case studies. Thanks to these authors, this volume presents an integration of invaluable and actionable knowledge.

In Chapter 2, Lindsey Lavaysse, Erica, and Tahira Probst kick off the discussion by focusing on the complexity for new parents of navigating workplace and care-taking roles. They place a spotlight on stereotype threat, or "the fear of confirming negative stereotypes about a group to which one belongs". Stereotype threat is not only prevalent, especially for women during pregnancy and for both parents on their return-to-work, but it can also increase over time. It has a harmful impact on individuals, including in terms of safety, career aspirations, and conflict between work and family responsibilities. Their recommendations for reducing the occurrence of stereotype threat concern how individuals cope with stereotype threat, how organizations discourage it and protect individuals, and how governments respond with legislation and guidance. There are good examples to learn from and also more to explore through research.

In Chapter 3, Helen Pluut and Sara De Hauw explore how new parents who return to work after childbirth can build social support networks at work and outside to "avoid falling prey to the conflicting demands of work and family". Social support is extremely beneficial for the parenting role, especially in view of the challenges of returning to work. They also highlight three important debates. First, that the sources of social support for mothers and fathers are different, often being aligned with prevailing gender roles and expectations. Second, that society and employers have an important role to play in an individual's work success and well-being, although there is currently a clear trend to place responsibility on the individual. Third, that social support "may also be too much of a good thing" and that in some situations different types of social support may even be harmful. The authors outline practical recommendations for helping new parents to build a social support network and key needs for future research.

In Chapter 4, Angela Martin, Sarah Dawkins, Vanessa Miles, Sarah Cotton, and Justine Alter explore practical strategies that new parents can use to support their return-to-work experience and adjust to the demands of balancing the work and family domains. These strategies focus on building and applying a range of psychological resources which are essential for adjusting to new demands and maintaining well-being and effective work performance. The authors bring the discussion to life with case studies and insights from work-family transition coaches or practitioners supporting new parents.

In Chapter 5, Marc Grau-Grau turns to the needs of new fathers. He outlines why the changing nature of fatherhood can be at odds with the 'ideal worker' and argues that working fathers also have specific needs on their return-to-work after having a new child. Discussions on inequality in the workplace have tended to focus on pregnant women and mothers, and fathers have so far been a relatively hidden group. There are ways to support new fathers, such as equality-promoting policies, which can also have a range of important secondary effects on gender equality and families, as Marc discusses.

In Chapter 6, Adrienne Burgess and Jeremy Davies offer important insights on the barriers and potential solutions for increasing fathers' uptake of parental leave. As they note, "for the men, the issue is not 'return-to-work' but leaving it." Gender culture and the gender pay gap are important barriers, but the top priority for encouraging fathers to take more parental leave is redesigning the parental leave system – "because gender inequality is grounded in it". They remind us how intertwined societal attitudes, institutions, and policy structures are.

In Chapter 7, Gayle Kaufman lays out the leading example of the Nordic countries, which are "perennially on lists of 'most gender-equal countries'" in promoting gender equality and integration between work and family domains. She discusses research that shows how equality in parental leave can positively affect gender equality in a range of areas: mothers' employment rates, the motherhood wage penalty, the share of domestic work, and fathers' involvement in childcare. The rich lessons that the Nordic model offers can be adapted to other countries, starting with parental leave and early childhood education provision.

In Chapter 8, Nina Junker, Alina Hernandez Bark, and Jamie Gloor focus on the impact of parenthood and specifically the impact of stereotypes of parenthood on career progression. Becoming a parent can kick-start a chain of effects that are based on stereotypes and that can lead to a motherhood penalty and/or a fatherhood bonus among other impacts. The authors shatter commonly held stereotypes by juxtaposing them with empirical research and place such stereotypes in the often-dependent context of culture, society, and changing times. They then offer suggestions on how working parents can buffer some of the negative stereotypes and biases by focusing on their values and on communicating their unique parenting-related skills.

In Chapter 9, Julia Yates discusses the career options in terms of job role and conditions that those returning from parental leave or a career break are faced with in light of their new family demands. She notes that for women especially, flexibility is not always an option and that "the parenting pay gap never goes away". She outlines ways to optimize these options, with illustrative scenarios from parents, and to achieve a fit between career development and family responsibilities. The practical implications extend beyond what parents can do to what employers, coaches, governments, and society can and ought to do.

In Chapter 10, Joanna Yarker, Hans-Joachim Wolfram, and Nina Junker focus on training and development needs and opportunities for those returning to work after parental leave. This is set within the background of a lack of evidence on the prevalence and impact of employment practices designed to support return-to-work. The discussion goes beyond work scheduling and flexible work practices, to focus on changes in behaviour, attitudes, and identity, and on the spillover experiences that parenthood comes with. They also apply insights from return-to-work after a long-term sickness absence to return-to-work after parental leave. This examination culminates in an insightful model that can be used to guide training and development practices focused on parental leave. Most usefully, they recommend a whole-organization approach and highlight that return-to-work training and development should be ongoing to meet employees' changing needs and experiences.

In Chapter 11, Danielle Boyer and Claude Martin present the characteristics of childcare services offered in France, "beyond the hypothetic free choices". France was one of the first countries "to explicitly make family matters an affair of the state since the end of the nineteenth century", where substantial public investment was allocated to early childcare, with notable positive impact on addressing inequalities, promoting employment, and supporting work-life balance. In addition to formal government policies and support, they note the role of informal support such as from family and grandparents and of employers allowing atypical working schedules. They talk about "fluidity between the different actors and solutions", underlining the importance of a collaborative approach to this complex issue that parents, employers, society, and governments face.

In Chapter 12, Hans van Dijk and Loes Meeussen turn the spotlight on the importance of developing and encouraging a diversity climate and an inclusive workplace culture for maintaining and enhancing work-family well-being. They argue that offering family-friendly organizational policies and practices is not enough; rather, most important is *how* these policies and practices are implemented and experienced, in the shared experience of the workplace. Focusing on inclusive workplace cultures, they discuss how the two components of inclusivity (i.e., belonging and authenticity) can be placed at risk during role changes to parenting. They explain how promoting a diversity climate through policies that enhance fairness and discrimination and policies that support synergy can support feelings of belongingness and authenticity, respectively. In essence, practices that foster inclusion are practices that foster the well-being of new parents.

In Chapter 13, Inés Martínez-Corts and Pablo Moreno-Beltrán focus on the importance of idiosyncratic deals (i-deals) between employers and employees for easing parents back into work. Although family-friendly policies are important, the shift to parenting is a personal challenge that is unique to each person. The combination of personal, work, and family circumstances means that accommodations that are appropriate to the needs and circumstances of new parents and that are in addition to policies designed for all employees may be necessary. As they note, i-deals "better solve the individuals' needs and motivations in accordance with the organizational goals" and can thus offer a win-win solution for helping parents to rebalance their work and family roles.

Finally, Chapter 14 is a synthesis of the invaluable learnings and practical recommendations that these twelve chapters collectively offer. Although principles and the values of equality, inclusivity, and respect are engraved in legislation, at least in the more developed countries, it is often difficult to see how they can be translated and enacted in practice. We outline what parents, employers, governments, and researchers can do and provide a number of additional reflections that can help us to gain perspective on the issues around parents' return-to-work.

A disclaimer

We would like to note two potential limitations with our efforts. First, we acknowledge that families come in all shapes and sizes (depending on the parents' gender; the type of family, such as nuclear or extended or single parent; whether the children are biological or adopted; whether it is a single-or dual-earner family, etc.) and that combinations of these factors imply a range of different challenges that families face. Therefore, it was not possible to cover all types of families, least because the evidence is still under development. The main focus of the book is on working parents, irrespective of these variations. However, two of the chapters focus on fathers and can help us to address gendered experiences and the fact that mothers and fathers have access to different resources and face different challenges in the same quest. Second, we acknowledge that work and family issues and the interpretation of these into practice vary across time and place, between and within different countries, and even different cultures within countries. It was not our intention nor was it possible to address all these issues, partly because of the limited space and partly because of the limited research and evidence covering time, place, and groups.

This book is for working parents and families and for those who look after them in an employer or policy-making capacity. As parenting affects millions of employees, thousands of organizations, and societies worldwide, we hope that this book will help to enact the values of equality, solidarity, and prosperity for our and our future generations. Please read this book with empathy and an open mind, draw from your own experiences, and help us to turn words into actions.

Notes

1 https://cla.umn.edu/about/directory/profile/phylmoen; https://cla.umn.edu/sociology/research/research-centers/life-course-center;www.theguardian.com/media/2018/aug/18/mishal-husain-interview-name-like-mine-career-only-possible-britain; www.flexiblework.umn.edu; www.flexiblework.umn.edu/MoenSloan_Network_News_InterviewSept-2009.pdf
2 https://ec.europa.eu/eurostat/statistics-explained/index.php/People_outside_the_labour_market
3 https://ec.europa.eu/info/policies/justice-and-fundamental-rights/gender-equality/equal-pay/gender-pay-gap-situation-eu_en
4 https://ec.europa.eu/info/policies/justice-and-fundamental-rights/gender-equality/equal-pay/gender-pay-gap-situation-eu_en
5 https://www.abc.net.au/news/2018-04-05/stay-at-home-dads-on-the-rise/9622498
6 www.bbc.co.uk/news/world-middle-east-49201019
7 www.bbc.co.uk/news/business-46399467; www.thesun.co.uk/fabulous/7883191/four-men-stay-at-home-dads/; https://www.bbc.co.uk/news/stories-44718727
8 https://www.theguardian.com/commentisfree/2017/may/15/sheryl-sandberg-mothers-childcare-has-to-change
9 www.bbc.co.uk/news/world-45638201

References

Barker, G., Greene, M., Nascimento, M., Segundo, M., Ricardo, C., Taylor, A., Aguayo, F., Sadler, M., Das, A., Singh, S., Figueroa, J. G., Franzoni, J., Flores, N., Jewkes, R., Morrell, R., & Kato, J. (2012). *Men who care: A multi-country qualitative study of men in non-traditional caregiving roles.* Washington, DC: International Center for Research on Women (ICRW); Rio de Janeiro: Instituto Promundo. Retrieved from https://promundoglobal.org/wp-content/uploads/2014/12/Men-Who-Care.pdf

Brenning, K., Soenens, B., Mabbe, E., & Vansteenkiste, M. (2019). Ups and downs in the joy of motherhood: Maternal well-being as a function of psychological needs, personality, and infant temperament. *Journal of Happiness Studies*, *20*(1), 229–250.

Grimshaw, D., & Rubery, J. (2015). *The motherhood pay gap: A review of the issues, theory and international evidence.* Working Paper No. 1/2015, International Labour Office. Retrieved from https://eige.europa.eu/resources/wcms_371804.pdf

Håkansson, C., Axmon, A., & Eek, F. (2016). Insufficient time for leisure and perceived health and stress in working parents with small children. *Work*, 55(2), 453–461.

International Labour Organisation (2014). *Maternity and paternity at work: Law and practice across the world.* Retrieved from www.ilo.org/global/publications/books/WCMS_242615/lang-en/index.htm

International Labour Organisation (2019). *Global Wage Report 2018/19: What lies behind gender pay gaps.* Retrieved from https://www.ilo.org/wcmsp5/groups/public/---dgreports/---dcomm/---publ/documents/publication/wcms_650553.pdf

Lewis, S., & Beauregard, T. A. (2018). The meanings of work-life balance: A cultural perspective. In R. Johnson, W. Shen, & K. M. Shockley (Eds.), *The Cambridge handbook of the global work-family interface* (pp. 720–732). Cambridge: Cambridge University Press.

Nottingham Civic Exchange. (2017, June). *Out of the ordinary: Exploring the lives of ordinary working families.* Nottingham Trent University. Retrieved from www.ntu.ac.uk/about-us/nottingham-civic-exchange/out-of-the-ordinary

PWC. (2016). *Women returners: The £1billion career break penalty for professional women.* Retrieved from www.pwc.co.uk/economic-services/women-returners/pwc-research-women-returners-nov-2016.pdf

Ruffell, B., Smith, D. M., & Wittkowski, A. (2019). The experiences of male partners of women with postnatal mental health problems: A systematic review and thematic synthesis. *Journal of Child and Family Studies*, *28*(10), 2772–2790.

The Fatherhood Institute (2014). *Why paternity leave matters for young children.* Retrieved from http://www.fatherhoodinstitute.org/wp-content/uploads/2014/11/Why-paternity-leave-matters-for-young-children.pdf

UK House of Commons Briefing Paper No. CBP06838. (2019, March 8). *Women and the economy.* Retrieved from www.parliament.uk/commons-library

World Economic Forum (2018). *The Global Gender Gap Report 2018.* Retrieved from http://www3.weforum.org/docs/WEF_GGGR_2018.pdf

2 New parents navigating the workplace

Pregnancy, stereotype threat, and work-family conflict

Lindsey M. Lavaysse, Erica L. Bettac, and Tahira M. Probst

In today's increasingly fast-paced global environment, many workers struggle juggling work and non-work roles (O'Brien, 2012; Williams & Alliger, 1994). Indeed, a report from the Families and Work Institute found that 47 percent of women and 60 percent of men with children under the age of 18 report experiencing conflict between their work/family roles (Aumann, Galinsky, & Matos, 2011). Such interference can be exacerbated in unsupportive working environments, where the lack of accommodating work-family policies (at the organizational and/or national level), as well as unsupportive supervision and management practices, place additional strain upon employees with family demands. It is therefore important for practitioners and researchers alike to better understand and be able to respond to employee work/family demands.

In this chapter, we consider the role of stereotypes regarding new parents in the workplace. Stereotypes are commonly held (but often erroneous) beliefs about entire groups of individuals (e.g., "all Asians are good at math"; "women are bad drivers"). This chapter specifically focuses on how stereotype threat – the fear of confirming negative stereotypes about a group to which one belongs – can influence how parents experience and react to work-family conflict. We start the chapter by briefly reviewing the concept of stereotype threat. Next, we discuss how stereotype threat affects employee- and work-related outcomes. We then turn our focus to pregnant employees and the emerging research on the role stereotype threat plays. Later, we discuss work-family conflict and how stereotype threat impacts those juggling work and family demands. Finally, we consider practical implications, what new parents can do to ease the work-family stereotype threat employees experience, and offer avenues for future research to explore.

Stereotype threat

When individuals perceive and feel at risk of confirming a negative stereotype about a social group (e.g., sex, race, religion, political affiliation, sexual orientation) to which they belong, *stereotype threat* is said to occur (Steele & Aronson, 1995; Steele, 1997). There are numerous social groups within our society with associated (often negative) stereotypes, including race, gender, nationality, disability status, relationship status, sexual orientation, age, political affiliation, religion, and socio-economic status. Such negative societal beliefs open the opportunity for stereotype threat. While stereotype threat has been shown (Nguyen & Ryan, 2008) to harm numerous affected groups, we focus specifically upon women at work who are impacted by stereotypes regarding women and associated groups (e.g., pregnant employees, working mothers), since this is where most of the extant literature has focused.

Prior research on stereotype threat

Empirical research – replicated under a variety of conditions and contexts – demonstrates that stereotype threat leads to decreased performance (Nguyen & Ryan, 2008). For example, stereotype threat has been linked with athletic performance based on race stereotypes (e.g., "white athletes aren't as skilled as black athletes"; Stone, Lynch, Sjomeling, & Darley, 1999), driving performance based on gender stereotypes (e.g., "women are worse drivers than men"; Yeung & von Hippel, 2008), childcare performance because of sexual orientation stereotypes (e.g., "gay men are dangerous to children"; Bosson, Haymovitz, & Pinel, 2004), memory performance due to age stereotypes (e.g., "older people are forgetful"; Hess, Auman, Colcombe, & Rahhal, 2003), and language skills based on lower socioeconomic status stereotypes ("poorer individuals lack intellectual ability"; Croizet & Claire, 1998).

While stereotype threat is clearly a potent stressor affecting many groups of individuals (women, racial minorities, lower socioeconomic classes, etc.), studies of stereotype threat within an organizational or workplace context are few and far between (Kalokerinos, von Hippel, & Zacher, 2014). However, as Streets and Nguyen (2014) postulated, stereotype threat may have implications for women in the workplace in regards to hiring and applications, career decisions, and career advancement.

Stereotypes of what it means to be feminine remain pervasive for working women and often contradict stereotypes of what it means to be a leader, manager, or authority figure (Chemers, 1997). Thus, efforts to understand stereotypes of women in leadership roles in relation to women's career advancement, rates of taking leadership positions, and decisions about career goals or aspirations have important implications. Early research found that when women make social comparisons with men, this can induce stereotype threat which is then related to decreased career aspirations (Von Hippel, Wiryakusuma, Bowden, & Shochet, 2011). Further, women experiencing stereotype threat made their communication style more masculine in an effort to debunk said stereotypes, which then had the unintended negative consequence of these women being perceived as less likeable and warm (Von Hippel et al., 2011). Commonly discussed stereotypes such as the "think leader, think male" or "women take care, men take charge" are harmful standards that might impact a woman in business and must be considered. Clearly, there is a double-edged sword for women in leadership roles directly fuelled by these stereotypes prevalent in society.

Pregnancy at work

Pregnancy is a visibly dynamic experience, meaning the pregnancy begins as an invisible identity for a period of time (i.e., the first trimester) and gradually transforms into a more visible identity during the third trimester. While some women show a "baby bump" signalling their pregnancy early on, others may not exhibit such visible telltale signs until further along in their pregnancy. Prior to a pregnancy becoming visible, women elect whether or not to disclose their pregnancy status at work. This identity management decision can be complicated by the woman's awareness of stereotypes associated with pregnancy status, including perceived inflexibility, incompetence, lack of commitment, and need for accommodations (Morgan et al., 2013). Research (e.g., Little, Major, Hinojosa, & Nelson, 2015) indicates that: a) these stereotypes are prevalent in the workplace, and b) women are generally aware of and concerned with how co-workers and/or supervisors perceive pregnant workers. Moreover, disclosing one's pregnancy is associated with greater perceived discrimination.

According to the stereotype threat model developed by Steele (1997), certain conditions trigger the onset of stereotype threat. For example, stereotype threat regarding working while pregnant would be salient while women are in the work setting. Steele (1997) further describes how efforts to counteract the negative stereotype can be draining. For example, pregnant employees may try to counteract negative stereotypes by pushing themselves to work harder, that is, supra-perform, while another strategy would be to put effort into concealing the pregnancy while at work (Gatrell, 2011b). Pregnancy has also been shown to be associated with working while ill (Gatrell, 2011a). These additional efforts at work or additional efforts to conceal can be exhaustive and lead to unsafe behaviours or adverse outcomes such as increased work-related accidents (Lavaysse, Probst, Leffler, & Castro, 2017).

During pregnancy, women undergo many psychological and physical changes. While the use of reasonable accommodations at work is legally protected, what is recommended by physicians during a prenatal appointment and what behaviors actually ensue while at work are often not the same (Swarns, 2014). Indeed, Lavaysse and colleagues (2017) found that not only do pregnant workers experience stereotype threat but also it increases over time as they progress through their pregnancy. Moreover, stereotype threat of pregnant workers significantly predicted poorer safety outcomes, specifically, a decline in safety motivation, and increased accidents, injuries, and under-reporting of accidents (Lavaysse et al., 2017). Thus, pregnancy-related stereotype threat appears to have clear negative implications for pregnant employees' safety. After a woman's pregnancy has concluded, she and/or her partner typically return to work, at which point, one (or both) of them are new working parents. How juggling the demands of parenthood and work responsibilities and whether this work-family conflict leads to associated stereotype threat is an area untouched by researchers thus far. Next, we briefly review the concept of work-family conflict and discuss how stereotypes (and stereotype threat) regarding workers with family responsibilities may be an impactful topic to explore.

Family-work stereotype threat

Defined as the process whereby one domain diminishes personal resources and impedes capabilities in the other, work-family conflict has been an increasing concern for modern society, with growing numbers of men and women reporting an imbalance among domains (Kossek, 2016; Ten Brummelhuis & Bakker, 2012). These increases can be attributed to multiple factors, including workload escalation, rising numbers of mothers in the workforce with children under the age of 18, substantial increases in elder caregiving needs, fathers' growing contribution in family caregiving responsibilities, as well as technological advancements (e.g., personal devices and smartphones) that maintain ties to work 24/7 (Kossek, 2016). As a result, blurring boundaries between work and non-work roles, as well as subsequent imbalances in work/family life, often occur (Brough & O'Driscoll, 2010).

Most scholars today refer to such interference as 'work-to-family conflict' (WFC) and 'family-to-work conflict' (FWC), whereby WFC conflict refers to the impact of work responsibilities on family and FWC conflict reflects the impact of family responsibilities upon work (Notten, Grunow, & Verbakel, 2017). While parents with children serve as the stereotypical prototype for those who experience work/family conflict, such interference arguably directly and indirectly afflicts much of the world's population (Kossek & Distelberg, 2009; Kossek & Ollier-Malaterre, 2013). Nearly everyone is a son, daughter, sister, or brother. Moreover, individuals living with friends who serve as a proxy family, single individuals, and childless couples also report experiencing WFC (Casper, Weltman, & Kwesiga, 2007). Additionally, scholars have found indirect effects of WFC crossing over to affect partners (Westman, 2001) and job colleagues (O'Neill et al., 2009).

Adverse reactions in response to WFC have been extensively documented in the literature and include elevated levels of heavy alcohol consumption, depression, anxiety, hypertension, and general poor physical health (Frone, Russell, & Cooper, 1997). In the work domain, WFC is associated with heightened stress, absenteeism, turnover intentions, and perceived violation in psychological contracts (Anderson et al., 2002; Anderson, Coffey, & Byerly, 2002; Taylor, DelCampo, & Blancero, 2009), as well as decreased attendance, work attitudes (e.g., job satisfaction and job commitment), and job performance.

While work- and health-related reactions to WFC conflict are well established, the literature has only begun to explore how employee experiences of stereotype threat in the WFC context (i.e., family-work stereotype threat; family-work ST) can exacerbate such outcomes. A recent investigation (Bettac, Probst, Lavaysse, Petitta, & Barbaranelli, 2019) revealed greater FTW conflict was related to increased work-related cognitive failures, greater perceived production pressure, and more accidents and injuries experienced at work. Moreover, these associations were strengthened among workers who feared confirming negative stereotypes about employees with family responsibilities, that is, employees with higher family-work ST. Such research suggests that a large segment of today's working population may be at risk not only because of the main effects of WFC conflict, but also because of interactive effects in conjunction with fears of confirming negative stereotypes associated with workers who have co-occurring family responsibilities.

Practical implications

New parents transitioning back into work

As noted previously, the birth of a child can lead to the occurrence of work-family conflict, as well as stereotype threat associated with fears of confirming negative assumptions about working parents. Therefore, it is important to consider variables that can facilitate a smooth transition back to the workplace. Schlossberg's transition theory (1981) is particularly relevant as it posits four factors which have a substantial influence on the way an individual perceives and copes with transition: 1) the situation, 2) the self, 3) the support available, and 4) strategies to aid in coping. Given that parenthood is a permanent change that alters self-identity and roles, it is considered a significant transition that requires proactive measures to alleviate the change. For example, upon initially entering the job role, new parents should be clear with themselves and their organization in expectations of returning to the job role, schedule constraints, and length of working hours (Moffett, 2018). By doing so, employed caregivers are able to tend to caregiving roles outside of work, thereby alleviating family spillover and decreasing occurrences of potential stereotyping and further, potential experiences of stereotype threat.

Organizational responses to new parents' return-to-work

Oftentimes, the competing interests of employers, working parents, and young children clash in the determining of work schedules, childcare arrangements, time-off, and overtime hours (Friedman, 2001). Moreover, balancing inter-role demands is particularly arduous for employees in organizations with unaccommodating work-family policies and/or who have inadequate resources in their work and life (Notten et al., 2017). Companies have subsequently offered flexibility in working schedules (e.g., working from home, telecommuting) and additional family-related benefits (e.g., paid leave, onsite childcare), often using such practices as part of a central strategy to attract, motivate, and retain key talent (Allen, Johnson, Kiburz, & Shockley, 2013). However, use of such benefits in an organization that is not openly supportive of their use (i.e., they are available but using them might label you) could lead to stereotype threat. Thus, it is important to gear organizational culture to be inclusive and accepting of those juggling multiple roles in order to reduce potential stereotype threat perceived as well as increase resource use. For example, across the 1990s and early 2000s, many German fathers did not feel comfortable taking paternal leave until federal incentives were enacted in January 2007 (e.g., highly competitive wage-replacement rates, additional benefits if both parents take leave; Erler & Erler, 2007); organizations might implement incentives to encourage use of policies or resources.

Indeed, scholars have increasingly emphasized the importance of family-friendly workplace cultures and supportive supervision and management practices (Friedman, 2001). In fact, reporting to a supportive supervisor has been linked to lower self-reported levels of conflict (Breaugh & Frye, 2008), higher levels of maintained balance (Greenhaus, Ziegert, & Allen, 2012), and even, several health benefits (Berkman, Buxton, Ertel, & Okechukwu, 2010). Family-supportive supervision has therefore been viewed as an "enhancement" to policies already in place, with the positive effects of supportive supervisors being strongest in organizations with robust work-family policies (Greenhaus et al., 2012). This enhancement may be additionally important in avoiding stereotype threat. For example, an employee juggling caring for children who has a family-supportive supervisor may be less likely to experience threat (regardless whether s/he experiences WFC conflict) than one whose supervisor is unsupportive. Further, organizations can seek to educate all employees about potential stereotype threat and provide a means to effectively cope with negative emotions (i.e., reappraising the situation or the meaning of their anxiety), both practical approaches shown to reduce detrimental effects (Johns, Schmader, & Martens, 2005).

Another effective practice involves organizations highlighting diverse role models (McIntyre, Paulson, & Lord, 2003). Doing so requires the organization to provide supportive networks (e.g., other employees with children/family member needs, current/recent expecting mothers) and that supervisors encourage participation in these mentoring programs and employee network groups (Friedman & Holtom, 2002). Supervisors might also maintain a diverse network of contacts, so they may be aware of potential role models (e.g., other workers who have successfully navigated the transition to parenthood and return-to-work) and connect new parents with those role models (Roberson & Kulik, 2007).

National responses to new parents' return-to-work

Because of increasingly conflicting work/family demands, policy changes have occurred at the national level in much of the industrialized world. While the extent of such policies varies from country to country and policies initially focused on the provision of maternal leave, these have expanded to include flexible work arrangements, leave for paid paternity, post-infant childcare, and care for elderly or other family members (O'Brien, 2012). Often, policy development and implementation have reflected cultural and political agendas as well as global processes, such as flexible labor markets, work intensification, and emerging child well-being norms, and increased the numbers of working mothers and caregiving fathers (Kamerman & Moss, 2009).

National policies may also counteract stereotypes and stereotype threat regarding caregiver roles. For example, women traditionally serve as the primary caretaker which may lead fathers to be reluctant to request time to attend to caretaking duties (Månsdotter, Fredlund, Hallqvist, & Magnusson, 2010). When faced with such a problem, Germany introduced a paternal leave system that incorporated paternal incentives for taking leave and subsequently saw a tripling in the proportion of fathers taking leave (Erler & Erler, 2007).

Through their implementation of policies, countries can help continue to shape gender norms of working parents and in turn potentially their experiences of stereotype threat. For example, countries, such as Germany, implemented incentives for paternal leave and experienced a tripling in the proportion of men taking such leave (Erler & Erler, 2007). Given the promising research in social psychology suggesting norms are modifiable (Rosenthal & Crisp, 2006; Knudson-Martin, 2011), and interventions targeting stereotypes can cause significant behavior change (Walton & Cohen, 2011), national policy-makers may be able to "intervene" and help form family caregiving norms through the offering of supportive work-family leave, time off, and as in Germany, the usage of such policies. Thus, familial roles may become salient at the national level and decrease occurrences of stereotyping and experiences of stereotype threat.

Research from the International Labour Organization (ILO) further extends this notion, as it suggests that for parenthood to become a normal fact of business life, national laws and policies that support work-family harmonization at minimal/no cost to employers should be combined with targeted support measures particularly taking into account the specific characteristics and needs of small and medium-sized enterprises (SMEs). Successful examples of this include the Mexican government, which subsidizes their maternity insurance scheme in addition to employers' and employees' contributions, thereby protecting low-income employers and employees, and the United Kingdom, which allows small firms to deduct statutory maternity payments from taxes to better support its employees (ILO, 2016). Actions such as these allow comprehensive family leave policy coverage (regardless of firm size) and prevent potential parent-related disruptions from work for both men and women (regardless of income level). Moreover, such widespread policy coverage facilitates the normalization of parenthood in the workplace and helps to reduce the perceptions (e.g., "I am the only parent taking leave in my department") that engender stereotype threat.

Future directions

While the nascent literature on family-work stereotype threat is compelling, workers have multiple social identities in addition to "parent". In recognition of this, academics and practitioners are increasingly responding to calls for research to acknowledge such intersectionality within the workplace. Intersectionality is the interaction of multiple social identities, such as race, religion, class, sexual orientation, and gender; these interactions form qualitatively unique experiences (Warner, 2008). Thus, just as there have been calls for more research on intersectionality in order to provide a more holistic understanding of workplace experiences for employees of diverse backgrounds (Sawyer, Salter, & Thoroughgood, 2013), it would be fruitful for family-work stereotype threat research to also consider other potentially co-occurring stereotype threats (e.g., stereotypes regarding being a parent, as well as a female or a racial minority).

Research on intersectionality (although, not in the workplace) has shown that intersectional individuals (i.e., individuals with multiple salient identities) have uniquely different experiences. For example, Livingston, Rosette, and Washington (2012), while assessing both race and sex, found that black and white women had fundamentally different experiences. Specifically, they explored the interaction of being a woman and black compared with being a woman and white, highlighting that not all women have the same experience simply because of their sex but that the nuance of combining race and sex makes for uniquely different experiences. This calls attention to the importance of studying multiple identities (i.e., intersectionality) simultaneously, which has yet to be thoroughly explored in the organizational context. Further, how stereotype threat may impact intersectional individuals is rarely explored, that is, combined stereotype threat resulting from one's simultaneous race, sex, and/or caregiving roles. For example, do women who are mothers experience similar levels of stereotype threat as women who are caregivers of an elderly parent in the workplace context? Do working mothers and fathers (both caregivers, different sex) have similar experiences of stereotype threat? Intriguingly, might fathers who attempt to shoulder more caregiving duties experience more stereotype threat than women who do the same because of differing cultural gender norms and expectations?

The stereotype threat literature has focused its impact upon single groups (i.e., women or African Americans). How stereotypes about multiple groups one individual may belong to simultaneously may impact one's level and experience of stereotype threat is unknown. That is, an intersectional employee may experience stereotype threat differently than what has been empirically explored. These differences might impact any number of employee outcomes, such as job satisfaction, job security, underemployment, turnover intention, motivation, mental and physical health, safety, productivity, and leadership aspirations.

Conclusions

In summary, this chapter discussed the complexity of juggling work and caretaking roles, with a specific focus on the impact of stereotype threat in the workplace. We briefly reviewed the concept of stereotype threat and how stereotype threat impacts employees, with a particular focus on pregnant employees and workers dealing with work-family conflict. Finally, we offer some practical recommendations for reducing the occurrence of stereotype threat as well as potential fruitful research directions to consider.

Key learnings from research	*Practical recommendations*
• Although stereotype threat is known to harm numerous affected groups, women (e.g., pregnant employees, working mothers) and men (e.g., working fathers) in the work setting are also largely impacted. • Stereotype threat is most salient within certain conditions (i.e., working while pregnant), and counteracting such threat is draining and can lead to actions to counteract the stereotype (i.e., pushing oneself to work harder while pregnant).	• New parents returning to work must be realistic in their expectations of returning to their job role, schedule constraints, and length of working hours to help ease their transition, alleviate family spillover, and reduce potential instances of stereotype threat. • Becoming a parent is a significant life change, and as such, organizations can help returning parents transition back into work life and decrease perceptions

(*Continued*)

(Continued)

Key learnings from research	Practical recommendations
• Research suggests a large segment of today's working population may be at risk not only because of the main effects of work and family conflict, but also the interactive effects in conjunction with fears of confirming negative stereotypes associated with workers who have co-occurring family responsibilities. • Intersectionality, or the interaction of social identities, poses a particularly important empirical consideration, as women and men of infant children and caretaking of elderly parents, for example, may experience stereotype threat differently.	of stereotype threat by offering flexibility in working schedules, paid leave, onsite childcare, as well as family-friendly workplace cultures, supportive supervisors, and supportive networks of other working parents. • Through their implementation of national work-family policies (e.g., paternal leave, leave wage replacement, parental leave incentives), countries can help continue to shape gender norms of working parents and in turn potentially their experiences of stereotype threat.

References

Allen, T. D., Johnson, R. C., Kiburz, K. M., & Shockley, K. M. (2013). Work–family conflict and flexible work arrangements: Deconstructing flexibility. *Personnel Psychology, 66*(2), 345–376.

Anderson, B. J., Vangsness, L., Connell, A., Butler, D., Goebel-Fabbri, A., & Laffel, L. M. B. (2002). Family conflict, adherence, and glycaemic control in youth with short duration type 1 diabetes. *Diabetic Medicine, 19*(8), 635–642.

Anderson, S. E., Coffey, B. S., & Byerly, R. T. (2002). Formal organizational initiatives and informal workplace practices: Links to work-family conflict and job-related outcomes. *Journal of Management, 28*(6), 787–810.

Aumann, K., Galinsky, E., & Matos, K. (2011). *The new male mystique.* National Study of the Changing Workforce, Families and Work Institute.

Berkman, L. F., Buxton, O., Ertel, K., & Okechukwu, C. (2010). Managers' practices related to work–family balance predict employee cardiovascular risk and sleep duration in extended care settings. *Journal of Occupational Health Psychology, 15*(3), 316.

Bettac, E. L., Probst, T. M., Lavaysse, L. M., Petitta, L., & Barbaranelli, C. (2019, February). *The impact of family-to-work conflict on workplace safety outcomes: The moderating impact of stereotype threat.* Poster presented at The Society for Personality and Social Psychology, Portland, OR.

Bosson, J. K., Haymovitz, E. L., & Pinel, E. C. (2004). When saying and doing diverge: The effects of stereotype threat on self-reported versus non-verbal anxiety. *Journal of Experimental Social Psychology, 40*(2), 247–255.

Breaugh, J. A., & Frye, N. K. (2008). Work–family conflict: The importance of family-friendly employment practices and family-supportive supervisors. *Journal of Business and Psychology, 22*(4), 345–353.

Brough, P., & O'Driscoll, M. P. (2010). Organizational interventions for balancing work and home demands: An overview. *Work & Stress, 24*(3), 280–297.

Casper, W. J., Weltman, D., & Kwesiga, E. (2007). Beyond family-friendly: The construct and measurement of singles-friendly work cultures. *Journal of Vocational Behavior, 70*(3), 478–501.

Chemers, M. M. (1997). *Leadership, change, and organizational effectiveness*. Santa Cruz, CA: University of California Santa Cruz.

Croizet, J. C., & Claire, T. (1998). Extending the concept of stereotype threat to social class: The intellectual underperformance of students from low socioeconomic backgrounds. *Personality and Social Psychology Bulletin, 24*(6), 588–594.

Erler, D., & Erler, W. (2007). The Germany report. In P. Moss & K. Wall (Eds.), *International review of leave policies and related research*. Retrieved from www.leavenetwork.org/fileadmin/user_upload/k_leavenetwork/annual_reviews/2007_annual_report.pdf

Friedman, D. E. (2001). Employer supports for parents with young children. *The Future of Children, 11*(1), 62.

Friedman, R. A., & Holtom, B. (2002). The effects of network groups on minority employee turnover intentions. *Human Resource Management: Published in Cooperation with the School of Business Administration, The University of Michigan and in alliance with the Society of Human Resources Management, 41*(4), 405–421.

Frone, M. R., Russell, M., & Cooper, M. L. (1997). Relation of work–family conflict to health outcomes: A four-year longitudinal study of employed parents. *Journal of Occupational and Organizational Psychology, 70*(4), 325–335.

Gatrell, C. J. (2011a). 'I'm a bad mum': Pregnant presenteeism and poor health at work. *Social Science & Medicine, 72*(4), 478–485.

Gatrell, C. J. (2011b). Policy and the pregnant body at work: Strategies of secrecy, silence and supra-performance. *Gender, Work & Organization, 18*(2), 158–181.

Greenhaus, J. H., Ziegert, J. C., & Allen, T. D. (2012). When family-supportive supervision matters: Relations between multiple sources of support and work–family balance. *Journal of Vocational Behavior, 80*(2), 266–275.

Hess, T. M., Auman, C., Colcombe, S. J., & Rahhal, T. A. (2003). The impact of stereotype threat on age differences in memory performance. *The Journals of Gerontology Series B: Psychological Sciences and Social Sciences, 58*(1), P3–P11.

International Labour Organization (ILO). (2016). *Women at work: Trends 2016*. International Labour Organization, Geneva, Switzerland. Retrieved from www.ilo.org/wcmsp5/groups/public/-dgreports/-dcomm/-publ/documents/publication/wcms_457317.pdf

Johns, M., Schmader, T., & Martens, A. (2005). Knowing is half the battle: Teaching stereotype threat as a means of improving women's math performance. *Psychological Science, 16*(3), 175–179.

Kalokerinos, E. K., von Hippel, C., & Zacher, H. (2014). Is stereotype threat a useful construct for organizational psychology research and practice? *Industrial and Organizational Psychology, 7*(3), 381–402.

Kamerman, S. B., & Moss, P. (2009). *The politics of parental leave policies: Children, parenting, gender and the labour market*. Bristol: The Policy Press.

Knudson-Martin, C. (2011). Changing gender norms in families and society: Toward equality amidst complexities and contradictions. In F. Walsh (Ed.), *Normal family processes* (4th ed., pp. 324–346). New York: Guilford.

Kossek, E. E. (2016). Implementing organizational work-life interventions: Toward a triple bottom line. *Community Work and Family, 19*(2), 242–256.

Kossek, E. E., & Distelberg, B. (2009). Work and family employment policy for a transformed work force: Trends and themes. In N. Crouter & A. Booth (Eds.), *Work-life policies* (pp. 1–51). Washington, DC: Urban Institute Press.

Kossek, E. E., & Ollier-Malaterre, A. (2013). Work-family policies: Linking national contexts, organizational practice and people for multi-level change. In S. Poelmans, J. Greenhaus, & M. Las Heras (Eds.), *New frontiers in work-family research: A vision for the future in a global world* (pp. 1–53). Basingstoke, UK: Palgrave Macmillan.

Lavaysse, L. M., Probst, T. M., Leffler, A., & Castro, K. (2017 June). *The impact of stereotype threat on workplace safety for pregnant employees.* Poster presented to the 12th Annual Meeting of Work, Stress, and Health, Minneapolis, MN.

Little, L. M., Major, V. S., Hinojosa, A. S., & Nelson, D. L. (2015). Professional image maintenance: How women navigate pregnancy in the workplace. *Academy of Management Journal, 58*(1), 8–37.

Livingston, R. W., Rosette, A. S., & Washington, E. F. (2012). Can an agentic Black woman get ahead? The impact of race and interpersonal dominance on perceptions of female leaders. *Psychological Science, 23*(4), 354–358.

Månsdotter, A., Fredlund, P., Hallqvist, J., & Magnusson, C. (2010). Who takes paternity leave? A cohort study on prior social and health characteristics among fathers in Stockholm. *Journal of Public Health Policy, 31*(3), 324–341.

McIntyre, R. B., Paulson, R. M., & Lord, C. G. (2003). Alleviating women's mathematics stereotype threat through salience of group achievements. *Journal of Experimental Social Psychology, 39*(1), 83–90.

Moffett, J. (2018). "Adjusting to that new norm": How and why maternity coaching can help with the transition back to work after maternity leave. *International Coaching Psychology Review, 13*(2), 62–76.

Morgan, K., Rahman, M., Atkinson, M., Zhou, S. M., Hill, R., Khanom, A. . . . Brophy, S. (2013). Association of diabetes in pregnancy with child weight at birth, age 12 months and 5 years: A population-based electronic cohort study. *PLoS One, 8*(11), e79803.

Nguyen, H. H. D., & Ryan, A. M. (2008). Does stereotype threat affect test performance of minorities and women? A meta-analysis of experimental evidence. *Journal of Applied Psychology, 93*(6), 1314.

Notten, N., Grunow, D., & Verbakel, E. (2017). Social policies and families in stress: Gender and educational differences in work-family conflict from a European perspective. *Social Indicators Research, 132*(3), 1281–1305. https://doi.org/10.1007/s11205-016-1344-z

O'Brien, M. (2012). *Work-family balance policies.* Background Paper. New York: UNDESA.

O'Neill, J. W., Harrison, M., Cleveland, J., Almeida, D., Stawski, R., & Crouter, A. (2009). Work–family climate, organizational commitment, and turnover: Multilevel contagion effects of leaders. *Journal of Vocational Behavior, 74*(1), 18–29.

Roberson, L., & Kulik, C. T. (2007). Stereotype threat at work. *Academy of Management Perspectives, 21*(2), 24–40.

Rosenthal, H. E., & Crisp, R. J. (2006). Reducing stereotype threat by blurring intergroup boundaries. *Personality and Social Psychology Bulletin, 32*(4), 501–511.

Sawyer, K., Salter, N., & Thoroughgood, C. (2013). Studying individual identities is good, but examining intersectionality is better. *Industrial and Organizational Psychology, 6*(1), 80–84.

Schlossberg, N. K. (1981). A model for analyzing human adaptation to transition. *The Counseling Psychologist, 9*(2), 2–18.

Steele, C. M. (1997). A threat in the air: How stereotypes shape intellectual identity and performance. *American Psychologist, 52*(6), 613.

Steele, C. M., & Aronson, J. (1995). Stereotype threat and the intellectual test performance of African Americans. *Journal of Personality and Social Psychology, 69*(5), 797.

Stone, J., Lynch, C. I., Sjomeling, M., & Darley, J. M. (1999). Stereotype threat effects on black and white athletic performance. *Journal of Personality and Social Psychology, 77*(6), 1213.

Streets, V. N., & Nguyen, H. H. D. (2014). Stereotype threat impacts on women in the workforce. In R. J. Burke & D. A. Major (Eds.), *Gender in organizations: Are men allies or adversaries to women s career advancement?* (pp. 270–290). Cheltenham, UK: Edward Elgar.

Swarns, R. L. (2014). Doctor says no overtime; Pregnant worker's boss says no job. *New York Times*.

Taylor, B. L., DelCampo, R. G., & Blancero, D. M. (2009). Work–family conflict/facilitation and the role of workplace supports for US Hispanic professionals. *Journal of Organizational Behavior, 30*(5), 643–664.

Ten Brummelhuis, L. L., & Bakker, A. B. (2012). A resource perspective on the work–home interface: The work–home resources model. *American Psychologist, 67*(7), 545.

Von Hippel, C., Wiryakusuma, C., Bowden, J., & Shochet, M. (2011). Stereotype threat and female communication styles. *Personality and Social Psychology Bulletin, 37*(10), 1312–1324.

Walton, G. M., & Cohen, G. L. (2011). A brief social-belonging intervention improves academic and health outcomes of minority students. *Science, 331*(6023), 1447–1451.

Warner, L. R. (2008). A best practices guide to intersectional approaches in psychological research. *Sex Roles, 59*(5–6), 454–463.

Westman, M. (2001). Stress and strain crossover. *Human Relations, 54*(6), 717–751.

Williams, K. J., & Alliger, G. M. (1994). Role stressors, mood spillover, and perceptions of work-family conflict in employed parents. *Academy of Management Journal, 37*(4), 837–868.

Yeung, N. C. J., & von Hippel, C. (2008). Stereotype threat increases the likelihood that female drivers in a simulator run over jaywalkers. *Accident Analysis & Prevention, 40*(2), 667–674.

3 Building the support network of new parents at work and outside

Helen Pluut and Sara De Hauw

Most of us spend a large proportion of our waking time at work, and many of us seek jobs that are exciting, challenging and fulfilling. For those of us with families, work does not only give meaning but also provides the means to take care of our families (e.g., afford school tuitions). Hence, work takes a central place in the lives of many, and this often remains so after becoming parents. Although the birth of a child is no doubt a game changer for handling the daily demands of the family, many new parents are motivated to return to work and re-engage with their careers. In fact, being a good parent can involve working, just as much as caring for the child(ren) at home, and it is therefore not uncommon that both partners choose to fulfill their family roles in career terms (e.g., by earning money or being a professional role model; Masterson & Hoobler, 2015). Subsequently, modern societies have witnessed a rise of households in which both parents hold jobs, often working full time, as indicated by household statistics from recent years from the Eurostat Labour Force Survey (2019) (up to 2018) and the OECD Family Database (2019) (up to 2014).

Combining the demands of high-pressured jobs with raising a new family is, however, not an easy task. Work can be stressful, and work-induced strain is often carried home and can diminish the quality of family life (Zedeck & Mosier, 1990). Parents may experience guilt when their work takes up more time than expected (Irak, Kalkişim, & Yildirim, 2019; Korabik, 2015), while thoughts and concerns about the family may act as a distraction and negatively impact parents at work (Smit, Maloney, Maertz, & Montag-Smit, 2016). In all such instances, parents experience conflict between work and family such that "the role pressures from the work and family domains are mutually incompatible in some respect" (Greenhaus & Beutell, 1985, p. 77).

On the other hand, combining work with family roles can also be an enriching experience for parents (Vieira, Matias, Lopez, & Matos, 2016). In a study by Ruderman, Ohlott, Panzer, and King (2002), female managers noted that being a mother helped them to develop their interpersonal skills and taught them to be more prone to individual differences, aiding them in better understanding, motivating and developing their employees. But also skills learned at work, such as conflict resolution, can be successfully applied at home, or being in a positive mood at home can make one more patient and helpful at work (Carlson, Kacmar, Holliday

Wayne, & Grzywacz, 2006). In other words, parents may also reap the benefits of being strongly engaged in both work and family roles and experience work-family enrichment to the extent that "experiences in one role improve the quality of life in the other role" (Greenhaus & Powell, 2006, p. 73).

Nevertheless, the question remains how parents who return to work after childbirth can avoid falling prey to the conflicting demands of work and family and instead capitalize on the richness that both their work and parental roles may bring. In this chapter, we look for answers in parents' social support network. More specifically, we firstly review the relevant literature on working parents' social support network, focusing on two main questions: 1) what are benefits of (different sources and types of) social support for working parents? and 2) what are challenges for return-to-work parents in building a social support network? After that, we identify three key debates that have arisen in society and the scientific literature regarding the social support of working parents. Our chapter ends with a discussion of emerging needs for research and practice in helping parents build a social support network. Finally, we offer an overview of the learnings and a list of recommendations for parents, organizational practitioners and scholars.

Benefits of social support for return-to-work parents

An impressive body of research has demonstrated that social support is a key resource that can prevent work-family conflict (e.g., French, Dumani, Allen, & Shockley, 2018; Kossek, Pichler, Bodner, & Hammer, 2011; Pluut, Ilies, Curşeu, & Liu, 2018) and enhance work-family enrichment (e.g., Nicklin & McNall, 2013; Odle-Dusseau, Britt, & Greene-Shortridge, 2012; Siu et al., 2015). Social support is hence an important interpersonal resource that individuals can call upon in both their work (e.g., supervisor support) and home (e.g., spousal support) environments (Van Daalen, Willemsen, & Sanders, 2006). Social support is often conceptualized as a multidimensional construct that involves caring and showing concern (emotional support), giving advice and making suggestions (informational support), lending a hand (instrumental support) and/or providing feedback relevant to self-evaluation (appraisal support) (Bowling et al., 2004; House, 1981).

Despite the proliferation of research indicating the beneficial effects of social support for the work-family well-being of employees, few studies have focused on social support for working parents in particular, and even less have examined social support in the context of returning to work after childbirth. Studies on employed parents confirm findings in the general population and show that social support can reduce work-family conflict and enhance work-family enrichment. Lu, Siu, Spector, and Shi (2009), for example, found among a sample of employed parents in China that family-friendly supervisors and co-workers reduced work-to-family conflict, while a supportive spouse and helpful co-workers enhanced work-family enrichment. In Turkey, emotional support from the spouse and supervisor reduced work-to-family conflict for employed mothers, and an empathic supervisor alleviated their employment-related guilt (Irak et al., 2019). In addition, Aryee, Srinivas, and Tan (2005) found that support outside of work (i.e., from the spouse, family and friends) was significantly related to family-to-work enrichment in a sample of full-time employed parents in India. Social support thus promotes the well-being of working parents because it assists them in successfully combining work and family roles.

The very few studies focusing on return-to-work parents indicate that social support can also help improve mothers' and fathers' well-being after childbirth. In one such study, Grice and colleagues (2007) found that single mothers have lower mental health than mothers who are married, showing the importance of spousal support. They also found that co-worker support results in better physical health of postpartum women who return to work. In another study, Lucia-Casademunt, Garcia-Cabrera, Padilla-Angulo, and Cuéllar-Molina (2018) showed that supervisor support in particular improves the job well-being of both mothers and fathers with children under the age of 1, especially when the organization itself does not offer family-friendly human resource practices. It appears that both family- and work-related support after the arrival of a child can help parents facilitate the return-to-work experience.

In a recent meta-analysis covering more than 1000 studies on social support and work-family conflict, French and colleagues (2018) showed that all sources of social support (spousal support, general family support, supervisor support, co-worker support and organizational support) have their unique added value in reducing work-family conflict. Therefore, it is recommended for return-to-work parents to invest in all sources of social support and as such create a broad support network, both at work and outside. When calling on support resources to deal with a specific situation, parents may take into account that sources of support tend to be most effective when stemming from the domain in which problems originate (domain specificity hypothesis; French et al., 2018). It might also be important to match the type of support (e.g., instrumental or emotional) to the type of demands they are facing at that moment (matching principle; De Jonge & Dormann, 2006).

Challenges for parents in building a social support network

The question then arises which elements determine what one's support system at work and outside looks like. And what challenges do parents returning to work after childbirth face in building a solid social support network? Though studies on the predictors of social support are scarce (see Bowling, Beehr, & Swader, 2005), we provide some initial insights here.

First, Lee and Duxbury (1998) showed that both the age of the child and the gender of the working parent matter. In their classical study, these authors found that parents with younger children receive more support from their spouses and friends than parents with older children. In addition, fathers primarily mention the support they receive from their spouses, while mothers rather rely on friends who are understanding of work and family issues. Thus, demographics are key predictors of social support for parents. In addition, there is evidence for personality effects, with individuals scoring high on agreeableness and extraversion receiving more social support from their co-workers (Bowling et al., 2005). This suggests that agreeable and extraverted parents might be better able to build a social support network at work. Attachment styles are also an important factor, as insecure people consider their partners less supportive during the transition to parenthood (Simpson, Rholes, Campbell, Trans, & Wilson, 2003).

But one of the most important determinants of how much social support you receive is actually how much social support you give. In a study among high school employees, Bowling and colleagues (2004) found strong evidence for a reciprocity hypothesis of social support, as their results indicated that the more employees helped out co-workers by, for example, assisting them with heavy workloads or listening to their problems, the more they received social support from their co-workers. Halbesleben and Wheeler's (2015) diary study confirmed the notion that co-workers reciprocate the support they receive from one another at work. Interestingly, Ten Brummelhuis and Greenhaus (2018) found such effects across the work-family boundary, but only among women. Receiving support at work made women – not men – more supportive toward their spouses, and receiving support from their spouses made women – not men – more helpful toward team members at work. These findings are in line with theory and research on gender differences in prosocial behavior (Eagly, 2009), which suggests that gender stereotypes (communion versus agency) prescribe that women are more helpful and supportive than men.

It remains an open question whether the reciprocity effects and gain cycles discovered in the general population generalize to parents because new parents who return to work find themselves in unprecedented situations. It is not self-evident that they give and receive social support from a broad network at work and outside. That is, building a support network may be particularly challenging for new parents, for several reasons.

First, as parents with young children suffer from sleep deprivation, positive marital interactions decrease markedly (Medina, Lederhos, & Lillis, 2009), leading to a significant decline in marital satisfaction after the birth of a first child (Mitnick, Heyman, & Smith Slep, 2009). Hence, the marital relationship of new parents is under strain, putting their spousal support system in jeopardy. The quality of the spousal support system may decrease even further when both partners return to work after the birth of their child. The evening interactions of dual-earner couples with young children typically take place after both parents have experienced a fully packed day. The relationship functioning of such couples may decline if they cannot contain the spill of stressful workday experiences. That is, workday stress tends to result in withdrawn and angry marital behaviors in the evening (Schulz, Cowan, Cowan, & Brennan, 2004). Hence, working parents should be wary of how their work affects the quality of nightly marital interactions. New parents are in dire need of supportive acts from each other, but at the same time their demanding lives take away the resources to do so, which makes the building of a strong spousal support system extra challenging for return-to-work parents (Feeney & Collins, 2015; Granrose, Parasuraman, & Greenhaus, 1992).

The transition to parenthood also brings about changes in leisure activities. Ekert-Jaffé and Grossbard (2015) observed that parents have less time for leisure than non-parents, especially parents with children under 3 years old. Claxton and Perry-Jenkins (2008) found that joint leisure activities with one's spouse decline over the first year of parenthood but recover gradually as the wife returns to work. They also found that new parents spend less time with friends, although they manage to resume these leisure activities over time. Engaging in leisure activities is important, as research shows that insufficient time for leisure leads to more stress and health complaints among working parents (Håkansson, Axmon, & Eek, 2016). It also enables new parents to build a strong friendship network from which they can draw social support.

Finally, also the support system at work might be affected by the new family situation of return-to-work parents. Of course, the birth of a child is joyful, and the many positive emotions of new parents can enrich their work lives in many ways (Lu et al., 2009). For instance, it has been shown that care tasks can be a source of fulfilment for working parents and in this way result in more helpful behaviors toward co-workers (Ten Brummelhuis, Van der Lippe, & Kluwer, 2010). Yet, collegiality at work is reduced when employees have young children (Ten Brummelhuis, Haar, & Van der Lippe, 2010; Ten Brummelhuis et al., 2010). It seems that "caring for [young] children . . . prevents employees from being fully involved in workplace social networks" (Ten Brummelhuis et al., 2010, p. 2841). This might be particularly so for men, as Ten Brummelhuis and Greenhaus (2018) found that family demands make men – not women – less helpful team members at work. They also found that after encountering high demands at work, men become less supportive to their spouses. Ten Brummelhuis and Greenhaus (2018) explained these findings based on social role theory, suggesting that men may feel less responsible than women for maintaining relationships at work and at home and for protecting those relationships from negative cross-domain influences. The key takeaway from Ten Brummelhuis and Greenhaus's (2018) study is that work and family domains are closely intertwined and influence parents' broader support network, probably in different ways for mothers and fathers.

Key debates

The first debate we have identified concerns gender. Though social support has proven to be beneficial to the work-family well-being of both men and women (e.g., French et al., 2018; Siu et al., 2015), the way in which mothers and fathers build a social support network seems to differ. Lee and Duxbury (1998) already noted in their study that while fathers mainly refer to the benefits of spousal support in successfully combining their work and family, mothers – more often than fathers – turn to friends and relatives to help them out. Also, in terms of providing support, gender differences can be noted that support the gender role perspective on prosocial behavior (see Ten Brummelhuis & Greenhaus, 2018). According to social role theory, different expectations exist about the degree to and manner in which men and women should show social support (Eagly, 2009). While women are expected to be nurturing and caring, men are expected to be rational and assertive. As a result, mothers will provide more spousal support than fathers because society expects them to. The question, however, remains to what degree these gender differences will still hold in the future (or even today) as the upcoming gender similarity model (Keene & Quadagno, 2004) proposes that behavioral shifts and new household arrangements lead to a more equal (expected) involvement of men and women in the work and family environments, eliminating any gender differences over time. Let's say, the jury is still out on the debate around gender.

Another important debate concerns the current trend in today's working world to shift the responsibility to the individual to create his/her own work success and well-being. New concepts, such as job crafting, protean careers, i-deals and so on, increasingly emphasize the agency of the individual in shaping his/her own job and career (see also De Vos & Van der Heijden, 2017). This chapter, however, clearly conveys the importance of other people, in terms of social support, and indicates that the pendulum should not divert too much to the individual; also society and employers have a significant role to play that should not be neglected. This responsibility may be shared among many actors, as research has shown that different sources of support do not compensate for one another but rather build on one another (French et al., 2018) or even enhance one another's effects (Greenhaus, Ziegert, & Allen, 2012). Hence, we believe that stronger performance and well-being can be obtained by combining individual and organizational efforts. Therefore, a more balanced debate focusing on shared responsibilities may be beneficial, in which questions may arise about the role of society and legislation.

Finally, though the majority of research has emphasized the beneficial effects of social support, several studies indicate that in some situations social support may not be helpful and may even worsen the receiver's psychological and physical health (Beehr, Bowling, & Bennett, 2010; Collins & Feeney, 2004; Deelstra et al., 2003). No doubt this can also apply to new parents returning to work. First, and most detrimental, are social support interactions that make the parents focus on how stressful it all is and how impossible it is to combine work with a newborn. Though such sympathetic comments may be intended to be helpful, according to the social information processing theory (Bateman, Griffin, & Rubinstein, 1987), they might focus the parents' attention on stressors they did not even think about yet, making them feel worse rather than better after the social interaction. Second, there may also be too much of a good thing. According to the stress-as-offense-to-the-self theory (Semmer, Jacobshagen, Meier, & Elfering, 2007), receiving too much social support that comes off as imposing may form a threat to parents' self-esteem, hurting their mental and physical health. Imagine, for instance, when all the instrumental support you get from your spouse or relatives in taking care of your newborn, in combination with supervisors or co-workers who spare you from extra work or hassles, actually makes you feel inadequate and incompetent in your new role as a parent. A final situation in which social support may be detrimental is when parents receive social support they do not need or that is unwanted (e.g., your own mother checking in every evening to see if everything is *still* okay with you and your newborn). According to the person-environment fit theory (Edwards, Caplan, & Harrison, 1998), receiving supplies in excess of one's needs can be stressful, and as such, receiving unwanted help can be detrimental to parents' health. Hence, debates on whether social support is always a good thing are still thriving.

Recommendations for research and practice and emerging needs

Despite these few examples in which social support can be detrimental, most research shows that social support is an important mechanism in facilitating work-family well-being and organizational performance. Both parents and the organizations that employ them can therefore benefit from building a strong social support network. At the end of the chapter, we summarize the key learnings from this chapter and the recommendations that follow for new parents and the organizations employing them.

Important for parents to realize is that a significant determinant of receiving support is the amount of support they provide to others (Bowling et al., 2005). Providing support initiates a support exchange system that easily goes beyond the tit-for-tat between provider and receiver and sparks a resource gain cycle that spills over not only to others within the same domain but also across the work-family boundary (Ten Brummelhuis & Greenhaus, 2018). However, as new parents are often pressed for time, research also shows that parents with young children engage less in helping behaviors at work (Ten Brummelhuis et al., 2010; Ten Brummelhuis et al., 2010), experience a drop in positive marital interactions (Medina et al., 2009), and spend less time with friends and on leisure activities (Claxton & Perry-Jenkins, 2008; Ekert-Jaffé & Grossbard, 2015). We would like to advice parents – to the extent possible – to keep engaging in supportive interactions within all three domains, as research has shown that different sources of social support enhance one another (Greenhaus et al., 2012). Hence, creating a diversified social support network is recommendable.

The same recommendation holds for organizations. As a recent meta-analysis has shown that organizational, supervisor and co-worker support all have unique positive effects on work-family well-being above and beyond each other (French et al., 2018), organizations are advised to invest in all three sources of social support and do not rely on one of them (e.g., a supportive supervisor) to compensate for a lack in others (e.g., no family-friendly organization). To aid return-to-work parents in finding a new work-family routine, organizations are thus strongly advised to go beyond formally describing a set of work-family policies and rather ensure that the current organizational climate, the supervisor and the co-workers are supportive of parents using these work-family policies. Several studies have already emphasized that informal work-family social support is more predictive of parents' work-family well-being than formal work-family policies (Behson, 2005; Dikkers et al., 2007). Similarly, French and colleagues' (2018) meta-analysis suggested that perceptions of social support may be more strongly associated with work-family conflict than support behaviors. Organizations should thus focus their efforts on developing broad perceptions of workplace support. Yet another meta-analysis (Kossek et al., 2011) showed that perceptions of specific *work-family* support (e.g., a supervisor helping to resolve concrete work-family conflicts or the organization enabling mothers to keep breastfeeding) have a larger impact than more general perceptions of support. Thus, we recommend organizations to do more than generally support return-to-work parents and really create a family-friendly organization that is borne by all supervisors and employees.

Conclusions

In this chapter, we have tried to formulate some recommendations for new parents and the stakeholders involved, but how to create a diversified and strong social support network for new parents is a question that is not easily answered. Our brief review of the research on this topic points to a number of issues that remain unaddressed to date. For instance, as social relations are changing and becoming more virtual, both at work (e.g., virtual teams) and outside (e.g., Facebook friends), questions arise about how these evolutions toward more digital relationships may impact social support networks. May they become more superficial and volatile, depleting the power of social support networks and enhancing the loneliness in our society? Or may our social support networks grow exponentially as a result of the digitalization and can only become richer? But also the way in which we define families has undergone a tremendous change over the past decades. Today, we do not only have single- and dual-career families but also all kinds of blended families with in-living grandparents, stepparents and -children, all with their own unique challenges. We encourage future studies on new parents that take into account these societal developments and how these may impact the social support networks of working parents. We also encourage scholars to engage with and further enrich the debates identified earlier in this chapter. But perhaps most important is to extend the small but growing body of research on social support for return-to-work parents. The following table offers recommendations for scholars on this point. We are convinced that this is a field of research that will offer many more insights that can help new parents navigate the return-to-work experience.

Key learnings from research	Practical recommendations		
	For parents	*For organizations*	*For society*
• Social support increases work-family enrichment and decreases work-family conflict and employment-related guilt. • Different sources of support build on and enhance one another's effects.	• Build a broad and diversified support network across life domains. • Call on many sources of social support (spouse, family members, co-workers, supervisors, friends, etc.).	• Invest in organizational, supervisor and co-worker support. • Go beyond formally describing a set of work-family policies and develop broad perceptions of a family-friendly organizational climate.	• Conduct additional research on the benefits of social support when returning to work after childbirth. • Test the matching principle for social support amongst return-to-work parents.

(Continued)

(Continued)

Key learnings from research	Practical recommendations		
	For parents	*For organizations*	*For society*
• Providing support triggers reciprocity. • The transition to parenthood challenges the marital relationship, interferes with leisure and reduces collegiality at work.	• Be aware of the specific challenges of becoming parents (and returning to work) and employ strategies to overcome them. • Keep engaging in supportive interactions within the family, leisure and work domains.	• View the (work-family) well-being of new parents who return to work as a shared responsibility. • Encourage and reward collegiality at work both formally and informally.	• Examine reciprocity effects and gain cycles among new parents. • Identify strategies for maintaining a broad support network during the transition to parenthood.

References

Aryee, S., Srinivas, E. S., & Tan, H. H. (2005). Rhythms of life: Antecedents and outcomes of work-family balance in employed parents. *Journal of Applied Psychology, 90*, 132–146.

Bateman, T. S., Griffin, R. W., & Rubinstein, D. (1987). Social information processing and group-induced shifts in responses to task design. *Group and Organization Management, 12*, 88–108.

Beehr, T. A., Bowling, N. A., & Bennett, M. M. (2010). Occupational stress and failures of social support: When helping hurts. *Journal of Occupational Health Psychology, 15*, 45–59.

Behson, S. J. (2005). The relative contribution of formal and informal organizational work-family support. *Journal of Vocational Behavior, 66*, 487–500.

Bowling, N. A., Beehr, T. A., Johnson, A. L., Semmer, N. K., Hendricks, E. A., & Webster, H. A. (2004). Explaining potential antecedents of workplace social support: Reciprocity or attractiveness? *Journal of Occupational Health Psychology, 9*, 339–350.

Bowling, N. A., Beehr, T. A., & Swader, W. M. (2005). Giving and receiving social support at work: The roles of personality and reciprocity. *Journal of Vocational Behavior, 67*, 476–489.

Carlson, D. S., Kacmar, K. M., Holliday Wayne, J., & Grzywacz, J. G. (2006). Measuring the positive side of the work-family interface: Development and validation of a work-family enrichment scale. *Journal of Vocational Behavior, 68*, 131–164.

Claxton, A., & Perry-Jenkins, M. (2008). No fun anymore: Leisure and marital quality across the transition to parenthood. *Journal of Marriage and Family, 70*, 28–43.

Collins, N. L., & Feeney, B. C. (2004). Working models of attachment shape perceptions of social support: Evidence from experimental and observational studies. *Journal of Personality and Social Psychology, 87*, 363–383.

De Jonge, J., & Dormann, C. (2006). Stressors, resources, and strain at work: A longitudinal test of the triple-match principle. *Journal of Applied Psychology, 91*, 1359–1374.

De Vos, A., & Van der Heijden, B. I. J. M. (2017). Current thinking on contemporary careers: The key roles of sustainable HRM and sustainability of careers. *Current Opinion in Environmental Stability, 28*, 41–50.

Deelstra, J. T., Peeters, M. C. W., Schaufeli. W. B., Stroebe, W., Zijlstra, F. R. H., & Van Doornen, L. P. (2003). Receiving instrumental support at work: When help is not welcome. *Journal of Applied Psychology, 88*, 324–331.

Dikkers, J. S. E., Geurts, S. A. E., Den Dulk, L., Peper, B., Taris, T. W., & Kompier, M. A. J. (2007). Dimensions of work-home culture and their relations with the use of work-home arrangements and work-home interaction. *Work & Stress: An International Journal of Work, Health & Organisations, 21*, 155–172.

Eagly, A. H. (2009). The his and hers of prosocial behavior: An examination of the social psychology of gender. *American Psychologist, 64*, 644–658.

Edwards, J. R., Caplan, R. D., & Harrison, R. V. (1998). Person-environment fit theory: Conceptual foundations, empirical evidence, and directions for future research. In C. L. Cooper (Ed.), *Theories of organizational stress* (pp. 28–67). Oxford: Oxford University Press.

Ekert-Jaffé, O., & Grossbard, S. (2015). Time cost of children as parents' foregone leisure. *Mathematical Population Studies, 22*, 80–100.

Eurostat Labour Force Survey (2019). *LFS series – specific topics: Household statistics.* Retrieved from https://ec.europa.eu/eurostat/web/lfs/data/database

Feeney, B. C., & Collins, N. L. (2015). A new look at social support: A theoretical perspective on thriving through relationships. *Personality and Social Psychology Review, 19*, 113–147.

French, K. A., Dumani, S., Allen, T. D., & Shockley, K. M. (2018). A meta-analysis of work-family conflict and social support. *Psychological Bulletin, 144*, 284–314.

Granrose, C. S., Parasuraman, S., & Greenhaus, J. H. (1992). A proposed model of support provided by two-earner couples. *Human Relations, 45*, 1367–1393.

Greenhaus, J. H., & Beutell, N. J. (1985). Sources of conflict between work and family roles. *Academy of Management Review, 10*, 76–88.

Greenhaus, J. H., & Powell, G. N. (2006). When work and family are allies: A theory of work-family enrichment. *Academy of Management Review, 31*, 72–92.

Greenhaus, J. H., Ziegert, J. C., & Allen, T. D. (2012). When family-supportive supervision matters: Relations between multiple sources of support and work-family balance. *Journal of Vocational Behavior, 80*, 266–275.

Grice, M. M., Feda, D., McGovern, P., Alexander, B. H., McCaffrey, D., & Ukestad, L. (2007). Giving birth and returning to work: The impact of work-family conflict on women's health after childbirth. *Annals of Epidemiology, 17*, 791–798.

Håkansson, C., Axmon, A., & Eek, F. (2016). Insufficient time for leisure and perceived health and stress in working parents with small children. *Work, 55*, 453–461.

Halbesleben, J. R. B., & Wheeler, A. R. (2015). To invest or not? The role of coworker support and trust in daily reciprocal gain spirals of helping behavior. *Journal of Management, 41*, 1628–1650.

House, J. S. (1981). *Work stress and social support.* Reading, MA: Addison-Wesley.

Irak, D. U., Kalkişim, K., & Yildirim, M. (2019). Emotional support makes the difference: Work-family conflict and employment related guilt among employed mothers. *Sex Roles.* https://doi.org/10.1007/s11199-019-01035-x

Keene, J. R., & Quadagno, J. (2004). Predictors of perceived work-family balance: Gender difference or gender similarity? *Sociological Perspectives, 47*, 1–23.

Korabik, K. (2015). The intersection of gender and work-family guilt. In M. J. Mills (Ed.), *Gender and the work-family experience* (pp. 141–157). Cham, Switzerland: Springer.

Kossek, E. E., Pichler, S., Bodner, T., & Hammer, L. B. (2011). Workplace social support and work-family conflict: A meta-analysis clarifying the influence of general and work-family-specific supervisor and organizational support. *Personnel Psychology, 64*, 289–313.

Lee, C. M., & Duxbury, L. (1998). Employed parents' support from partners, employers, and friends. *The Journal of Social Psychology, 138*, 303–322.

Lu, J.-F., Siu, O.-L., Spector, P. E., & Shi, K. (2009). Antecedents and outcomes of a four-fold taxonomy of work-family balance in Chinese employed parents. *Journal of Occupational Health Psychology, 14*, 182–192.

Lucia-Casademunt, A. M., Garcia-Cabrera, A. M., Padilla-Angulo, L., & Cuéllar-Molina, D. (2018). Returning to work after childbirth in Europe: Well-being, work-life balance, and the interplay of supervisor support. *Frontiers in Psychology, 9,* 68.

Masterson, C. R., & Hoobler, J. M. (2015). Care and career: A family identify-based typology of dual-earner couples. *Journal of Organizational Behavior, 36,* 75–93.

Medina, A. M., Lederhos, C. L., & Lillis, T. A. (2009). Sleep disruption and decline in marital satisfaction across the transition to parenthood. *Families, Systems, & Health, 27,* 153–160.

Mitnick, D. M., Heyman, R. E., & Smith Slep, A. M. (2009). Changes in relationship satisfaction across the transition to parenthood: A meta-analysis. *Journal of Family Psychology, 23,* 848–852.

Nicklin, J. M., & McNall, L. A. (2013). Work-family enrichment, support, and satisfaction: A test of mediation. *European Journal of Work and Organizational Psychology, 22,* 67–77.

Odle-Dusseau, H. N., Britt, T. W., & Greene-Shortridge, T. M. (2012). Organizational work-family resources as predictors of job performance and attitudes: The process of work-family conflict and enrichment. *Journal of Occupational Health Psychology, 17,* 28–40.

OECD Family Database. (2019). *The labour market position of families, LMF2.2: Patterns of employment and the distribution of working hours for couples with children.* Retrieved from www.oecd.org/els/family/database.htm

Pluut, H., Ilies, R., Curşeu, P. L., & Liu, Y. (2018). Social support at work and at home: Dual-buffering effects in the work-family conflict process. *Organizational Behavior and Human Decision Processes, 146,* 1–13.

Ruderman, M. N., Ohlott, P. J., Panzer, K., & King, S. N. (2002). Benefits of multiple roles for managerial women. *Academy of Management Journal, 45,* 369–386.

Schulz, M. S., Cowan, P. A., Cowan, C., & Brennan, R. T. (2004). Coming home upset: Gender, marital satisfaction, and the daily spillover of workday experience into couple interactions. *Journal of Family Psychology, 18,* 250–263.

Semmer, N. K., Jacobshagen, N., Meier, L. L., & Elfering, A. (2007). Occupational stress research: The stress-as-offense-to-self perspective. In J. Houdmont & S. McIntyre (Eds.), *Occupational health psychology. European perspectives on research, education and practice* (pp. 41–58). Nottingham, UK: Nottingham University Press.

Simpson, J. A., Rholes, W. S., Campbell, L., Trans, S., & Wilson, C. L. (2003). Adult attachment, the transition to parenthood, and depressive symptoms. *Journal of Personality and Social Psychology, 84,* 1172–1187.

Siu, O. L., Bakker, A. B., Brough, P., Lu, C-Q., Wang, H., Kalliath, T. . . . Timms, C. (2015). A three-wave study of antecedents of work-family enrichment: The roles of social resources and affect. *Stress & Health, 31,* 306–314.

Smit, B., Maloney, P. W., Maertz, C. P., & Montag-Smit, T. (2016). Out of sight, out of mind? How and when cognitive role transition episodes influence employee performance. *Human Relations, 69,* 2141–2168.

Ten Brummelhuis, L. L., & Greenhaus, J. H. (2018). How role jugglers maintain relationships at home and at work: A gender comparison. *Journal of Applied Psychology, 103,* 1265–1282.

Ten Brummelhuis, L. L., Haar, J. M., & Van der Lippe, T. (2010). Collegiality under pressure: The effects of family demands and flexible work arrangements in the Netherlands. *The International Journal of Human Resource Management, 21,* 2831–2847.

Ten Brummelhuis, L. L., Van der Lippe, T., & Kluwer, E. S. (2010). Family involvement and helping behavior in teams. *Journal of Management, 36,* 1406–1431.

Van Daalen, G., Willemsen, T. M., & Sanders, K. (2006). Reducing work-family conflict through different sources of social support. *Journal of Vocational Behavior, 69*, 462–476.

Vieira, J. M., Matias, M., Lopez, F. G., & Matos, P. M. (2016). Relationships between work-family dynamics and parenting experiences: A dyadic analysis of dual-earner couples. *Work & Stress: An International Journal of Work, Health & Organisations, 30*, 243–261.

Zedeck, S., & Mosier, K. L. (1990). Work in the family and employing organization. *American Psychologist, 45*, 240–251.

4 Practical strategies for work-family resources management in the return-to-work experiences of new parents

Angela Martin, Sarah Dawkins, Vanessa A. Miles, Sarah J. Cotton, and Justine Alter

Maintaining personal and family well-being and effective work performance following the return to work from parental leave is a major life transition challenge (Martin, Cooklin, & Dawkins, 2015). Research has consistently demonstrated that even when government policies are in place to support the transition to becoming a working parent, the employment context is not always supportive, and organisations vary considerably in how well these policies are implemented (Skinner, Hutchinson, & Pocock, 2012). Key dimensions of organisational culture related to attitudes, norms, gender role beliefs (Allen et al., 2001), structural/operational constraints in different work settings and professions (e.g., Heiligers & Hingstman, 2000) and the extent to which family-supportive supervisor behaviours are present (Hammer et al., 2009) all affect how well employees cope, adjust and thrive during this transition.

At an individual level, returning parents can face discrimination, negative attitudes and a lack of working time flexibility (Australian Human Rights Commission [AHRC], 2014) as well as the financial burden of childcare (Wilkins, 2017), all whilst battling sleep deprivation and the increased risk of mental health issues (COPE, 2017). Meanwhile, organisations must bear the costs of backfilling roles whilst operating under the uncertainty of when/whether the parent will return, and above-average attrition rates for those who do (AHRC, 2014). Addressing these issues in workplaces is essential to making progress on gender equality and promoting employee/family well-being.

However, even in the most supportive organisational context, dealing with conflicts between work and family priorities in the early parenting period (both work to family and family to work) requires drawing on and managing a variety of temporal, social, psychological and financial resources. Whilst it is undeniable that many organisational contexts require significant culture change, capability development and improved supervision practices when it comes to better work/ family support (Kossek & Hammer, 2008), the focus of this chapter is to explore the strategies *parents* returning from parental leave can use to help ease and support their transition.

Mentoring provided within an organisation has been associated with reduced work-family conflict (Nielson, Carlson, & Lankauc, 2001) and the practice of externally provided executive coaching services has increasingly needed to focus on work-family issues (O'Neil, Hopkins, & Bilimoria, 2015) as women enter more leadership roles and social expectations of the role of fathers changes (Burnett, Gatrell, Cooper, & Sparrow, 2013). Mentoring and/or coaching, both during planning for parental leave and after the return to work, is one strategy for proactively supporting the transitions of individual parents. Such support can help new parents to optimally manage available resources following the return to work from parental leave.

As children grow older, demands and challenges can change, but early development of a strong mindset and repertoire of strategies early in the transition to becoming a working parent can establish a work-family 'hygiene' approach that can be adjusted throughout the career, promoting resilience to different forms of work-family conflict that may emerge in different situations. In addition, supporting new parents to develop these mindsets and skills may also promote work-family enrichment, a construct concerned with the benefits of combining work and family roles via transfer of resources from one domain to the other (Grzywacz, Carlson, Kacmar, & Wayne, 2007). For example, learning to focus on what is most important and most valued by the organisation is something new parents may need to do from a time management perspective (part-time roles, etc.). However, this skill of 'essentialism' (McKeown, 2014) can also enhance performance across the career, particularly as careers advance into management and leadership roles.

The concept of resources, not just time and money, but forms of psychological and social capital as well, plays a central part in understanding how well parents adjust to these new demands. This chapter is structured by providing an overview of conservation of resources theory and discussing its connection to a key psychological resource, psychological capital, and how it is developed. This frames an analysis of excerpts from an interview with highly experienced parental leave coaching providers, designed to illustrate practical strategies related to identifying, developing and leveraging a range of resources that support the transition to becoming a working parent. Finally, implications for future research and practice are discussed.

Stress, coping and resources – applied to parental leave transitions

Lazarus and Folkman (1984) developed the transactional theory of stress and coping in which the extent to which a person appraises events as stressful is a function of the personal and social coping resources they can draw upon in formulating responses to a stressor or potential stressor. It usefully recognises the role of environmental factors in coping processes but has been criticized for its overemphasis on perception of environment rather than actual environmental contingencies.

Conservation of resources (COR) theory developed by Hobfoll (1988) also linked coping and resources but furthered stress theory by arguing that people strive to retain, protect and build resources and that what is threatening to them is the potential or actual loss of these valued resources. In COR theory, *psychological stress* is defined as "a reaction to the environment in which there is (a) the threat of a net loss of resources, (b) the net loss of resources, or (c) a lack of resource gain following the investment of resources" (Hobfoll, 1989, p. 516).

Hobfoll (1989) defined resources as objects (e.g., rare or expensive status symbols), personal characteristics (e.g., self-esteem, mastery), conditions (e.g., marriage, job tenure) or energies (e.g., time, money, knowledge) that are valued by the individual or that serve as a means for attainment of resources. Social relations are also regarded as a resource when they provide or facilitate the preservation of valued resources, but they also can detract from individuals' resources.

According to COR theory, transitions are a series of linked events. When these chains of events entail *multiple loss events* (e.g., divorce leading to income loss, breakup of other relationships, and childcare difficulties), they are likely to prove stressful (Hobfall, 1989). Importantly, both *perceived* and *actual* loss or lack of gain of resources motivate individuals to strive to minimize net loss of resources.

Individuals may employ personal resources to offset net loss. Personal characteristics are resources to the extent that they generally aid stress resistance by supporting a positive sense of self and a view that one can master or at least see through stressful circumstances. Individuals may also conserve resources by reinterpreting threat as challenge or by reappraising the value of resources that are threatened or that have been lost. Normative tendencies regarding how resources are evaluated and what constitutes loss guide individuals' assessments of their environments and their selves. They also deploy resources in their environment to offset loss. Replacement is the most direct way this is accomplished, but the resource "fit" with the demands can also affect outcomes. Loss spirals can also develop when lacking the resources to offset loss. Managing the deployment of resources for coping is also stressful in itself. Individuals employ resources in the coping process which often depletes these resources: "energy is expended, favors are used up, and self-esteem is risked, all in the service of offsetting loss of other potential loss. If the resources expended in coping outstrip the resultant benefits, the outcome of coping is likely to be negative" (Hobfoll, 1998, p. 518).

In this chapter we examine how resources are deployed towards specific problems, how they are lost and replaced or rebuilt during the transition to becoming a working parent. In particular, we focus on the following major resource areas identified in contemporary work-family literature (Hobfoll, Halbesleben, Neveu, & Westman, 2018):

- *Temporal* (e.g., time-based initiatives such as schedule flexibility)
- *Geographical/technological* (e.g., work from home, co-working spaces with crèches)
- *Social* (e.g., peer support, mentors, broader family networks, neighbourhood)
- *Financial* (e.g., cost benefit analysis of income both short and long term [superannuation impact of lost time in workforce], outsourcing costs of childcare and domestic unpaid work)
- *Psychological* (e.g., strengths-based training, early intervention regarding perinatal mental health)

Psychological capital (PsyCap) is an example of a psychological resource which we explore further later and that may promote an individual's capacity to cope with the challenges and stressors associated with a return-to-work process following parental leave.

Psychological capital and the work-family interface

PsyCap reflects an individual's positive developmental psychological state, in which the specific resources of hope, efficacy, resilience and optimism enhances a person's ability to copy with challenges, stress or strain (Luthans, Avey, Avolio, Norman, & Combs, 2006). In situations in which demands cannot be reduced, psychological resources such as PsyCap can provide a buffer to the negative relationship between job demands and employee outcomes (Bakker, Hakanen, Demerouti, & Xanthopoulou, 2007). Research has shown that PsyCap is an important predictor of job performance, satisfaction, work-family enrichment, organizational commitment and psychological well-being (e.g., Avey, Reichard, Luthans, & Mharte, 2011; Lee, Seo, Jeung, & Kim, 2017; Mishra, Bhatnagar, Gupta, & Wadsworth, 2017).

A growing body of literature is emerging which specifically explores the impact of PsyCap on how employees manage the competing demands of work and family roles. For example, in one study PsyCap was found to mediate the relationship between work-family conflict and burnout among Chinese doctors (Wang, Liu, Wang, & Wang, 2012). In longitudinal research, Siu (2013) reported that PsyCap was positively related to employee psychological well-being and work-family balance outcomes. Other research has shown that PsyCap moderated the relationship between work-family conflict and depressive symptoms among nurses (Hao, Wu, Liu, Li, & Wu, 2015). It is theorised that PsyCap may foster employee work-family psychological resources, thereby improving psychological well-being, which in turn enhances functioning in both the work and family domains.

To date, and somewhat surprisingly, the potential benefits of PsyCap in supporting new parents navigate the return to work following parental leave has not yet been investigated in the literature. Drawing on COR theory outlined earlier, we suggest that PsyCap may be an important psychological resource to foster among parents transitioning back to work following parental leave. Recent research has applied COR to the study of PsyCap by suggesting that the hope, optimism, resilience and efficacy are psychological resources which individuals can draw upon to optimise performance and functioning across the work and family domains, and importantly, to enhance psychological well-being (Avey, Luthans, & Jensen, 2009; Avey, Luthans, Smith, & Palmer, 2010).

As outlined previously, COR theory differentiates between two mechanisms designed to conserve resources: (1) the seeking of new resources which will aid energetic activation towards the pursuit of goals (resource gain orientation); and (2) the propensity to prevent resource loss and thus retain a sufficient buffer of resources (resource loss orientation; Hobfall, 1989). In considering each of the individual PsyCap components, we suggest that self-efficacy, hope and optimism reflect psychological resources which foster a resource gain orientation, in that they provide the necessary confidence, pathways and positive expectations to propel an individual towards work-family goal achievement.

In contrast, resilience reflects a resource loss orientation, in that it preserves momentum towards work-family goal achievement by enabling recovery from unfavourable events, challenges or stressors. Thus, resilience may be negatively related to feelings of work-family conflict/family-work conflict, as it enables individuals to prevent further resource loss, and thereby recover and rebound from setbacks and preserve towards their work-family goals.

Conversely, each of the gain-oriented psychological resources (hope, efficacy, optimism) may be more positively associated with feelings of work-family enrichment/family-work enrichment, as these resources enable the attainment of new resources, which activate energetic activation towards work-family goal orientation, thereby enhancing feelings of enrichment across the work-family domains.

To further understand and illustrate how parents may use these various forms of resources in adaptive ways that support their transition back to work after becoming a parent, and to assist readers to see connections between research and practice, we use an extract from an interview. The interview was conducted by the lead author with two subject matter experts who practice in the field through Transitioning Well, a company that provides work-life integration strategy, education and coaching services.

Insights of parental leave return from work-life transition coaching providers

ANGELA: Today we're focusing on helping parents with smart and creative management of the resources available to them to support their transition back to paid work after parental leave. I will start by asking you what are the most common resources in your coaching that you see people become more aware of?

SARAH: The primary one is the social support that people have available to them both at work and external to work

ANGELA: So people are generally well aware of that as a resource?

JUSTINE: Yes, we believe it takes a village to raise a child, and whether that means at work or outside of work, we focus on what do your supports look like? If you don't have them . . . let's say, for example, you're an ex-pat or you have family outside of where you're living, how can you create that? In the workplace we look at what support programs are available, internal networks they may have in terms of connecting mums together. This is a growing area – bringing in the idea of mentoring and what that means inside the workplace.

SARAH: This idea of mentoring/peer support is an incredible opportunity to support the parental leave transition in the workplace . . . an opportunity to build a support network of peers who are at similar stages in the transition, and connect them. . . .

ANGELA: That's a great idea. So that's something that the organisation could do, but also a person returning could initiate their organisation to start providing that.

JUSTINE: Organisations often have no budget to support these networks so it can be one woman saying, 'I know there's a real need here and I'm going to start it'.

SARAH: There is a good ground-up atmosphere happening. The problem we have is when organisations don't devote any resources to it, it can fall flat.

ANGELA: Are there any other kinds of things that are to do with the resource of support outside of work? How do people mobilise support in their personal networks?

JUSTINE: I'm just thinking of some of my clients who've really had no one, and the mother's group hasn't worked out. Some will make friends for life and other people will say, 'I just didn't connect'. I'm talking about those who are isolated, where they don't have family or friends, so it's about creating a whole new world for yourself.

ANGELA: So, using different strategies to find the right kind of people to connect with.

JUSTINE: Exactly.

SARAH: I think it's also important to consider that while not everyone has a partner, for those that do – how do we have the conversations about distribution of home duties and roles. . . .

ANGELA: . . . . how radically those dynamics change, and in your relation-ship what a shock and surprise it can be. So, you help with relationship strategies focused on the childcare and domestic stuff. . . .

JUSTINE: Yes, it's about roles and identity in terms of becoming parents, how you're going to both actually parent and what does that mean in terms of sharing stuff, including the 'mental overload', which is a huge topic of discussion at the moment . . . birthday presents, packing the swimming bag, knowing that it's photo day, you know that mental stuff – I think it's inherently still been on the woman and changing that is hard.

SARAH: I think what also needs to be highlighted is when people are on leave, they are often picking up a lot of 'slack' at home and so in the transition back from leave, there's a critical point that needs to be set up well. Before you go back to paid work, start having conversations with your partner around 'look things are going to be different now; I'm not going to be able to do everything I did, so what does that mean?'

ANGELA: What about psychological resources, so people's styles of how they think and respond to events?

JUSTINE: I think a huge one is control . . . a lot of the women we work with tend to be Type A and learning to let go and focus on the things that you can actually control as opposed to trying to control everything is a huge shift in their thinking along with the confidence piece. . . .

ANGELA: So you help build their confidence?

JUSTINE: Yeah. It's a big part of our coaching; it's asking open questions, getting them to have the ah-hah moment to know their own self-worth, to ask the right questions so they do come back and go 'actually you know what, I was so scared of having that conversation with my manager but it was the best thing I did'. We often get feedback . . . the session with you gave me the ability to have that conversation.

ANGELA: Thinking about psychological capital, in addition to self-efficacy, there's also hope, optimism and resilience.

SARAH: One of the other coaching tools is helping to build realistic optimism. We do a lot of cognitive behavioural therapy (CBT) . . . we introduce a simplified version of CBT called the 'Three C's'.

JUSTINE: Catch it, check it, change it (see case study 2).

ANGELA: So we've talked a bit about psychological resources; financial resources is the other big one.

JUSTINE: Yeah, one question we ask is how dependent is your family on your income? That paves the way for a conversation including your attitude towards money . . . and how that changes since having a baby. A very big part of coaching is to help people have the conversations, because we all know that money can become a problem once you become a family.

SARAH: . . . even people being aware of what people can access both through their employer and the government is important.

ANGELA: Any examples of what people maybe were able to access that they didn't know about, so where knowledge is the resource?

JUSTINE: . . . the Keep in Touch days (Australian, Fair Work Act). Many people don't know that they can use ten paid keep in touch days to do a bit of work when they're on leave.

SARAH: This has huge implications not just financial, but also for staying connected to the business while you're on leave to help facilitate the return . . . a lot of men also don't know that they've got any entitlement to parental leave or flexible work arrangements.

JUSTINE: It comes under a bigger heading, I think, of flexible working; would you agree?

SARAH: A hundred percent. You've also got the situation where some people are working say three days a week and getting paid three days a week yet working five days a week.

ANGELA: I just read an article on that this morning, on false part-timers syndrome . . . OK, so, other resources, time for example, are there smart ways to manage time during this period that you go through with people?

SARAH: Yes, we build what we call work-life transition tactics . . . for example, we only have twenty-four hours seven days a week, so we get people to look at their values. . . .

ANGELA: Values . . .

SARAH: . . . to help them inform their yes's and their no's, because ultimately you have to make hard calls on where you spend your time when you become a parent, because you don't have as much time.

JUSTINE: What are your absolute non-negotiables? For example, I need to be home on my work days in time to put my kid to bed and read a story. Actually, the session I had this morning we talked about wanting to get home earlier so how will she make that work? Go in earlier because those three days it's important to her to do that bottle feed when she gets home. And does that mean she needs to log on after the baby goes to sleep on those days? Is she prepared to do that? What does that look like? We work a lot around that space.

SARAH: This is often referred to as the 'second shift'.

ANGELA: . . . and how do you care for your own well-being . . . if you make up the work time at night, how that impacts your sleep if you get up in the night for the baby as well.

SARAH: Rather than self-care . . . we use the term self-advocacy. Because as working parents, you are always advocating for someone else.

ANGELA: One of the things touched on in the literature relates to the threat of loss and the actual loss of resources. . . .

SARAH: I think it's important to talk about reframing the loss because a lot of people struggle when they come back. They can't just stay at work like they used to in meeting a deadline; there can be some loss and grief around that for people. It takes some adjustment. . . .

JUSTINE: . . . expanding on that is the loss of spontaneity, so that feeling of before you were a parent, if you wanted to go for work drinks you could. If you wanted to just meet your husband for a dinner out rather than cooking, you did . . . but the confines of the routine of working parenthood is a difficult one. You really do learn to know what's important and what's not.

ANGELA: Prioritizing. And people creating strategies that suit their priorities.

SARAH: How we integrate work and family life is different for everyone, not one tool fits everyone, so it needs to be a conscious choice about what's right for you. We talk a lot about getting out of automatic pilot, helping people to create the space, and give them the opportunity, to reflect and make some decisions about how they approach it.

ANGELA: Create a personalised plan, but it's very values based?

SARAH: Very values based, yeah.

JUSTINE: So the beauty of this transition is giving you the gift to do that. It makes you stop and reflect on that and if done well, you're paving the way for success through all the transitions to come later on. A much more meaningful career and life, together, enriched by this process.

SARAH: Our observation is that if you do this piece well, it can set up the routines and rhythms for the rest of your work-life integration.

The major themes explored in the interview regarding smart use of resources that support the parental leave transition (support, strengths, mentoring, self-efficacy, identity, cognitive and domestic load, finances, legal entitlements) are connected with recent research literature in Table 4.1 to guide readers interested in further scholarly exploration of these issues. We also explore some of the issues further by highlighting two Transitioning Well case studies. Finally, in the conclusion to this chapter, we explore in further detail how themes raised in the interview around resource management relate to furthering both research and practice.

Table 4.1 Connecting key themes related to parents' use of resources in the transition back to work after parental leave with recent research findings and concepts

Theme	*Research examples*
The importance of support at work	Work-family specific support from supervisors has been shown to reduce the extent to which daily workload leads to work-family conflict (Goh, Ilies, & Wilson, 2015). Support from work may be even more helpful for reducing work-family conflict than family support, particularly if the employee perceives the organisation to be supportive (French, Dumani, Allen, & Shockley, 2018).
Using values/ strengths to manage the transition	Strengths interventions directly affect general self-efficacy (Van Woerkom & Meyers, 2019) and short- and long-term increases in psychological capital (Meyers & Van Woerkom, 2017).
Mentoring	Mentoring has been shown to benefit outcomes such as performance and career satisfaction (Underhill, 2006) and to reduce work-family conflict (de Janasz, Behson, Jonsen, & Lankau, 2013).
Self-efficacy of women returning to work	New working mothers engage different tactics involving both cognitive and behavioural adjustments to help reduce maternal and professional identity and efficacy uncertainty. Adjustments to reduce identify uncertainty include revising one's self-concept ("I've come to the realisation I can't be super-woman anymore") and/or establishing a prioritisation between their professional and maternal identities. Tactics to reduce uncertainty regarding efficacy include learning from role models and from early work-return experiences, for example, trial work days (Ladge & Greenberg, 2015).
Self-worth, identity, integrating motherhood and career	Whilst motherhood restricts the time available to invest in careers, it simultaneously enhances the capacity to perform well. To do this, women must establish priorities, develop strategies to meet needs in both the work and family spheres, to set boundaries around the demands of those two spheres, and to renegotiate the priorities, strategies and boundaries as the needs of the workplace and their children change over time (Laney, Carruthers, Hall, & Anderson, 2014).
Distribution of home duties and 'mental housework'	Inequality in the distribution of home duties is typically felt more acutely by women than men, and mothers report lower satisfaction in the relationship with their partners when they under-benefit in parenting divisions of labour (Schieman, Ruppanner, & Milkie, 2018).

Theme	Research examples
	Feeling disproportionately responsible for 'mental housework' (i.e. keeping track of everyday needs, demands and schedules of all family members, including being vigilant of children's emotional needs) is associated with strains on mothers' personal well-being as well as lower satisfaction with the relationship with their partner (Ciciolla & Luthar, 2019).
Proactively managing financial impact	Having shared goals and values about money is a strong predictor of relationship satisfaction (Archuleta, 2013).
Awareness/use of entitlements	Australian research regarding entitlements: Paid Parental Leave (PPL), Dad & Partner Pay (DAPP), Keep in Touch (KIT) days (Martin et al., 2014).
	• 58% of women taking PPL in 2013 were not aware of KIT days • Among coupled families who had a single baby born in April 2013 and where the father was working around the time of the baby's birth: • 36% of dads/partners took DAPP • 23% of working fathers said they had not heard about DAPP • Uptake was significantly higher amongst casually employed and self-employed fathers (~50% for both groups), reflecting their very limited access to employer-paid leave of any kind • Only 6% of fathers who applied for DAPP were aware of the provision that allowed employers to top-up DAPP to fathers' normal earnings, and only 1% said they had been paid a top-up

Transitioning Well case study 1

About a year ago we began supporting a new mum in a very supportive workplace. She had returned to work full time after parental leave but was struggling with her load and the immense pressure she felt at having to 'juggle it all'. She felt her only way out was a resignation. We were called in at this point to start the parental leave transition coaching process. She was mentally and physically exhausted and clearly in need of psychological support. In this case her health meant she could not continue to be at work. Her organisation did not accept her resignation; rather it insisted she take a leave of absence. She took another period of time off and focussed on her health and well-being. She spent time with her baby and sought the help she so desperately needed. She returned to work a couple of weeks ago, and we met with her to recommence the coaching program. We almost didn't recognise her. She looks healthy and happy. She has returned part time and will be ramping up slowly. We discussed the importance of having clear boundaries and non-negotiables so that she can show up in both work and life. It's a good news story with a positive outcome on all fronts. But the good news story in this case is uncommon. Not the story itself but the fact she has returned to the same workplace. What we see in a far more common form is women leaving, taking time off and if they return at all it's to another company. There are very few companies that actually realise that although the parental transition is challenging, it is also just that, a transition. And transition, when supported, will be quicker and with positive outcomes for all. The bottom line for business is that everyone wins when you have support procedures in place.

Transitioning Well case study 2

As part of our coaching we provide our clients with tools and strategies to support them with the parental leave transition. One tool we commonly use is a simplified version of cognitive behavioural therapy (CBT) called the three C's. It is used as a way of addressing the common thinking traps we can fall into, and as a way of helping clients to move towards more realistic and helpful thinking. One example of this is the belief that one new mum held around believing that she "should be able to manage it all". We know that there is a common misconception that "women should work as if they don't have children and parent as if they don't work". In our coaching we allow clients to firstly **'Catch'** the unhelpful thought, secondly to **'Check'** it (i.e. stop and think about what you're thinking – is it really true? Do you have any evidence to back it up?) and finally work with them to **'Change'** it (i.e. substitute it for a more realistic thought). By using the three C's tool with the foregoing example, it helped the client challenge her belief that "she should be able to manage it all" by looking at the evidence around this statement and the unrealistic/irrational nature of it. By changing this thought to something more helpful along the lines of "I can only do what I can do" or "nobody can manage it all the time", we worked with her to find practical examples of what managing it all actually means and better ways of thinking about her return-to-work experience. This is just one way of providing a strategy to help sift through unhelpful thoughts which can impede upon transition.

Implications for research and practice

As policy-makers continue to develop, implement and evaluate the system-level changes that are needed to support parents and their employing organisations to manage work-family conflict and promote work-family enrichment, collaboration among practitioners and researchers, such as the one embodied in the author team for this chapter, is critical.

Practitioners can assist working parents to understand and use the types of strategies we have discussed in this chapter through in-house training provision, through coaching programs such as those developed by our expert informants at Transitioning Well or via Employee Assistance Program support directed specifically towards managing the work-family interface. They can also assist managers and leaders to create working conditions that optimise new parents' transitions and improve processes and outcomes for organisations and help promote and/or facilitate evaluation of relevant interventions (Allen & Martin, 2017).

Researchers can increase the practical utility of their studies by increasing focus on interventions and 'what works'. Working with practitioners to discover and implement 'actionable' research outcomes is critical to research translation. As noted by a leading scholar, "we need research on interventions for practitioners to consult on potential solutions for organizational problems. There is a role for both academics and practitioners to play in conducting and publishing more research that is actionable" (Spector, 2019). Interventions promoting positive work-life transitions for new parents at work are an important area of focus in the well-being at work literature. A specific area of intervention research, that of Psychological Capital, resonates with many of the themes discussed in the interview about psychological resources and appears very pertinent for future research. Here we expand on this.

Psychological capital intervention research

The Psychological Capital Intervention (PCI; Luthans, Avey, Avolio, & Peterson, 2010) involves a series of exercises for each individual component of PsyCap (i.e. hope, efficacy, resilience and optimism), along with more integrative reflective exercises which are aimed at incorporating the development of the individual component training into an understanding and operationalisation of overall PsyCap (Luthans et al., 2010). Research has established the efficacy of the PCI in relation to enhanced PsyCap and improved job performance (Luthans et al., 2010). It has also been reported that the PCI can deliver quantifiable returns on investment. Preliminary utility analyses have estimated robust return of investment (ROI) in excess of 200% (see Luthans, Youssef, & Avolio, 2007).

The intervention centres on individuals identifying important and personally meaningful work-related goals which are framed to enhance 'agentic capacity' (Bandura, 2008). The goals are then 'stepped' into subgoals (Snyder, 2000), with the individual encouraged to generate multiple pathways to achieve the goal by identifying personal assets and strengths, and reflecting on past accomplishments and successes. Multiple goal pathway generation is theorized to increase participants' resilience as it enables them to 'bounce back' by selecting an alternative pathway, if an original pathway is blocked or met with challenge (Luthans et al., 2010). The final element of the PCI is directed towards optimism development by increasing participants' self-awareness of negative cognitions they may possess when faced with a challenge or problem at work. Based upon cognitive behavioural theory, the optimism development phase aims to counter negative cognitive distortions by encouraging participants to identify and challenge negative cognitions and replace these with more positively oriented and realistic expectations.

The practices reflected in the PCI (e.g., identifying meaningful goals and subgoals, acknowledging personal strengths) outside of work may foster work-family development, as a facet of enrichment (Morganson, Litano, & O'Neill, 2014). Thus, PsyCap gained via training is a form of work-family capital that promotes further 'gain spirals'. The exercises of the PCI could be adapted so as to encourage new parents to devise a specific work-family goal (e.g., to build up to working a three-day week), identify potential obstacles/challenges that may prevent attainment of the work-family goals (e.g., child is unwell, lack of childcare options), develop a list of personal assets and resources that can aid work-family goal achievement (e.g., flexible work hours, family support), and identify and challenge negative expectations and cognitions related to the work-family goal (e.g., "I am not going to be as effective at work now that I a parent"). Additionally, the small-group workshop-style format of the PCI could promote vicarious learning and modelling between new parents, who could share experiences and learn from one another regarding experiences of transitioning back to work following parental leave. Hence, we suggest the framework of the PCI is amenable to adaptation for a work-family focus, and specifically, a focus on the return-to-work transition following parental leave.

Given that psychological resources are critical to managing the transition that is the subject of this book, we see psychological capital as an important resource-boosting intervention for supporting new parents' return-to-work. Hence, research on the utility of interventions to develop/enhance PsyCap before and after parental leave appears to be a particularly promising direction for future research.

Conclusions

In this chapter we have explored a range of strategies new parents can use to support their return-to-work and positive adjustment to the changed work/family interface with new boundaries and related challenges to manage. By presenting multiple examples of 'resource management' we also provide work-family scholars with a deeper understanding of how conservation of resources theory and the construct of psychological capital are applied to real-world examples from new parents and the practitioners supporting them.

Key learnings from research	*Practical recommendations*
Resources that can support the transition back to work for new parents include time, money, technology, social networks and supports, psychological strengths.	All of these can be deployed in managing the transition optimally. Coaching can support new parents to break these down and consider strategies to manage them.
Resource loss offset and gain strategies are part of the transition and important for all stakeholders to understand.	Analysing these processes specifically before and after the transition can help to inform appropriate action plans and problem-focused coping strategies.
Psychological capital is a major resource to explore in the work-family management arena.	Interventions that aim to develop psychological capital during this transition can potentially reduce work-family conflict and increase work-family enrichment.

References

Allen, T. (2001). Family-supportive work environments: The role of organizational perceptions, *Journal of Vocational Behavior, 58*(3), 414–435.

Allen, T., & Martin, A. (2017). The work-family interface: A retrospective look at 20 years of research in JOHP. *Journal of Occupational Health Psychology, 22*(3), 259–272.

Archuleta, K. L. (2013). Couples, money, and expectations: Negotiating financial management roles to increase relationship satisfaction. *Marriage & Family Review, 49*(5), 391–411.

Australian Human Rights Commission. (2014). *Supporting working parents: Pregnancy and return to work national review*. Retrieved from https://www.humanrights.gov.au/our-work/sex-discrimination/projects/supporting-working-parents-pregnancy-and-return-work-national

Avey, J. B., Luthans, F., & Jensen, S. (2009). Psychological capital: A positive resource for combating stress and turnover. *Human Resource Management, 48*, 677–693.

Avey, J. B., Luthans, F., Smith, R. M., Palmer, N. F. (2010). Impact of positive psychological capital on employee wellbeing over time. *Journal of Occupational Health Psychology, 15*, 17–28.

Avey, J. B., Reichard, R. J., Luthans, F., & Mharte, K. H. (2011). Meta-analysis of the impact of positive psychological capital on employee attitudes, behaviors, and performance. *Human Resource Development Quarterly, 22*(2), 127–152.

Bakker, A. B., Hakanen, J. J., Demerouti, E., & Xanthopoulou, D. (2007). Job resources boost work engagement, particularly when job demands are high. *Journal of Educational Psychology, 99*, 274–284.

Bandura, A. (2008). An agentic perspective on positive psychology. In S. J. Lopez (Ed.), *Positive psychology: Exploring the best in people* (Vol. 1, pp. 167–196). Westport, CT: Greenwood Publishing.

Burnett, S. B., Gatrell, C. J., Cooper, C. L., & Sparrow, P. (2013). Fathers at work: A ghost in the organizational machine. *Gender, Work and Organizations, 20*(6), 632–646.

Ciciolla, L., & Luthar, S. S. (2019). Invisible household labor and ramifications for adjustment: Mothers as captains of households. *Sex Roles*, 1–20.

COPE. (2017). *Mental health care in the perinatal period: Australian clinical practice guideline.* Retrieved from https://www.clinicalguidelines.gov.au/portal/2586/mental-health-care-perinatal-period-australian-clinical-practice-guideline

de Janasz, S., Behson, S. J., Jonsen, K., & Lankau, M. J. (2013). Dual sources of support for dual roles: How mentoring and work-family culture influence work-family conflict and job attitudes. *International Journal of Human Resource Management, 24*(7), 14.

French, K. A., Dumani, S., Allen, T. D., & Shockley, K. M. (2018). A meta-analysis of work–family conflict and social support. *Psychological Bulletin, 144*(3), 284–314.

Goh, Z., Ilies, R., & Wilson, K. S. (2015). Supportive supervisors improve employees' daily lives: The role supervisors play in the impact of daily workload on life satisfaction via work–family conflict. *Journal of Vocational Behavior, 89*, 65–73.

Grzywacz, J. G., Carlson, D. S., Kacmar, K. M., & Wayne, J. H. (2007). A multi-level perspective on the synergies between work and family. *Journal of Occupational and Organizational Psychology, 80*(4), 559–574.

Hammer, L. B., Kossek, E. E., Yragui, N. L., Bodner, T. E., & Hanson, G. C. (2009). Development and validation of a multidimensional measure of Family Supportive Supervisor Behaviors (FSSB). *Journal of Management, 35*(4), 837–856. doi:10.1177/0149206308328510

Hao, J., Wu, D., Liu, L., Li, X., & Wu, H. (2015). Association between work-family conflict and depressive symptoms among Chinese female nurses: The mediating and moderating role of psychological capital. *International Journal of Environmental Research & Public Health, 12*, 6682–6699.

Heiligers, P. J. M., & Hingstman, L. (2000). Career preferences and the work–family balance in medicine: Gender differences among medical specialists, *Social Science & Medicine, 50*, 1235–1246.

Hobfoll, S. E. (1988). *The series in health psychology and behavioral medicine. The ecology of stress.* London: Hemisphere Publishing Corp.

Hobfall, S. E. (1989). Conservation of resources: A new attempt at conceptualizing stress. *American Psychologist, 44*, 513–524.

Hobfoll, S., Halbesleben, J., Neveu, J. P., & Westman, M. (2018). Conservation of resources in the organizational context: The reality of resources and their consequences. *Annual Review of Organizational Psychology & Organizational Behavior, 5*, 103–128.

Kossek, E., & Hammer, L. (2008). Work/life training for supervisors gets big results. *Harvard Business Review*, November, 36.

Ladge, J. J., & Greenberg, D. N. (2015). Becoming a working mother: Managing identity and efficacy uncertainties during resocialization. *Human Resource Management, 54*(6), 977–998.

Laney, E. K., Carruthers, L., Hall, M. L., & Anderson, T. (2014). Expanding the self: Motherhood and identity development in faculty women. *Journal of Family Issues, 35*(9), 1227–1251.

Lazarus, R. S., & Folkman, S. (1984). *Stress, appraisal, and coping*. New York: Springer.

Lee, J. Y., Seo, Y., Jeung, W., & Kim, J. (2017). How ambidextrous organizational culture affects job performance: A multilevel study of the medicating effect of psychological capital. *Journal of Management & Organization, 25*(6), 860–875. https://doi.org/10.1017/jmo.2017.38

Luthans, F., Avey, J. B., Avolio, B. J., Norman, S. M., & Combs, G. M. (2006). Psychological capital development: Toward a micro-intervention. *Journal of Organizational Behavior, 27*, 387–393.

Luthans, F., Avey, J. B., Avolio, B. J., & Peterson, S. (2010). The development and resulting performance impact of positive psychological capital. *Human Resource Development Quarterly, 21*(1), 41–66.

Luthans, F., Youssef, C. M., & Avolio, B. J. (2007). *Psychological capital: Developing the human competitive edge*. Oxford, UK: Oxford University Press.

Martin, A., Cooklin, A., & Dawkins, S. (2015). A multilevel intervention model for promoting work-family enrichment during early parenting. In R. Burke, K. Page, & C. Cooper (Eds.), *Flourishing in life, work, and careers* (pp. 119–140). Cheltenham, UK: Edward Elgar.

Martin, B., Baird, M., Brady, M., Broadway, B., Hewitt, B., Kalb, G. . . . Xiang, N. (2014). *Paid parental leave evaluation: Final report*. Canberra: Department of Social Services.

McKeown, G. (2014). *Essentialism: The disciplined pursuit of less*. New York: Random House.

Meyers, M. C., & Van Woerkom, M. (2017). Effects of a strengths intervention on general and work-related well-being: The mediating role of positive affect. *Journal of Happiness Studies, 18*(3), 671–689.

Mishra, P., Bhatnagar, J., Gupta, R., & Wadsworth, S. (2017). How work-family enrichment influence innovative work behavior: Role of psychological capital and supervisory support. *Journal of Management and Organization, 25*(1), 58–80. https://doi.org/10.1017/jom.2017.23

Morganson, V. J., Litano, M. L., & O'Neill, S. K. (2014). Promoting work-family balance though positive psychology: A practical review of the literature. *The Psychologist-Manager Journal, 17*(4), 221–244.

Nielson, T. D., Carlson, D., & Lankauc, M. J. (2001). The supportive mentor as a means of reducing work–family conflict. *Journal of Vocational Behavior, 59*(3), 364–381.

O'Neil, D. A., Hopkins, M. M., & Bilimoria, D. (2015). A framework for developing women leaders: Applications to executive coaching. *Journal of Applied Behavioural Science, 51*(2), 253–276.

Schieman, S., Ruppanner, L., & Milkie, M. A. (2018). Who helps with homework? Parenting inequality and relationship quality among employed mothers and fathers. *Journal of Family and Economic Issues, 39*(1), 49–65.

Siu, O. L. (2013). Psychological capital, work well-being, and work-life balance among Chinese employees: A cross-lagged analysis. *Journal of Personnel Psychology, 12*, 170–181.

Skinner, N., Hutchinson, C., & Pocock, B. (2012). *The big squeeze: Work, life and care in 2012 – The Australian work and life index*. Adelaide, SA: Centre for Work & Life.

Snyder, C. R. 2000. *Handbook of hope*. San Diego, CA: Academic Press.

Spector, P. (2019). *Bridging the academic-practice divide*. Retrieved 12 June 2019 from http:// paulspector.com/career-and-professional-issues/bridging-the-academic-practice-divide/

Underhill, C. M. (2006). The effectiveness of mentoring programs in corporate settings: Ameta-analytical review of the literature. *Journal of Vocational Behavior, 68*(2), 292–307.

Van Woerkom, M., & Meyers, M. C. (2019). Strengthening personal growth: The effects of a strengths intervention on personal growth initiative. *Journal of Occupational and Organizational Psychology, 92*(1), 98–121.

Wang, Y., Liu, L., Wang, J., & Wang, L. (2012). Work–family conflict and burnout among Chinese doctors: The mediating role of psychological capital. *Journal of Occupational Health, 54*, 232–240.

Wilkins, R. (2017). *The household, income and labour dynamics in Australia survey: Selected findings from waves 1 to 15*. Melbourne Institute, Applied Economic & Social Research, The University of Melbourne.

5 Return-to-work for fathers

A group with specific needs?

Marc Grau-Grau

Fatherhood as a transformative event

Reconfiguration of priorities

Becoming a parent is one of the most transformative experiences in an adult's life. Although this transformative experience has different and special meanings for each person, in general terms, it seems that fatherhood and motherhood come along with a reconfiguration of priorities and new daily dynamics, which in turn imply new dilemmas and new sources of conflict, but also new sources of enrichment (Greenhaus & Powell, 2006; Miller, 2017; Parker & Wang, 2013; Smith Russell, 1974).

These sources of enrichment, especially the ones related to fatherhood, have recently attracted the attention of policy-makers, the media and scholars from a wide variety of disciplines, such as medicine (Kotelchuck & Lu, 2017; Yogman & Garfield, 2016), sociology (Dermott, 2008; Kaufman, 2013), economy (Cools, Fiva, & Kirkebøen, 2015) and history (Bailey, 2010), among others. The benefits of fatherhood involvement are numerous, and although researchers have mainly focused on the impact of fathers on children's development (Flouri, 2005; Lamb, 2004; Sarkadi, Kristiansson, Oberklaid, & Bremberg, 2008), new evidence suggests that fatherhood involvement also has a positive impact on couples' satisfaction (Evertsson, Boye, & Erman, 2015) and gender equality (Schober, 2013), as well as fathers themselves (Eggebeen, Dew, & Knoester, 2010) and their jobs (Grau-Grau, 2017), as a result of fathers being more likely to have more altruistic relationships compared with men who have never been fathers.

Nevertheless, another significant part of the vibrant research about fathers has been focused on understanding the changing nature of fatherhood during the past decades, which has evolved from 'the moral teacher', to 'the distant breadwinner', and more recently from 'the sex role model' to 'the new nurturant father' (Lamb, 2000). Fathers are no longer seen purely as breadwinners. According to a recent study, 93% of Europeans agree that "men should take as much responsibility as women for home and children", and 78% agree that "fathers are as well-suited to look after their children as mothers" (Knight & Brinton, 2017). These new expectations, probably explained by the rise of dual-earner couples, which urge men to be more involved at home, at least in post-industrial societies, together with an increase in the caregiving ambition (Bear, 2019) of some men, have redefined in many contexts the importance of fatherhood in men's lives.

Returning to work: a new normal

Even though parenthood is probably the most transformative experience in an adult's life, together with the increasing importance of fatherhood in men's identity, the vast majority of fathers have one thing in common when they become fathers: they shortly return to work.

Despite the hidden costs of this imminent return-to-work, such as feelings of exclusion, frustration and exhaustion, which are described by very few scholars (Ives, 2014; Miller, 2010, 2011), the literature has largely centred on the positive side of fatherhood in men 's work trajectories, which is known as the *fatherhood premium*. It is indeed relevant to understand how parenthood is intertwined with work trajectories, and empirical evidence suggests that becoming a parent has opposite effects on men's and women's careers. While women seem to suffer a *motherhood penalty* in terms of hiring, salary and promotion (Budig & England, 2001; Correll, Benard, & Paik, 2007; Glauber, 2007), men apparently enjoy a *fatherhood premium* in their careers (Glauber, 2008; Hodges & Budig, 2010; Killewald & Gough, 2013; Knoester & Eggebeen, 2006), which is associated with an increase in hourly wages, annual earnings and promotions. Although the reasons that explain these opposite consequences for fathers and mothers are complex, varied and not always easy to disentangle, in short, and in organizational terms, it seems that the attributes associated with fatherhood are ostensibly closer to the notion of the *ideal worker* (Williams, 2001) than the ones associated with motherhood.

The notion of the *ideal worker* has not changed essentially in the past decades (Davies & Frink, 2014). An abstract (Acker, 1990) or ideal worker (Williams, 2001) is a person who is defined by having very few or minimal caring activities that require time, attention and energy, which could potentially distract him or her from their main activity: work. This existing notion of the ideal worker, which is shared by many contemporary organizations, is based on a scarcity approach (Goode, 1960), which assumes that time, energy and attention are limited. Thus, according to this approach, the more roles a person holds, the less of an ideal worker they will become.

In the case of fathers, it seems that despite their profound sense of having achieved something especial with their own paternity, the notion of the ideal worker described earlier and the ideals of hegemonic masculinity (Connell, 2005) continue to frame, guide and model men's expectations to be a breadwinner (Miller, 2010). These contrasting experiences generate a (new) and constant feeling of confusion, ambiguity, ambivalence and "asynchronicity" (Rotundo, 1985), which can be summarized as a clear gap between conduct and culture (Dermott, 2008; LaRossa, 1988).

Why are fathers a group with specific needs if they "have it all"?

Anyone can easily argue that if working fathers are a privileged group, who continue to enjoy the *fatherhood premium* in their organizations, why should it be necessary to consider them as a group with specific needs? The goal of this section is to present at least three main reasons why working fathers need to be considered a group with specific needs when they return to work after having a child. These three reasons can be summarized as: 1) fathers and fatherhood seem to be *in transition*, which implies a dynamic process of which organizations and governments need to be aware; 2) working fathers, far from being a homogenous group, are a heterogenous group (like men, women and all the human groups), and it seems that the fatherhood premium is experienced by "some" fathers, but not necessarily by involved fathers, a distinction that is not used with mothers, because it is assumed that mothers are always involved; and 3) because involved fathers seem to experience many barriers, especially regarding the use of parental leave and flexible polices for caring reasons, which can be summarized as a lack of legitimacy.

Fathers are in transition

Fathers are *in transition*. We are witnessing, in post-industrial societies, how the nature of what it means to be a father has evolved from a pure breadwinner with minimal care responsibilities, to an active *carer* with still important economic responsibilities, with some significant differences depending on the context (Blum et al., 2018; Bosch, Las Heras, Russo, Rofcanin, & Grau-Grau, 2018; Gregory & Milner, 2008). However, recent economic, demographic, technologic and cultural changes in post-industrial societies have modified the way in which people and families work, with important implications for men. One of the major social changes in the past decades has been the massive entry of women to the (paid) labour market, which has prompted men to reconsider their position in terms of care and home. Among other recent changes (Parker, 2015; Parker & Livingston, 2018), new studies have identified: 1) the rise of dual-income partners; 2) fathers being much more involved in childcare than they were some decades ago; 3) work-family balance being a new challenge for many working fathers, with similar levels of work-family conflict as mothers (Harrington, Van Deusen, & Humberd, 2011); 4) a substantial part of the population agreeing that it is equally important for babies to bond with their mother and their father; and 5) fathers seeing parenting as central to their identity. With this new situation, organizations and governments, as key actors of our contemporary times, should be aware of the *transitionality* of the nature of fatherhood. This relatively new call to fathers to be more nurturing, together with the prevalence of the notion of the ideal worker (Las Heras, Chinchilla, & Grau-Grau, 2019), which implies long hours and a strong focus on the paid work, generates new dilemmas, tensions and asynchronicities among working fathers, which seems to affect their full development due to potentially high levels of frustration (Ives, 2014).

Fathers are a (very) heterogenous group

The second reason why fathers should be considered a special group is that far from being a hegemonic group with univocal descriptions, fathers (and men) are a very heterogenous group. Gerson (2004), in fact, suggested that scholars should go beyond the two absolute categories of men and women, and use a gender lens to understand the heterogeneity within gender groups. Following Gerson's call, some scholars have made an effort to describe the different types of fathers that coexist at the same time. In short, scholars have found three types of fathers, which can be briefly and abstractly summarized as old fathers (breadwinners with low participation at home), fathers in transition (fathers who want to be involved at home but are not as involved as they want to be because of cultural, organizational and personal barriers), and new dads (active fathers who are as involved as they want to be). This triple categorization has taken different names in the literature, with small differences: traditional, conflicted and egalitarian (Harrington, Fraone, & Lee, 2017); old dads, new dads and superdads (Kaufman, 2013); traditional, transitionals and superdads (Cooper, 2000); conservatists, sharers and carers (Hanlon, 2012); and gender hegemonic order conformers, borderers and deviants (Tanquerel & Grau-Grau, 2019). Considering these typologies of fatherhood might be relevant for organizations and governments to understand the degree to which each group enjoys a *fatherhood premium* (Killewald, 2012), suffers a *flexibility stigma* (Rudman & Mescher, 2013) or has a true impact on their children's development or gender equality. For instance, it is interesting to understand the role played by the group in the middle (e.g., borderers, transitionals). Far from being neutral, a recent study (Tanquerel & Grau-Grau, 2019) suggests that with their invisible strategies, and by passing as an ideal worker to avoid stigma and to enjoy the *fatherhood premium*, fathers in the middle group are (unconsciously) reinforcing the hegemonic masculinity in the organizations, which means that they are complicit with the first group of fathers (e.g., traditional, old fathers, HGO conformers).

Fathers experience hidden barriers

Finally, a third reason why fathers should be considered a group with specific needs when they return to work after having a baby is that they systematically report hidden barriers that do not allow them to be as active as they may want to be. In other words, these barriers keep the distance between the new culture and the old conduct (Dermott, 2008; LaRossa, 1988). In a recent study (Tanquerel & Grau-Grau, 2019), various macro-meso-micro barriers experienced by working fathers were identified. The contextual barriers (macro level) comprised two sub-barriers: "poor political support" and "our common past", referring to the traditional view of masculinity and fatherhood, which can still be present in many men's attitudes and behaviors. The organizational barriers (meso level) comprised three main sub-barriers, which were labeled "poor management support", "poor peer support" and "anticipation of career consequences", which prevent fathers from using parental leave or other flexible arrangements. Finally, two main internalized barriers (micro level) were identified: the internalization of the ideal worker image and the internalization of traditional gender norms. A novelty of this study is the link between the categorization of fathers presented in the previous section and the perception of such barriers. According to Tanquerel and Grau-Grau (2019), the main difference between "new dads" and "fathers in transition" and "old dads" is that the new dads (or deviants) are the only group who have not internalized the notion of the ideal worker and traditional gender norms. In a similar vein, Haas and Hwang (2019) have done excellent work on disentangling how workplace culture and workplace structures are important barriers for fathers. As an example, the authors describe that *men's leave-taking was not a strategic concern for organizations*, providing five clear signs perceived by participants: 1) 'organizations lacked formal policy in regard to supporting fathers' leave-taking', 2) 'champions of fathers' leave-taking were absent', 3) 'there was no discussion about fathers' leave-taking', 4) 'management assumed that the law was sufficient encouragement for fathers to take leave', and 5) 'there was a limited understanding of what companies might gain by promoting fathers' leave-taking' (p. 65).

The access-use gap: from a problem perspective to a solution perspective

Understanding the barriers that (some) fathers might experience when considering work-family balance is important but not sufficient to reverse the perplexing underutilization of flexible work arrangements offered by organizations (Williams, Blair-Loy, & Berdahl, 2013) and the lack of use of parental-leave policies offered by governments (Blum, Koslowski, Macht, & Moss, 2018) to contemporary working fathers. To increase the use of flexible policies by fathers, it is important, firstly, to understand the *gendered practices* in gender-neutral policies (Moran & Koslowski, 2019), which means to understand the gender-specific practices when using flexible policies. In other words, it means to examine the gender differences in the use of neutral, flexible policies. Secondly, it is also important to move from a problem-focused perspective to a solution-focused perspective (Brandth & Kvande, 2019).

When policy design is crucial

Brighouse and Olin Wright (2008) proposed three kinds of publicly supported parental leave that can transform gender equality: 1) equality-impeding policies (e.g., unpaid leave), 2) equality-enabling polices (e.g., paid leave for families) and 3) equality-promoting policies (e.g., paid parental leave for individuals rather than families). According to the authors, the third type of policy, which is in fact a form of incentive or stimulation, is the only way to really change gender norms and reduce gender inequality in the private realm. These types of policies, which can be moderate (e.g., use-it-or-lose-it leave for fathers) or radical (e.g., amount of leave available to mothers was contingent on the amount of leave taken by father), create incentives that put pressure on men to move towards a more egalitarian distribution at home. Governments have made important efforts towards providing gender-neutral leave polices, but the reality is that the gendered practices embedded in each context lead to the uneven use of such policies between fathers and mothers. Thus, in a situation in which fathers want to be more active than they really can be (Parker & Livingston, 2018) and they have the option to use gender-neutral policies (Blum et al., 2018) but they do not use them because of a lack of legitimacy, it seems that the most appropriate solution is to rethink the way in which policies are designed in order to offer non-transferable and individualized and paid policies to the target population.

From entitlements to capabilities: Norway as a mirror

Brandth and Kvande (2019) suggest that research should move from describing the barriers to identifying the conditions for change. Their analyses of the father's quota in Norway since its introduction in 1993 found that today this individual, non-transferrable and well-paid policy has become a mature institution, and its use has become the norm among employed fathers. However, they alerted scholars that policies alone are not enough, and that it is important to understand each context in detail. In the Norway case, not only was the design of the policy adequate, but it was also accompanied by a very fertile context with high levels of cooperation between social partners and state authorities, and by the Norwegian workplace context, which is known as a micro-democracy, where those employed are considered the citizens of the company and have "the opportunity to influence how the company is organized and managed" (p. 46). In summary, Norway has become a leading country, not only because of its well-designed policies, which follow the suggestions of Brighouse and Olin Wright (2008), but also for having an adequate context, which allows for increasing the sense of entitlement to take parental leave among working fathers.

Practical recommendations

This chapter has examined why working fathers are a group with specific needs when they return to work after having a child and also identified some reasons why fathers, even though they are interested in using parental leaves and flexible polices in order to be more active, are reluctant to use such policies. This final section aims to present practical recommendations regarding what scholars, work organizations and governments can do to foster the use of policies and to ease fathers' return-to-work in order to achieve authentic work-family well-being.

Academia: gains, interventions and unexplored contexts

Despite the benefits of fatherhood involvement for gender equality, children's development and fathers themselves and their jobs, it seems that organizations have a limited understanding of what companies gain by promoting fatherhood involvement. Two types of research outputs could help at this point: 1) to prepare business cases to clearly demonstrate the benefits of fatherhood involvement for organizations and 2) to conduct interventions to compare the benefits for organizations of employing fathers vs. involved fathers. Scholars should also provide new empirical evidence not only about the barriers experienced by working fathers, but also about the *institution conversion factors* (Moran & Koslowski, 2019), which are defined as those aspects of employment that "can transform the knowledge of entitlement to work-family policies into the utilization of such policies, from policy to practice" (p. 122). Finally, it is necessary to conduct new research in unexplored contexts like the Global South, where the understanding of the changing nature of fatherhood and its implications is still very limited.

Organizations: new gaze, spaces, incentives and resources

Organizations play a crucial role because of the strong identification of many working fathers with the (old) notion of the ideal worker (Las Heras et al., 2019). A first suggestion for organizations is to encourage them to go beyond the scarcity approach, which assumes that time, energy and attention are limited, which in turn implies that abstract or ideal workers, which are unidimensional workers, are better than what I call *polyhedral* people – individuals with many faces (*poly*: many, *hedron*: faces, in classic Greek) – to a new expansion approach (Marks, 1977; Sieber, 1974), which assumes that time, energy and attention can be expandable. Thus, this new approach suggests that every person develops skills, abilities and resources in one role, which can be positively transferred to another one, enriching and improving the life of that person. So, according to this perspective, a person with more roles might be more productive than a unidimensional worker. Renewing this organizational gaze over working parents, both for mothers and fathers, is crucial for those organizations that want to offer authentic work-family well-being to their collaborators. Organizations should also comprehend that offering gender-neutral policies is not the best way to encourage men to use such policies because of the *gendered* practices in organizations and homes. If employers really believe that fatherhood involvement is beneficial for them, then they should design policies with a clear incentive and stimulus for fathers. We would also encourage organizations to open up new spaces and debates about masculinity and fatherhood in their workplaces. It would also be interesting to offer training programmes to managers and supervisors, in order to understand the benefits of an authentic work-family balance for men and women. When fathers take parental leave, empirical evidence suggests that this leave is short and part time, taken during quiet periods and in close contact with work, and that co-workers pick up the extra work (Haas & Hwang, 2019). Scholars suggest that companies should not consider co-workers as the way to deal with the extra work, because adding extra work to co-workers negatively affects the image of parental leave. If it is a priority and a strategic goal, new resources should be provided to hire temporary personnel.

Governments: innovations, debates and invisible productivity

Finally, governments, as organizations, should understand that gender-neutral polices are not the best solution if the goal is to foster the participation of men in childcare and household duties. As Brighouse and Olin Wright (2008) proposed, equality-promoting policies (offered to individuals rather than families, which are non-transferrable and well paid) are the most efficient way to encourage leave-taking by men. Governments should be not afraid to offer innovative policies, like in Iceland, which offers three months for mothers and three months for fathers, and, when fathers use this, rewards the family with three extra months (3+3+3). Today, daddy quotas have become a norm in some countries, especially in northern Europe (see also Chapter 11). However, the use of longer leave is still uncommon (O'Brien, 2009; Escot, Fernández-Cornejo, & Poza, 2014). New efforts could be made to encourage the use of longer leave and to reduce the gendered practices in such types of leave. Governments could also provide new spaces for men to discuss, debate and reflect on fatherhood. New governmental initiatives could also provide a new gaze through media campaigns of what it is to be "productive" in the twenty-first century. Usually, we only linked productivity with paid work, but fathers can also be productive at home. More research about the invisible rewards from fathers at home is also needed. Finally, governments, through their own health systems, should encourage the involvement of fathers from the perinatal period.

Key learnings from research	*Practical recommendations*
It seems that *organizations have a limited understanding of what companies gain* by promoting fatherhood involvement.	*Academia:* Two types of research outputs could help at this point: 1) to prepare *business cases* to clearly demonstrate the benefits of fatherhood involvement for organizations and 2) to conduct *interventions* to compare the benefits for organizations of employing fathers vs. involved fathers.
The *understanding* of the changing nature of fatherhood and its implications in non-European or American *contexts is still very limited.*	*Academia:* It is necessary to conduct *new research in unexplored contexts like the Global South.*
When fathers take parental leave, empirical evidence suggests that this *leave is short and part time, taken during quiet periods* and in close contact with work, and that *co-workers pick up the extra work.*	*Organizations:* Companies should not consider co-workers as the way to deal with the extra work, because adding extra work to co-workers negatively affects the image of parental leave. If the use of paternal leave is a priority and a strategic goal for companies, *new resources should be provided to hire temporary personnel.*
The *classic notion of ideal worker is still prevalent* in many contemporary organizations.	*Organizations: Renewing this organizational gaze over working parents*, both for mothers and fathers, is crucial for those organizations that want to offer authentic work-family well-being to their collaborators.

(*Continued*)

(Continued)

Key learnings from research	Practical recommendations
Gender-neutral policies are not the best solution if the goal is to foster the participation of men in childcare and household duties.	*Governments: Equality-promoting policies* (offered to individuals rather than families, which are non-transferrable and well paid) *are the most efficient way* to encourage leave-taking by men.
The *use of longer leave is still uncommon* among working fathers.	*Governments:* New efforts could be made to *encourage the use of longer leave* and to reduce the gendered practices in such types of leave. Governments could also provide new spaces for men to discuss, debate and reflect on fatherhood.
Involved fatherhood is positive for gender equality and couple satisfaction, and for fathers themselves and their jobs, but above all, it *is crucial for the social and cognitive development of children.*	*Governments:* Governments, through their own health systems, should *encourage the involvement of fathers from the perinatal period.*

References

Acker, J. (1990). Hierarchies, jobs, bodies: A theory of gendered organizations. *Gender & Society, 4*(2), 139–158.

Bailey, J. (2010). "A very sensible man": Imagining fatherhood in England c.1750–1830. *History, 95*(319), 267–292.

Bear, J. (2019). The caregiving ambition framework. *Academy of Management Review, 44*(1), 99–125. https://doi.org/10.5465/amr.2016.0424

Blum, S., Koslowski, A., Macht, A., & Moss, P. (2018). *International review of leave policies and research 2018.* Retrieved from www.leavenetwork.org

Bosch, M. J., Las Heras, M., Russo, M., Rofcanin, Y., & Grau-Grau, M. (2018). How context matters: The relationship between family supportive supervisor behaviours and motivation to work moderated by gender inequality. *Journal of Business Research, 82*, 46–55.

Brandth, B., & Kvande, E. (2019). Workplace support of fathers' parental leave use in Norway. *Community, Work & Family, 22*(1), 43–57. https://doi.org/10.1080/13668803.2018.1472067

Brighouse, H., & Olin Wright, E. (2008). Strong gender egalitarianism. *Politics & Society, 36*(3), 360–372. https://doi.org/10.1177/0032329208320566

Budig, M. J., & England, P. (2001). The wage penalty for motherhood. *American Sociological Review, 66*(2), 204–225.

Connell, R. W. (2005). *Masculinities* (2nd ed.). Cambridge: Polity Press.

Cools, S., Fiva, J. H., & Kirkebøen, L. J. (2015). Causal effects of paternity leave on children and parents. *The Scandinavian Journal of Economics, 117*(3), 801–828. https://doi.org/10.1111/sjoe.12113

Cooper, M. (2000). Being the "go-to guy": Fatherhood; masculinity; and the organization of work in Silicon Valley. *Qualitative Sociology, 23*(4), 379–405.

Correll, S. J., Benard, S., & Paik, I. (2007). Getting a job: Is there a motherhood penalty? *American Journal of Sociology, 112*(5), 1297–1339. https://doi.org/10.1086/511799

Davies, A. R., & Frink, B. D. (2014). The origins of the ideal worker: The separation of work and home in the United States from the market revolution to 1950. *Work and Occupations, 41*(1), 18–39. https://doi.org/10.1177/0730888413515893

Dermott, E. (2008). *Intimate fatherhood: A sociological analysis.* London, UK: Routledge.

Eggebeen, D. J., Dew, J., & Knoester, C. (2010). Fatherhood and men's lives at middle age. *Journal of Family Issues, 31*(1), 113–130. https://doi.org/10.1177/0192513X093 41446

Escot, L., Fernández-Cornejo, J. A., & Poza, C. (2014). Fathers' use of childbirth leave in Spain. The effects of the 13-day paternity leave. *Population Research and Policy Review, 33*(3), 419–453.

Evertsson, M., Boye, K., & Erman, J. (2015). *Fathers on call-A study on the sharing of care work among parents in Sweden: A mixed methods approach.* Retrieved from www.familiesandsocieties. eu/wp-content/uploads/2015/02/WP27EvertssonEtAl2015.pdf

Flouri, E. (2005). *Fathering and child outcomes.* West Sussex, UK: John Wiley & Sons Ltd.

Gerson, K. (2004). Understanding work and family through a gender lens. *Community, Work & Family, 7*(2), 163–178.

Glauber, R. (2007). Marriage and the motherhood wage penalty among African Americans, Hispanics, and Whites. *Journal of Marriage and Family, 69*(4), 951–961.

Glauber, R. (2008). Race and gender in families and at work the fatherhood wage premium. *Gender & Society, 22*(1), 8–30.

Goode, W. J. (1960). A theory of role strain. *American Sociological Review, 25*(4), 483–496.

Grau-Grau, M. (2017). *Work-family enrichment experiences among working fathers: Evidence from Catalonia.* Edinburgh, UK: University of Edinburgh.

Greenhaus, J. H., & Powell, G. N. (2006). When work and family are allies: A theory of work-family enrichment. *Academy of Management Review, 31*(1), 72–92. https://doi. org/10.5465/AMR.2006.19379625

Gregory, A., & Milner, S. (2008). Fatherhood regimes and father involvement in France and the UK. *Community, Work and Family, 11*(1), 61–84.

Haas, L., & Hwang, C. P. (2019). Policy is not enough: The influence of the gendered workplace on fathers' use of parental leave in Sweden. *Community, Work & Family, 22*(1), 58–76. https://doi.org/10.1080/13668803.2018.1495616

Hanlon, N. (2012). Care in masculinities studies. In *Masculinities, care and equality* (pp. 1–28). London: Palgrave Macmillan. https://doi.org/10.1057/9781137264879_1

Harrington, B., Fraone, J., & Lee, J. (2017). *The new dad: The career caregiving conflict.* Chestnut Hill, MA: Boston College Center for Work & Family.

Harrington, B., Van Deusen, F., & Humberd, B. (2011). *The New Dad: Caring, Committed and Conflicted.* Chestnut Hill, MA: Boston College Center for Work & Family.

Hodges, M. J., & Budig, M. J. (2010). Who gets the daddy bonus?: Organizational hegemonic masculinity and the impact of fatherhood on earnings. *Gender & Society, 24*(6), 717–745. https://doi.org/10.1177/0891243210386729

Ives, J. (2014). Men, maternity and moral residue: Negotiating the moral demands of the transition to first time fatherhood. *Sociology of Health & Illness, 36*(7), 1003–1019. https:// doi.org/10.1111/1467-9566.12138

Kaufman, G. (2013). *Superdads: How fathers balance work and family in the 21st century.* New York: NYU Press.

Killewald, A. (2012). A reconsideration of the fatherhood premium: Marriage, coresidence, biology, and fathers' wages. *American Sociological Review, 78*(1), 96–116. https://doi. org/10.1177/0003122412469204

Killewald, A., & Gough, M. (2013). Does specialization explain marriage penalties and premiums? *American Sociological Review, 78*(3), 477–502.

Knight, C. R., & Brinton, M. C. (2017). One egalitarianism or several? Two decades of gender-role attitude change in Europe, *122*(5), 1485–1532. Retrieved from www.journals.uchicago.edu.proxy.library.uu.nl/doi/pdfplus/10.1086/689814

Knoester, C., & Eggebeen, D. J. (2006). The effects of the transition to parenthood and subsequent children on men's well-being and social participation. *Journal of Family Issues*, *27*(11), 1532–1560. https://doi.org/10.1177/0192513X06290802

Kotelchuck, M., & Lu, M. (2017). Father's role in preconception health. *Maternal and Child Health Journal*, *21*(11), 2025–2039. https://doi.org/10.1007/s10995-017-2370-4

Lamb, M. E. (2000). The history of research on father involvement: An overview. *Marriage & Family Review*, *29*(2–3), 23–42. https://doi.org/10.1300/J002v29n02

Lamb, M. E. (2004). *The role of the father in child development*. Hoboken, NJ: John Wiley & Sons.

LaRossa, R. (1988). Fatherhood and social change. *Family Relations*, *37*(4), 451–457.

Las Heras, M., Chinchilla, N., & Grau-Grau, M. (2019). *The new ideal worker organizations between work-life balance, gender and leadership*. Berlin, Germany: Springer.

Marks, S. (1977). Multiple roles and role strain: Some notes on human energy, time and commitment. *American Sociological Review*, *42*(6), 921–936.

Miller, T. (2010). It's a triangle that's difficult to square: Men's intentions and practices around caring, work and first-time fatherhood. *Fathering*, *8*(3), 362–378. https://doi.org/10.3149/fth.0803.362

Miller, T. (2011). Falling back into gender? Men's narratives and practices around first-time fatherhood. *Sociology*, *45*(6), 1094–1109. https://doi.org/10.1177/0038038511419180

Miller, T. (2017). *Making sense of parenthood: Caring, gender and family Lives*. Cambridge, UK: Cambridge University Press.

Moran, J., & Koslowski, A. (2019). Making use of work–family balance entitlements: How to support fathers with combining employment and caregiving. *Community, Work & Family*, *22*(1), 111–128. https://doi.org/10.1080/13668803.2018.1470966

O'Brien, M. (2009). Fathers, parental leave policies, and infant quality of life: International perspectives and policy impact. *The Annals of the American Academy of Political and Social Science*, *624*(1), 190–213.

Parker, K. (2015). *5 facts about today's fathers*. Retrieved 10 March 2016 from http://pewrsr.ch/1kryvpJ

Parker, K., & Livingston, G. (2018). *7 facts about American dads*. Retrieved from www.pewresearch.org/fact-tank/2018/06/13/fathers-day-facts/

Parker, K., & Wang, W. (2013). *Modern parenthood. Roles of moms and dads converge as they balance work and family*. Washington, DC: Pew Research.

Rotundo, E. A. (1985). American fatherhood: A historical perspective. *American Behavioral Scientist*, *29*(1), 7–23.

Rudman, L. A., & Mescher, K. (2013). Penalizing men who request a family leave: Is flexibility stigma a femininity stigma? *Journal of Social Issues*, *69*(2), 322–340. https://doi.org/10.1111/josi.12017

Sarkadi, A., Kristiansson, R., Oberklaid, F., & Bremberg, S. (2008). Fathers' involvement and children's developmental outcomes: A systematic review of longitudinal studies. *Acta Paediatrica*, *97*(2), 153–158. https://doi.org/10.1111/j.1651-2227.2007.00572.x

Schober, P. S. (2013). The parenthood effect on gender inequality: Explaining the change in paid and domestic work when British couples become parents. *European Sociological Review*, *29*(1), 74–85. https://doi.org/10.1093/esr/jcr041

Sieber, S. D. (1974). Toward a theory of role accumulation. *American Sociological Review*, *39*(4), 567–578.

Smith Russell, C. (1974). Transition to parenthood: Problems and gratifications. *Journal of Marriage and Family*, *36*(2), 294–302.

Tanquerel, S., & Grau-Grau, M. (2019). Unmasking work-family balance barriers and strategies among working fathers in the workplace. *Organization*. https://doi.org/10.1177/1350508419838692

Williams, J. C. (2001). *Unbending gender: Why work and family conflict and what to do about it.* New York: Oxford University Press.

Williams, J. C., Blair-Loy, M., & Berdahl, J. L. (2013). Cultural schemas, social class, and the flexibility stigma. *Journal of Social Issues, 69*(2), 209–234.

Yogman, M., & Garfield, C. F. (2016). Fathers' roles in the care and development of their children: The role of pediatricians. *Pediatrics, 138*(1), e20161128. https://doi.org/10.1542/peds.2016-1128

6 Fathers and leave for parenting

How can we increase uptake?

Adrienne Burgess and Jeremy Davies

Our approach in this chapter is gendered. We consider fathers' aspirations and behaviour to be rooted in, and shaped by, traditional structures of gendered social institutions, especially government and the labour market, which assume that fathers have limited caregiving responsibilities (Haas & Russell, 2015) and which overlook their contribution to the health and psychosocial well-being of their families (Clapton, 2009). We adopt a gendered approach because the practice of parenting is overwhelmingly gendered, and it has long been understood that applying a gender-neutral approach to a gendered situation not only fails to dismantle gender inequalities but also exacerbates them (Buchy & Basaznew, 2005).

We draw mainly on policy and research in the UK, partly because we are based there and partly because the UK system is an exemplar of a jurisdiction that effectively prohibits fathers' early care-taking, thereby undermining women's economic and social advancement (Women & Equalities Committee, 2018) and confirming parenting as a remorselessly gendered activity. However, we also draw on international examples.

But before we explore barriers and catalysts relating to fathers' leave-taking, our objective needs clarification. In Germany, leave-taking by fathers has been introduced primarily as 'social investment': fathers are to contribute to the care of children so that the mother is better supported and family life runs more pleasantly. In Sweden, by contrast, the primary objective has long been gender equality (Auth & Martinek, 2017) (see also Chapter 7). It is that last objective which informs our interest in the topic and our recommendations in this chapter.

The power of the gender culture

Fathers' and mothers' decision-making relating to work and care is powerfully impacted by the 'gender culture' that frames it (Gasser, 2015). A 'progressive' or 'egalitarian' gender culture supports a dual earner model in which both partners have career trajectories and spend time away from the workplace to care for children, whereas a 'traditional' gender culture supports a male primary-earner model (Kil, Neels, & Vergauwen, 2016) and reserves leave for caretaking mainly for women. Swiss researchers have formalized indicators of these two approaches into an index, which has proven to be a high-ranking predictor of fathers' time spent on interactive care (Gasser, 2015).

Socio-cultural norms are key and, in the UK, are still largely traditional as far as parenting is concerned. In young children's picture books, fathers are significantly less likely to appear than mothers, to be mentioned at all, to be depicted in or around the home or involved in any kind of domestic activity, to appear with their children or be involved in physical contact with them or be portrayed as expressing any emotion (Adams, Walker, & O'Connell, 2011). Parenting guides (Gregory & Milner, 2008), magazines (Sunderland, 2000, 2006) and government parenting information (Clapton, 2014) cast fathers in a clearly secondary role to mothers, often emphasizing men's alleged lack of 'natural' parenting skills. The gender composition of the Early Childhood Education and Care Workforce (which includes staff working in nurseries, preschool centres and kindergartens, as well as self-employed childminders) of which only 1.8% of nursery nurses and assistants are male (Bonetti, 2019), sends out a clear signal that caring for children is women's work (Cameron, 2006). Health, education and family services focus on mothers' caregiving to the exclusion of fathers' (Burgess & Davies, 2017) and even service providers who are theoretically seeking to engage with fathers communicate unconscious beliefs about their non-relevance (Symonds, 2015). An analysis of newspaper articles about 'home dads' (also known as 'stay-at-home-dads' or 'primary caregiver fathers') found that, even there, the traditional hegemonic masculine ideal remained a 'forceful presence' (Locke, 2014). And while an analysis of high-profile 'family' films found some fathers undertaking more 'maternal' roles, other gender stereotypes remained in place: mothers did not take up paternal roles (Chang-Kredl, 2015). In video games, traditional hegemonic patriarchal values were inherent in all the representations of fatherhood studied (Lucat, 2017). The Advertising Standards Authority points to the widespread representation of fathers as bumbling and incompetent (ASA, 2017), and a government minister who had hoped to introduce more equal parental leave in the early 2000s found herself hamstrung by the dominant media narrative, which at the time focused on 'absent fathers' who allegedly 'refused to pay child support' (Hewitt, 2014, cited by Moss & O'Brien, 2019).

Public attitudes, which shape and are shaped by the gender culture, are critical. According to the most recent British Social Attitudes Survey, 54% of the population (Taylor & Scott, 2018) think mothers should take all or most of the parenting leave, with only 30% believing couples should share it equally (the rest were not decided; none stated that fathers should take all or most of it). When asked to rate preferentially a number of care options for preschoolers, including the 'home-dad' option in a previous BSA survey, respondents awarded 'home dads' the lowest approval rating of all (Scott & Clery, 2013).

Redesigning parenting leave

An important determinant of the gender culture is parenting leave design. In the UK, this is strongly 'maternalist'. Employed British mothers are entitled to 52 weeks' maternity leave (39 paid; the first six weeks at 90% of salary), plus holiday accrued, while fathers get two weeks' paternity leave, paid at a statutory rate of £140.98 per week, or 90% of salary, whichever is lower. The only other paid statutory leave a British father can access is maternity leave and pay transferred to him by his partner under limited circumstances. This transferred maternity leave was mis-named by the administration that introduced it as 'shared parental leave' ('SPL') – mis-named, because the universally agreed definition of parental leave is a 'quota' of leave to which each parent is individually and separately entitled (Moss & O'Brien, 2019). 'SPL', being transferred maternity leave, requires both partners' work histories and leave eligibilities to be taken into account, with the result that only a minority of couples (3:7) actually qualifies, and take-up will necessarily be low. When introducing the system, the government itself estimated likely take-up as being in the range of 2–8% (Moss & O'Brien, 2019). Nothing since has indicated that it was wrong: a 2019 Freedom of Information request to HMRC established that, in 2018, only 3.8% of eligible fathers had used the entitlement.[1] (With such low take-up predicted, one might wonder why the government bothered with the policy at all.)

Constraints on fathers' uptake of SPL are legion. As well as eligibility limitations, the complexity of the system renders it incomprehensible to many parents (and even to some employers), and this in itself is a barrier to take-up (Hacohen, Likki, Londakova, & Rossiter, 2018). Next – and again partly because of the complexity – awareness of the policy is extremely low (Hacohen et al., 2018), and fathers who don't know about it are unlikely to ask for it. Fourth, because the mother can use the leave herself, there is no incentive for the father to use any; substantial uptake of parenting leave by fathers is only found where the leave is lost to the family if the father does not take it (Moss & O'Brien, 2019).

Other than ineligibility, the greatest barrier to take-up is undoubtedly the level of shared parental *pay* (Working Families, 2019). An eligible father is paid by the state at a *maximum* of £148.60 per *week* (as with paternity pay). This is far lower than the minimum wage and even lower than an unemployment benefit. Fathers' take-up would be increased if their employers were to 'top up' the pay level, but enhancing the pay is left to the employers' discretion, and so far they have been less likely to 'top up' shared parental pay than to top up maternity (or even paternity) pay (Working Families, 2016).

The parent who earns more than their partner will hardly ever take substantial leave, because this will penalize their family financially. In the UK, as elsewhere, the substantial gender pay gap ensures that almost all men earn more than their female partner when becoming parents, a divergence which grows as new mothers take almost all the leave and then drop out of the workforce or work shorter hours: among UK families with at least one working parent, only one mother in five (22%) brings home even *half* the family income and, even in households in which both parents are in paid work, only one third of the mothers contribute half or more (Cory & Stirling, 2015).

Iceland's parenting leave design most nearly promotes gender equality. To care for young children, Iceland provides three months of relatively well-paid leave to mothers and the same to fathers, plus three months for the family to share as they will (Eydal & Gíslason, 2016). The three 'daddy/mummy months' are not transferable: they are 'use-it-or-lose-it' periods of leave, which, if not taken by the eligible individual, are lost to the family. In Iceland, the gender pay gap is recognised as inhibiting fathers' use of leave and is being addressed as a separate and related issue. The country has the narrowest gender pay gap in the world (World Economic Forum, 2019), and 80% of Icelandic fathers of newborns now take substantial leave (Eydal & Gíslason, 2016).

But a government reserving well-paid leave for fathers is, in itself, no guarantee of success. In Japan, fathers have an individual, non-transferable, entitlement to 11 months' paid leave to be taken in the first year, yet uptake remains negligible. This may be largely because mothers in Japan are also entitled to 11 months, so the family is not significantly disadvantaged if the father does not use his leave.[2] Workplace hostility in Japan to fathers' taking leave is said to be endemic and is likely to be erecting significant barriers (Nakazato, 2019). Japan's level of gender inequality is one of the worst in the developed world and continues to deteriorate (World Economic Forum, 2019).

Shifting workplace culture

This brings us to the final common barrier to fathers' use of leave for parenting: workplace culture. While the 'right' policy (well-paid leave for new fathers in the first year) must be in place within an organization, this is only the beginning. Leadership must be from the top, with middle management trained to address male as well as female employees' parenthood. Line managers' attitudes and behaviour may be particularly influential (Burnett, Gatrell, Cooper, & Sparrow, 2013; Hatter, Vinter, & Williams, 2002), but these may well be negative: managers tend to hold traditional views (Burnett et al., 2013), whilst line managers align themselves with what they perceive to be their employer's perspective (this tendency, unless challenged by clear leadership, to emphasize presenteeism and cost reduction), rather than with that of an employee father (Seddon, 2010). A qualitative UK study found that line managers expect mothers, but not fathers, to arrange their working hours to suit the needs of their young families (Smithson, Lewis, Cooper, & Dyer, 2004). And a study that used a 'vignette' method to assess managers' attitudes to fictitious fathers and mothers with equivalent skills and qualifications seeking part-time employment for family reasons, found the fathers were regarded with greater suspicion and judged less committed to their work (Kelland, 2017).

For work/family policies to support fathers' caretaking they must be *differentially* promoted to men inside an organization, as in wider society. A Belgian employer who did so recorded a dramatic increase in male employees taking up parental leave (EU, 2008). Additionally, evaluation needs to 'drill down' into the detail. For example, when flexible working was available to male and female employees in accountancy firms, both sexes availed themselves of the opportunity to a similar extent. However, analysis revealed that women who worked flexibly or part time typically did so to facilitate caring commitments at around age 30, damaging their career prospects. Men who worked flexibly typically did so ten years later, and not primarily for family care, with no negative impact on career/salary as seniority had already been achieved. This gendered pattern of take-up left management attitudes and the gender pay gap in the organization unchanged (Smithson et al., 2004).

Leading from the top

What else can be done to transform organizational culture? A small number of mainly high-profile and major employers (including Aviva, Hewlett Packard Enterprise, Volvo, Diageo) are "leap frogging" inadequate government policies to offer fully paid six months' parenting leave to both male and female employees. In Aviva, take-up internationally has been substantial, with extensive media coverage helping to change the company culture, so that take-up by fathers is perceived to have the organization's blessing. But these companies are outliers and do not impact policies in smaller and medium-sized companies, or in the 'gig' economy. For change to happen, government must take the lead. As one researcher puts it: 'If the state doesn't demand it, then the corporate sector won't do it unless they see a market advantage. Social policies only ever come in from the state – once they are in, things start to change slowly' (Browne, 2015).

To date, the UK government has resisted calls from such august bodies as the Women and Equalities Select Committee (Women & Equalities Committee, 2016, 2018) and the Trades Union Congress[3] to re-design its parenting leave system and introduce a substantial 'fathers' quota' of well-paid 'use-it-or-lose-it' leave for fathers to care for their children *solo* in the first year. Both *solo* and 'the first year' are important. Care-taking patterns established early on are moderately likely to endure (Norman, Elliot, & Fagan, 2014), and once a father has cared for his child 'home alone' for an extended period, his greater contribution to 'housework and childcare' tends to endure (Bünning, 2017; O'Brien & Wall, 2017). Mothers are more willing to return to work before the end of the first year, if their child is being cared for by his or her father (Barnes, Leach, Sylva, Stein, & Malmberg, 2006); and the mother's return-to-work boosts her earnings in the short and longer term. In Sweden, it has been estimated that with each additional month of parental leave taken by the father, the mother's earnings increase by 6.7% (Johannson, 2010). And in the UK, a survey of 773 working fathers found 47% of those who worked flexibly and shared substantially in childcare duties reported that their partner had progressed in her career since having children, compared with only 26% where the father had not worked flexibly or contributed much to childcare (Frith, 2016). Within a family, the ratio of the length of the mother's vs. the father's leave is crucial: when this is small, the mother's earnings are boosted; when it is large, they are not (Andersen, 2018).

Hope for the future

There is hope. Already, younger people in the UK are far more positive than older people about the idea of new parents sharing leave equally (Scott & Clery, 2013), and a recent survey found 25% of employed fathers said that in their company, taking three months' leave would not impact negatively on their careers (Birkett &

Forbes, 2019). The introduction of statutory, well-paid 'daddy months' in the UK would quickly impact on public attitudes. In Germany, for example, following the introduction of a 'father's quota' of well-paid 'use-it-or-lose-it' parenting leave, a study of grandparents' attitudes found they had quickly become far more positive about fathers' caregiving (Unterhofer & Wrohlich, 2017).

The UK government now requires larger companies to report annually on their gender pay gap, and moves are afoot to require them to make visible, on their websites, their parenting leave regimes and other family-related policies. In the recommendations of our 'Cash or Carry' report (Burgess & Davies, 2017), we called for this reporting to be extended to include data on fathers' and mothers' use of leave and other 'family-friendly' policies within the organization, so that the 'care gap' can be identified. Once such data are collected and published, progress can be measured and the mere introduction of it would change the national conversation on gender, work and care.

Changes in other domains which affect families' experiences of parenting are also important. Addressing the gender imbalance of the early childhood education and care workforce is an example: fathers will feel welcome and accepted as caregivers only when male professionals regularly undertake this role. Such men's presence in the workforce will change public attitudes – including those of children, whose perception of normative caretaking will be transformed. The Fatherhood Institute's MITEY (Men in the Early Years) campaign, which has received 'seed funding' from the Department of Education, is beginning to address this.[4]

Cultural stereotypes that discount or belittle men's capacities as caretakers are also being challenged through regulation. New guidance on gender-stereotyping from the Advertising Standards Authority (ASA, 2018) promises to rule 'unacceptable' advertisements that depict 'a man or a woman failing to achieve a task specifically because of their gender, e.g., a man's inability to change nappies'. It is now time for the Equalities and Human Rights Commission to follow this lead and rule such gender stereotyping unacceptable in the next edition of the Equalities Act Guidance. Once belittling male caretaking is recognized as a form of sex discrimination, such instruments as the Gender Equality Impact and Risk Assessments will need to include it, as will unconscious bias training. This will have a profound impact on organizational practices and cultures in both public and private sectors.

Conclusions

In this chapter we have outlined domains, often interlinked, which erect barriers to fathers' leave-taking: the gender pay gap; parenting leave design and remuneration; public attitudes; workplace cultures and cultural narratives. While all need to be tackled, in our view re-design of the parenting leave system is the most important because gender inequality is grounded in it. Until fathers have their own right to well-paid leave to care for their young children *solo* – ideally when their partner is in work, education or training – fathers' uptake of parenting leave will remain limited, and gender equality a distant dream.

Key learnings from research	*Practical recommendations*
• Prevailing 'gender cultures' have a powerful impact on mothers' and fathers' decision-making around work and care. Socio-cultural norms are key and, in the UK, are still largely traditional as far as parenting is concerned. • An important determinant of the gender culture is parenting leave design. In the UK, this is strongly 'maternalist'. • Ineligibility, low pay, complexity and lack of awareness are all obstacles to men's take-up of shared parental leave – which is, importantly, mis-named as it is, in fact, a form of transferable maternity leave. • The gender pay gap is a key factor that must be considered in parenting leave design. The higher earner in a family will hardly ever take substantial leave, because this will penalize their family financially; in the vast majority of cases, the (expectant) father is the higher earner.	• The parenting leave systems which are most effective in encouraging gender equality are those which give each parent substantial (but not excessive), well-paid leave in the first year, which is individual to them and lost to the family if not taken. The UK government should introduce a substantial 'fathers' quota' of well-paid 'use-it-or-lose-it' leave for fathers to care for their children *solo* in the first year. • The government's policy of requiring larger companies to report on their gender pay gaps should be extended to include data on fathers' and mothers' use of leave and other 'family-friendly' policies within the organization, so that the 'care gap' can be identified. • State-funded family services should be required to deliver mainstream services that address themselves squarely at fathers as well as mothers; a key step towards achieving this should be for the government to focus on correcting the gender imbalance of the early childhood education and care workforce. • The Equalities and Human Rights Commission should take its lead from the Advertising Standards Authority and make clear that gender stereotyping about men's (lack of) capacity as caregivers is unacceptable, in the next edition of the Equalities Act Guidance.

Notes

1 http://hrnews.co.uk/%EF%BB%BFdads-want-bigger-childcare-roles-but-just-1-in-10-take-shared-parental-leave/
2 Wage replacement during the second six months of a parent's leave in Japan is 50%, compared with 75% for the first six months, so the family should be better remunerated if the father takes the second half of the leave.
3 www.tuc.org.uk/news/tuc-calls-overhaul-shared-parental-leave
4 https://miteyuk.org/

References

Adams, M., Walker, C., & O'Connell, P. (2011). Invisible or involved fathers? A content analysis of representations of parenting in young children's picturebooks in the UK. *Sex Roles*, *65*(3–4), 259–270. https://doi.org/10.1007/s11199-011-0011-8. Retrieved from www.academia.edu/838078/Invisible_or_involved_fathers_A_content_analysis_of_representations_of_parenting_in_young_children_s_picturebooks
Andersen, S. H. (2018). Paternity leave and the motherhood penalty: New causal evidence. *Journal of Marriage and Family*, *80*(5), 1125–1143. https://doi.org/10.1111/jomf.12507. Retrieved from https://onlinelibrary.wiley.com/doi/abs/10.1111/jomf.12507

ASA. (2017). *Depictions, perceptions and harm: A report on gender stereotypes in advertising.* London: Advertising Standards Authority. Retrieved from www.asa.org.uk/asset/FA0CDD1A-6453-42FF-BD2892D70C53C5E7/

ASA. (2018). *Advertising guidance on depicting gender stereotypes likely to cause harm or serious or widespread offence.* London: Advertising Standards Authority. Retrieved from www.asa.org.uk/uploads/assets/uploaded/f39a881f-d8c9-4534-95f180d1bfe7b953.pdf

Auth, D., & Martinek, H. (2017). Social investment or gender equality? Aims, instruments, and outcomes of parental leave regulations in Germany and Sweden. In D. Auth, J. Hergenhan, & B. Holland-Cunz (Eds.), *Gender and family in European economic policy: Developments in the new millennium* (pp. 153–176). Cham, Switzerland: Springer International Publishing. https://doi.org/10.1007/978-3-319-41513-0_8

Barnes, J., Leach, P., Sylva, K., Stein, A., & Malmberg, L.-E. (2006). Infant care in England: Mothers' aspirations, experiences, satisfaction and caregiver relationships. *Early Child Development and Care, 176*(5), 553. http://doi.org/10.1080/03004430500317408

Birkett, H., & Forbes, S. (2019). *Research findings from The Equal Parenting Project – Dr Holly Birkett and Dr Sarah Forbes, University of Birmingham.* Paper presented at the Equal Parenting Campaign Forum, London.

Bonetti, S. (2019). *The early years workforce in England: An analysis using the Labour Force Survey.* London: Education Policy Institute. Retrieved from https://epi.org.uk/publications-and-research/the-early-years-workforce-in-england/

Browne, J. (2015). The corporate father. In W. Chavkin, J.-A. Navarro, & M. C. Inhorn (Ed.), *Globalized fatherhood.* Oxford: Berghahn Books.

Buchy, M., & Basaznew, F. (2005). Gender-blind organizations deliver gender-biased services: The case of Awasa Bureau of Agriculture in Southern Ethiopia. *Gender, Technology and Development, 9*(2), 235–251. https://doi.org/10.1177/097185240500900204. https://journals.sagepub.com/doi/abs/10.1177/097185240500900204

Bünning, M. (2017). What happens after the "daddy months"? Fathers' involvement in paid work, childcare, and housework after taking parental leave in Germany. *European Sociological Review, 31*(6), 738–748. https://doi.org/10.1093/esr/jcv072

Burgess, A., & Davies, J. (2017). *Cash or carry? Fathers combining work and care in the UK (Full Report).* Marlborough: Fatherhood Institute. Retrieved from www.fatherhoodinstitute.org/wp-content/uploads/2017/12/Cash-and-carry-Full-Report-PDF.pdf

Burnett, S. B., Gatrell, C. J., Cooper, C. L., & Sparrow, P. (2013). Fathers at work: A ghost in the organizational machine. *Gender, Work and Organization, 20*(6), 632–646. http://doi.org/10.1111/gwao.12000

Cameron, C. (2006). Men in the nursery revisited: Issues of male workers and professionalism. *Contemporary Issues in Early Childhood, 7*(1), 68–79. https://doi.org/10.2304/ciec.2006.7.1.68

Chang-Kredl, S. (2015). Constructing childcare in three American comedic films. *Child Care in Practice, 21*(4), 324–339. https://doi.org/10.1080/13575279.2015.1027174

Clapton, G. (2009). How and why social work fails fathers: Redressing an imbalance, social work's role and responsibility. *Practice, 21*(1), 17–34. https://doi.org/10.1080/09503150902745989

Clapton, G. (2014). *Where's dad? A father-focused exploration of national and local authority publicity for family services.* Edinburgh, UK: University of Edinburgh.

Cory, G., & Stirling, A. (2015). *Who's breadwinning in Europe? A comparative analysis of maternal breadwinning in Great Britain and Germany.* London: Institute for Public Policy Research. Retrieved from www.ippr.org/files/publications/pdf/whos-breadwinning-in-europe-oct2015.pdf?noredirect=1

EU. (2008, October 22–23). *Seminar reports*. Paper presented at the Parental Leave System in Iceland, Reykjavik.

Eydal, G. B., & Gíslason, I. V. (2016). Iceland. In A. Koslowski & S. Blum (Eds.), *12th international review of leave policies and related research 2016*. International Network on Leave Policies and Research. Retrieved from www.leavenetwork.org/fileadmin/Leavenetwork/Annual_reviews/2016_Full_draft_20_July.pdf

Frith, B. (2016, December 5). Women progress when childcare duties are shared more equally. *HR (Magazine)*. Retrieved from www.hrmagazine.co.uk/article-details/women-progress-when-childcare-duties-are-shared-more-equally

Gasser, M. (2015). The role of gender culture in predicting fathers' time-use: Evidence from subnational disparities in Switzerland. *Family Science, 6*(1), 259–269. https://doi.org/10.1080/19424620.2015.1082333

Gregory, A., & Milner, S. (2008). Fatherhood regimes and father involvement in France and the UK. *Community, Work & Family, 11*(1), 61–84. https://doi.org/10.1080/13668800701419391

Haas, L., & Russell, G. (2015). The social construction of men as caring fathers: Implications for gender equality. In M. Flood & R. Howson (Eds.), *Engaging men in building gender equality*. Newcastle upon Tyne, UK: Cambridge Scholars Publishing.

Hacohen, R., Likki, T., Londakova, K., & Rossiter, J. (2018). *Return to work: Parental decision making* London: H.M. Government. Retrieved from https://assets.publishing.service.gov.uk/government/uploads/system/uploads/attachment_data/file/705898/Return_to_work-parental_decision_making.pdf

Hatter, W., Vinter, L., & Williams, R. (2002). *Dads on dads: Needs and expectations at home and at work*. Manchester: Equal Opportunities Commission. Retrieved from www.fatherhoodinstitute.org/uploads/publications/281.pdf

Hewitt, P. (2014). Gender equality. In C. Clarke (Ed.), *The 'Too Difficult' box: The big issues politicians can't crack*. London: Biteback Publishing.

Johannson, E.-A. (2010). *The effect of own and spousal parental leave on earnings*. Uppsala, Sweden: Institute of Labour Market Policy Evaluation. Retrieved from www.ifau.se/globalassets/pdf/se/2010/wp10-4-The-effect-of-own-and-spousal-parental-leave-on-earnings.pdf

Kelland, J. (2017). *'Fatherhood forfeits' and 'motherhood penalties' – An exploration of UK management selection decision making of parent applicants*. Paper presented at the CIPD Applied Research Conference 2016: The Shifting Landscape of Work and Working Lives, London. Retrieved from www.cipd.co.uk/Images/fatherhood-forfeits-and-motherhood-penalties_2016-an-exploration-of-uk-management-selection-decision-making-on-parent-applicants_tcm18-20005.pdf

Kil, T., Neels, K., & Vergauwen, J. (2016). Gender inequality in the division of housework over the life course: A European comparative perspective. In K. M. Dimitri Mortelmans, E. Alofs, & B. Segaert (Eds.), *Seminar, London School of Economics*. London: Elgar Online.

Locke, A. (2014). Masculinity, subjectivities & caregiving in the British press: The case of the stay-at-home father. In E. Podnieks (Ed.), *Pops in pop culture: Fatherhood, masculinity, and the new man*. London: Palgrave Macmillan.

Lucat, B. (2017). *Playing with patriarchy: Fatherhood in BioShock: Infinite, the last of us, and the witcher 3: Wild Hunt*. Paper presented at the DiGRA 2017, Melbourne.

Moss, P., & O'Brien, M. (2019). United Kingdom: Leave policy and an attempt to take a new path. In P. Moss, A.-Z. Duvander, & A. Koslowski (Eds.), *Parental leave and beyond: Recent international developments, current issues and future directions*. Bristol: Policy Press.

Nakazato, H. (2019). Japan: Leave policy and attempts to increase fathers' take-up. In A.-Z. Duvander, A. Koslowski, & Peter Moss (Ed.), *Parental leave and beyond: Recent international developments, current issues and future directions*. Bristol: Policy Press.

Norman, H., Elliot, M., & Fagan, C. (2014). Which fathers are the most involved in taking care of their toddlers in the UK? An investigation of the predictors of paternal involvement. *Community, Work and Family, 17*(2), 163–180. https://doi.org/10.1080/13668803.2013.862361

O'Brien, M., & Wall, K. (2017). *Comparative perspectives on work-life balance and gender equality: Fathers on leave alone* (Vol. 6). London: Springer.

Scott, J., & Clery, E. (2013). *Gender roles: An incomplete revolution?* London: National Centre for Social Research. Retrieved from www.bsa.natcen.ac.uk/latest-report/british-social-attitudes-30/gender-roles/introduction.aspx

Seddon, V. (2010). *Fathers' experiences of paid work, care, and domestic labour.* PhD Thesis. Cardiff: Cardiff University. Retrieved from https://orca.cf.ac.uk/54130/1/U516706.pdf

Smithson, J., Lewis, S., Cooper, C., & Dyer, J. (2004). Flexible working and the gender pay gap in the accountancy profession. *Work, Employment and Society, 18*(1), 115–135. https://doi.org/10.1177/0950017004040765

Sunderland, J. (2000). Baby entertainer, bumbling assistant and line manager: Discourses of fatherhood in parentcraft texts. *Discourse and Society, 11*(2), 249–274. Retrieved from https://is.muni.cz/el/1423/jaro2010/GEN141/um/Sunderland_parentcraft_texts.pdf

Sunderland, J. (2006). 'Parenting' or 'mothering'? The case of modern childcare magazines. *Discourse and Society, 17*(4), 503–528. https://doi.org/10.1177/0957926506063126

Symonds, J. (2015). *'Have you got a partner as well?' Engaging fathers and other carers with parenting services: A study using conversation analysis.* PhD Thesis. University of Bristol. Retrieved from http://ethos.bl.uk/OrderDetails.do?uin=uk.bl.ethos.686417

Taylor, E. A., & Scott, J. (2018). Gender: New consensus or continuing battleground? In D. Phillips, J. Curtice, M. Phillips, & J. Perry (Eds.) *British social attitudes: The 35th report.* London: The National Centre for Social Research. Retrieved from www.bsa.natcen.ac.uk/latest-report/british-social-attitudes-35/gender.aspx

Unterhofer, U., & Wrohlich, K. (2017). *Fathers, parental leave and gender norms.* Berlin: DIW Berlin, German Institute for Economic Research. Retrieved from http://ftp.iza.org/dp10712.pdf

Women & Equalities Committee. (2016). *Gender pay gap.* London: House of Commons. Retrieved from www.publications.parliament.uk/pa/cm201516/cmselect/cmwomeq/584/58402.htm

Women & Equalities Committee. (2018). *Fathers and the workplace.* London: House of Commons. Retrieved from https://publications.parliament.uk/pa/cm201719/cmselect/cmwomeq/358/358.pdf

Working Families. (2016). *Modern families' index 2016.* London: Working Families. Retrieved from www.workingfamilies.org.uk/wp-content/uploads/2016/02/Modern-Families-Index-2016.pdf

Working Families. (2019). *Modern families index 2019.* London: Working Families. Retrieved from www.workingfamilies.org.uk/wp-content/uploads/2019/01/BH_MFI_Report_2019_Full-Report.PDF.FINAL_.pdf

World Economic Forum. (2019). *The global gender gap report 2018.* World Economic Forum. Retrieved from www3.weforum.org/docs/WEF_GGGR_2018.pdf

7 Work-family integration and gender equality

How Nordic countries lead the way

Gayle Kaufman

The five Nordic countries – Denmark, Finland, Iceland, Norway, and Sweden – are perennially on lists of "most gender-equal countries" (Zalis, 2018). Compared with the rest of the world, the Nordic countries have high rates of maternal employment and relatively small gender gaps in employment rates and usual weekly work hours (OECD, 2018). Nordic countries also demonstrate high gender empowerment and more equal division of domestic labor (Knudsen & Wærness, 2008). Why are Nordic countries more gender equal? It is likely due to their effective government-based work-family policies. In particular, the Nordic countries are known for their parental leave policies and the very effective father quotas (Haas & Rostgaard, 2011). According to Matysiak and Węziak-Białowolska's (2016) index of conditions for work and family reconciliation, Sweden is on top followed by Iceland, Denmark, Norway, and Finland. Parental leave and other work-family policies are important because patterns of gender inequality in employment and pay often emerge or increase when people have children. Therefore, policies that promote mothers' labor force participation and fathers' involvement at home will go a long way in minimizing gender inequality. This chapter focuses on work-family integration and gender equality in Nordic countries. First, I provide a brief overview of types of work-family policies in the Nordic countries. Second, I examine research on the links between work-family policies and gender equality. Third, I include some recommendations for other countries based on the Nordic model.

Work-family policies in Nordic countries

All five Nordic countries spend more than 3 percent of their GDP on family benefits, which is higher than the OECD average of two percent and considerably higher than the US rate of only 0.6 percent (OECD, 2017). Often there is an explicit recognition that family policy must consider that "the welfare of the family is based upon equality between men and women and on shared responsibility for the tasks within it" (Arnalds, Eydal, & Gíslason, 2013, p. 324). Perhaps the most influential policy in promoting a better balance between work and family is parental leave. In particular, well-compensated parental leave and leave set aside specifically for fathers, sometimes called the "daddy quota," have been effective in increasing fathers' leave uptake. While Sweden was the first country to introduce parental leave in 1974, Norway was the first country to introduce the father's quota in 1993. In 2018, Norway increased their quota to 15 weeks (Brandth & Kvande, 2018b), while Iceland and Sweden each reserve three months of leave for fathers (Duvander & Haas, 2018; Eydal & Gíslason, 2018).

Feldman and Gran (2016) evaluated paternity leave policies in 44 countries based on their promotion of gender equity. The measure used a number of factors, including duration of paternity, parity of maternity and paternity leave, incentives for fathers to take paternity or parental leave, and wage replacement. Based on this classification, Finland, Iceland, Norway, and Sweden are high-equity countries, with Sweden and Norway being the two countries that registered the most equitable score. According to Ray et al. (2010), Sweden scores highest on their gender equality index, based on father's portion of leave, wage replacement, and incentives for fathers to take leave, with Finland and Norway tied for second.

An overwhelming majority of Nordic fathers take at least some parental leave, and much of the increase in uptake is due to policies like the daddy quota that are tailored to increase gender equality. In Norway, approximately 90 percent of fathers take at least some parental leave, and there is evidence that fathers respond to the quotas by taking a greater number of leave days off (Brandth & Kvande, 2018b). Duvander and Johansson (2012) find that the introduction of the first non-transferrable month in Sweden decreased mothers' parental leave by 26 days and increased fathers' leave by 10 days, narrowing the gap in use. Partners are also influential in Swedish men's greater share of leave (Kaufman & Almqvist, 2017). Changes in parental leave in Iceland led to a more equal division of parental leave between mothers and fathers. The policy had an immediate effect, with 82 percent of fathers taking leave in 2001, the first year that non-transferable leave was available. The average number of days fathers take leave has also increased as more was introduced, from 39 days in 2001 when one month was set aside for fathers to 68 days in 2002 when two months were set aside for fathers to 97 days in 2003 when three months were set aside for fathers (Arnalds et al., 2013). Likewise, the increase in paternity leave from one month to nine weeks in Finland seems effective – whereas one third of fathers took the extra six weeks in 2013, half of fathers used the extra leave in 2016 (Salmi, Närvi, & Lammi-Taskula, 2018). Denmark lags behind the other countries in men's leave-taking. While 80 percent of eligible Danish fathers take some paternity leave, most do not extend their leave beyond two weeks. The Danish government has an ongoing campaign entitled "Operation Dad's Leave" (2017–2020) that seeks to promote men's greater use of parental leave (Bloksgaard & Rostgaard, 2018).

Early childhood education and care (ECEC) is another important policy that promotes better work-family integration. In particular, childcare is affordable because of public funding, and it is widely available, with no gap between parental leave and the start of ECEC. Denmark has by far the highest use of formal childcare arrangements, with more than 70 percent of children ages 0–2 years old in childcare (all other countries are below 50 percent). Childcare is widely accepted as "there is a tendency to see childcare as much as an offer to the children in their development as democratic citizens, as an offer to the parents to have their children cared for while they are working" (Plantenga & Remery, 2009, p. 40). Parents are entitled to ECEC starting when their child is 6 months old, and a recent policy change in August 2018 requires children in certain "vulnerable" areas to attend from age 1 (Bloksgaard & Rostgaard, 2018).

Norway ranks high on preschool services (Elizalde-San Miguel, Díaz Gandasegui, & García, 2019). In Sweden, public childcare is provided for children as it "constitutes an important part of the social infrastructure which is to further gender equality in the division of paid and unpaid work" (Plantenga & Remery, 2009, p. 40). Iceland lags behind in this area as there is no legal entitlement to ECEC in Iceland, and there is a care gap between the end of parental leave at nine months and the usual starting age for preschool (Eydal & Gíslason, 2018). While there is some variation across countries, the Nordic countries generally lead the way in providing well-paid parental leave, reserving time for each parent through quotas, and ensuring the availability of publicly provided early childhood education and care following parental leave.

Gender equality

The Nordic countries' emphasis on work-family integration allows them to create a more supportive environment for gender equality. Here I focus on women's employment and careers as well as men's involvement at home. Nordic women are better able to combine work and family, and having children does not seem to derail women's careers. Rønsen and Sundström (2002) examine the early impact of parental leave and early childcare programs in Finland, Norway, and Sweden between 1972 and 1992. They find that these programs had a positive impact on women's employment following birth. Other research shows that because of public provision of childcare, having a young child (ages 0–3) has a minimal negative effect on women's employment rates in Denmark and even a slightly positive effect in Sweden (Pettit & Hook, 2005). In Norway, most mothers who take parental leave return to work within the first year, and it is very rare for a mother not to return to work after two years (Rønsen & Kitterød, 2015). It is not unusual for Norwegian women with high-level careers to have families as well, which exemplifies the supportive nature of Nordic work-family policies (Seierstad & Kirton, 2015).

Furthermore, evidence from a Swedish cohort study shows that women's wages are not negatively affected by parental leave (Albrecht, Edin, Sundström, & Vroman, 1999). More recent research similarly concludes that parental leave has only small wage effects on mothers and fathers (Evertsson, 2016). In fact, Evertsson (2016) asserts that the similar impact of taking 20 weeks of parental leave on women and higher-educated men's wages should encourage couples to divide parental leave more equally. What may be even more astounding is that men's use of parental leave in the Nordic context benefits women's earnings. The motherhood wage penalty, the common pattern of lower earnings for mothers, decreased in response to family policies in Norway so much so that there was no difference between mothers and non-mothers in wages by the mid-1990s (Petersen, Penner, & Høgsnes, 2014).

Nordic mothers may be able to integrate work and family better because of their partners' greater involvement at home. Kotsadam and Finseraas (2011) use a natural experimental design to determine whether Norway's introduction of the daddy quota influenced the division of labor at home. They find that those who had a child after the reform were more likely to equally share housework and less likely to experience conflicts over the division of labor than those who had a child before the reform. Icelandic couples also emphasize the importance of sharing work and family roles (Ingólfsdóttir & Gíslason, 2016). In Finland, dual-career couples and female-career couples divide housework and paid work fairly evenly, with the man's share of both falling between 40 and 60 percent (Känsälä & Oinas, 2016).

Similarly, Almqvist, Sandberg, and Dahlgren (2011) find that Swedish fathers who take parental leave engage in more childcare and show a greater understanding of their partner's lived experiences, which may explain why men's use of parental leave is associated with lower risks of union dissolution (Oláh, 2001). Norwegian studies also show positive consequences of sharing parental leave, with fathers who take leave developing childcare skills, competency, and awareness of children's needs (Brandth & Kvande, 2018a). Evidence from Iceland also shows greater gender equality in caregiving following the 2000 introduction of three months of paternity leave, especially among couples in which fathers take more leave (Arnalds et al., 2013). In particular, case studies of Swedish fathers who took parental leave of six months or more show changes in attitudes and behavior surrounding gender equality, with greater emphasis on equal parenting and the benefits of caregiving for fathers themselves (Johansson, 2011). Another study of Swedish fathers shows a positive relationship between number of parental leave days taken and fathers' share of childcare, hours spent on childcare, and solo responsibility with the child (Haas & Hwang, 2008). A clear majority of Swedish adults think the best option when a child is less than a year old is to have both the mother and father work, with about 40 percent thinking both should work part time (Mussino, Tervola, & Duvander, 2019). Egalitarian attitudes are so engrained in Swedish culture that family transitions such as marriage, divorce, and children have little effect on young adults' support for gender equality (Kaufman, Bernhardt, & Goldscheider, 2017).

It is normative for Nordic fathers to take parental leave (Brandth & Kvande, 2019). And Nordic fathers spend more time with their children than fathers in other European countries (Gauthier & DeGusti, 2012). Previous research in Nordic countries shows that length of paternity leave increases father's involvement, and this continues after the leave is over (Arnalds et al., 2013; Evertsson, Boye, & Erman, 2018). Almqvist and Duvander (2014) find that Swedish fathers who take longer leave share housework and childcare more equally with their partners. And longer leave results in more equal parent-child relationships, with children being able to relate equally well to both parents as opposed to more with the mother and less with the father.

Daddy quotas increase gender equality. For example, the division of parental benefit to care for sick children became more equal after daddy months were introduced in Sweden. After the first month in 1995, mothers took fewer days of leave and, after the second month in 2002, fathers took more days of leave, compared with before the quotas (Duvander & Johansson, 2019). Before the policy was introduced in Iceland, 36 percent of parents of children born in 1997 divided care evenly when their child reached 3 years old. In comparison, 59 percent of parents of children born in 2009 divided care evenly when their child reached age 3. The latter figure is 70 percent for parents who live together (Arnalds et al., 2013).

Through research on fathers on leave alone in Nordic countries, we can see that the image of fathers as carers is normative. Particularly after taking parental leave, fathers see work as less important and a family-friendly workplace as more important (Duvander, Haas, & Thalberg, 2017; Lammi-Taskula, 2017). Interestingly, men may be changing their work habits to adjust to their partner and family's needs. For example, Duvander and Jans (2009) find a negative relationship between Swedish fathers' parental leave use and their weekly work hours, with those fathers who took at least two months of leave working 3.5 hours less per week relative to fathers who did not use parental leave.

Conclusions

This chapter has highlighted work-family policies and gender equality in Nordic countries. Iceland, Norway, Sweden, and Finland are yet again at the top of the World Economic Forum's 2018 global gender gap index (with Denmark at 13). These countries provide generous parental leave and publicly funded childcare for when parents return to work. Perhaps the most effective policies are those aimed at increasing men's involvement at home, such as through the daddy quotas. Indeed, Nordic fathers increasingly feel entitled to parental leave as they take on the role of caregiver (Brandth & Kvande, 2019). Men's shift toward family is a much-needed step in the second part of the gender revolution (Goldscheider, Bernhardt, & Lappegård, 2015).

However, the Nordic countries are not perfect and must still consider policies that will keep making progress toward gender equality. There is some evidence that certain policies are not as supportive of gender equality. For example, the home-care allowance system in Finland decreases mother's return to employment following birth (Rønsen & Sundström, 2002). This policy seems to contradict others that support maternal employment. While there are greater political divisions concerning the father's quota and gender equality in Denmark, Finland, and Norway, Sweden and Iceland have consistently embraced and institutionalized the father's quota as a way to support gender equality and the dual-earner/dual-carer model (Eydal et al., 2015). Nevertheless, in Iceland, where fathers generally took three months of parental leave in the mid-2000s, movement toward gender equality stalled and potentially reversed when the economic recession resulted in lower parental leave pay and therefore shorter leaves, particularly among higher-income fathers (Sigurdardottir & Garðarsdóttir, 2018). Certainly, limited funding may be the primary barrier to enacting such policies. However, funding parental leave and early childhood education and care is likely to pay off as increases in women's employment rates are associated with a stronger economy through increased economic growth, higher productivity, and higher incomes (Lagarde & Ostry, 2018). Therefore, efforts must be made to fully fund these policies to prevent regression to older, gendered patterns.

The Nordic countries provide a model for other countries that want to promote gender equality through increasing women's employment rates and men's participation in household and child care. A good starting point would be to develop parental leave and early childhood education and care (ECEC) policies. First, Nordic parental leave policies are generous in terms of duration of leave, wage replacement, and job security. Yet, a key element of the Nordic success story in achieving high levels of gender equity is the father quota. Therefore, countries should attempt to achieve parity in parental leave through individual entitlements and/or father quotas. Second, the Nordic countries further support gender equality and child well-being by ensuring that children have a safe and enriching place to go once parental leave ends. Countries should provide affordable ECEC for all children.

Gender equality should be promoted. Countries with higher levels of gender equality are healthier and happier than less-equal countries (Looze, Huijts, Stevens, Torsheim, & Vollebergh, 2018; Van de Velde, Huijts, Bracke, & Bambra, 2013). Gender equality is also good for the economy as increases in women's employment rates in the Nordic countries has led to greater economic growth over the past few decades (OECD, 2018). While not perfect, the Nordic countries seem to provide the best example we have of work-family integration and gender equality.

Key learnings from research	*Practical recommendations*
Positive impact of parental leave on gender equality:	Recommendations for parental leave and early childhood education and care (ECEC)
• Increase in women's employment rates • Decrease in motherhood wage penalty • Increase in men's domestic work • Increase in father's involvement	Parental leave: • Duration of six months for each parent • Individual entitlement/father quota • High wage replacement • Job protection Early childhood education and care: • Legal entitlement to ECEC for all children • Publicly funded/low fees • No gap between end of parental leave and beginning of ECEC

References

Albrecht, J. W., Edin, P., Sundström, M., & Vroman, S. B. (1999). Career interruptions and subsequent earnings: A reexamination using Swedish data. *The Journal of Human Resources, 34,* 294–311.

Almqvist, A., & Duvander, A.-Z. (2014). Changes in gender equality? Swedish fathers' parental leave, division of childcare and housework. *Journal of Family Studies, 20,* 19–27.

Almqvist, A., Sandberg, A., & Dahlgren, L. (2011). Parental leave in Sweden: Motives, experiences, and gender equality amongst parents. *Fathering, 9*, 189–206.

Arnalds, A. A., Eydal, G. B., & Gíslason, I. V. (2013). Equal rights to paid parental leave and caring fathers: The case of Iceland. *Icelandic Review of Politics and Administration, 9*, 323–344.

Bloksgaard, L., & Rostgaard, T. (2018). Denmark country note. In S. Blum, A. Koslowski, A. Macht, & P. Moss (Eds.), *International review of leave policies and research 2018*. Retrieved from www.leavenetwork.org/lp_and_r_reports/

Brandth, B., & Kvande, E. (2018a). Masculinity and fathering alone. *Men and Masculinities, 21*, 72–90.

Brandth, B., & Kvande, E. (2018b). Norway country note. In S. Blum, A. Koslowski, A. Macht, & P. Moss (Eds.), *International review of leave policies and research 2018*. Retrieved from www.leavenetwork.org/lp_and_r_reports/

Brandth, B., & Kvande, E. (2019). Fathers' sense of entitlement to ear-marked and shared parental leave. *The Sociological Review, 67*(5), 1154–1169.

Duvander, A.-Z., & Haas, L. (2018). Sweden country note. In S. Blum, A. Koslowski, A. Macht, & P. Moss (Eds.), *International review of leave policies and research 2018*. Retrieved from www.leavenetwork.org/lp_and_r_reports/

Duvander, A.-Z., Haas, L., & Thalberg, S. (2017). Fathers on leave alone in Sweden: Toward more equal parenthood? In M. O'Brien & K. Wall (Eds.), *Comparative perspectives on work-life balance and gender equality*. London: Springer.

Duvander, A.-Z., & Jans, A. (2009). Consequences of fathers' parental leave use: Evidence from Sweden. *Finnish Yearbook of Population Research, 44*, 49–62.

Duvander, A.-Z., & Johansson, M. (2012). What are the effects of reforms promoting fathers' parental leave use? *Journal of European Social Policy, 22*, 319–330.

Duvander, A.-Z., & Johansson, M. (2019). Does fathers' care spill over? Evaluating reforms in the Swedish parental leave program. *Feminist Economics, 25*, 67–89.

Elizalde-San Miguel, B., Díaz Gandasegui, V., & García, M. T. S. (2019). Family policy index: A tool for policy makers to increase the effectiveness of family policies. *Social Indicators Research, 142*, 387–409.

Evertsson, M. (2016). Parental leave and careers: Women's and men's wages after parental leave in Sweden. *Advances in Life Course Research, 29*, 26–40.

Evertsson, M., Boye, K., & Erman, J. (2018). Fathers on call? A study on the sharing of care work between parents in Sweden. *Demographic Research, 39*, 33–60.

Eydal, G. B., & Gíslason, I. V. (2018). Iceland country note. In S. Blum, A. Koslowski, A. Macht, & P. Moss (Eds.), *International review of leave policies and research 2018*. Retrieved from www.leavenetwork.org/lp_and_r_reports/

Eydal, G. B., Gíslason, I. V., Rostgaard, T., Brandth, B., Duvander, A., & Lammi-Taskula, J. (2015). Trends in parental leave in the Nordic countries: Has the forward march of gender equality halted? *Community, Work and Family, 18*, 167–181.

Feldman, K., & Gran, B. K. (2016). Is what's best for dads best for families? Paternity leave policies and equity across forty-four nations. *Journal of Sociology & Social Welfare, 43*, 95–119.

Gauthier, A. H., & DeGusti, B. (2012). The time allocation to children by parents in Europe. *International Sociology, 27*, 827–845.

Goldscheider, F., Bernhardt, E., & Lappegård, T. (2015). The gender revolution: A framework for understanding changing family and demographic behavior. *Population and Development Review, 41*, 207–239.

Haas, L., & Hwang, P. (2008). The impact of taking parental leave on fathers' participation in childcare and relationships with children: Lessons from Sweden. *Community, Work and Family, 11*, 85–104.

Haas, L., & Rostgaard, T. (2011). Fathers' rights to paid parental leave in the Nordic countries: Consequences for the gendered division of leave. *Community, Work and Family, 14,* 177–195.

Ingólfsdóttir, E. S., & Gíslason, I. V. (2016). Gendered solutions to the care gap issue in Iceland. *NORA – Nordic Journal of Feminist and Gender Research, 24,* 220–233.

Johansson, T. (2011). Fatherhood in transition: Paternity leave and changing masculinities. *Journal of Family Communication, 11,* 165–180.

Känsälä, M., & Oinas, T. (2016). The division of domestic work among dual-career and other dual-earner couples in Finland. *Community, Work and Family, 19,* 438–461.

Kaufman, G., & Almqvist, A. (2017). The role of partners and workplaces in British and Swedish men's parental leave decisions. *Men and Masculinities, 20,* 533–551.

Kaufman, G., Bernhardt, E., & Goldscheider, F. (2017). Enduring egalitarianism? Family transitions and attitudes toward gender equality in Sweden. *Journal of Family Issues, 38,* 1878–1898.

Knudsen, K., & Wærness, K. (2008). National context and spouses' housework in 34 countries. *European Sociological Review, 24,* 97–113.

Kotsadam, A., & Finseraas, H. (2011). The state intervenes in the battle of the sexes: Causal effects of paternity leave. *Social Science Research, 40,* 1611–1622.

Lagarde, C., & Ostry, J. D. (2018, December 4). *When more women join the workforce, everyone benefits.* World Economic Forum. Retrieved from www.weforum.org/agenda/2018/12/economic-gains-from-gender-inclusion-even-greater-than-you-thought/

Lammi-Taskula, J. (2017). Fathers on leave alone in Finland: Negotiations and lived experiences. In M. O'Brien & K. Wall (Eds.), *Comparative perspectives on work-life balance and gender equality.* London: Springer.

Looze, M. E., Huijts, T., Stevens, G. W. J. M., Torsheim, T., & Vollebergh, W. A. M. (2018). The happiest kids on earth. Gender equality and adolescent life satisfaction in Europe and North America. *Journal of Youth and Adolescence, 47,* 1073–1085.

Matysiak, A., & Węziak-Białowolska, D. (2016). Country-specific conditions for work and family reconciliation: An attempt at quantification. *European Journal of Population, 32,* 475–510.

Mussino, E., Tervola, J., & Duvander, A. (2019). Decomposing the determinants of fathers' parental leave use: Evidence from migration between Finland and Sweden. *Journal of European Social Policy, 29,* 197–212.

OECD. (2017). *Family benefits public spending.* Retrieved from www.oecd.org/social/family/child-well-being/data/policies/

OECD. (2018). *Is the last mile the longest? Economic gains from gender equality in Nordic countries.* Paris: OECD Publishing.

Oláh, L. (2001). Gender and family stability: Dissolution of the first parental union in Sweden and Hungary. *Demographic Research, 4,* 29–96.

Petersen, T., Penner, A. M., & Høgsnes, G. (2014). From motherhood penalties to husband premia: The new challenge for gender equality and family policy, lessons from Norway. *American Journal of Sociology, 119,* 1434–1472.

Pettit, B., & Hook, J. (2005). The structure of women's employment in comparative perspective. *Social Forces, 84,* 779–801.

Plantenga, J., & Remery, C. (2009). *The provision of childcare services: A comparative review of 30 European countries.* European Commission. Retrieved from https://eurogender.eige.europa.eu/system/files/the_provision_childcare_services.pdf

Ray, R., Gornick, J. C., & Schmitt, J. (2010). Who cares? Assessing generosity and gender equality in parental leave policy designs in 21 countries. *Journal of European Social Policy, 20,* 196–216.

Rønsen, M., & Kitterød, R. H. (2015). Gender-equalizing family policies and mothers' entry into paid work: Recent evidence from Norway. *Feminist Economics, 21*, 59–89.

Rønsen, M., & Sundström, M. (2002). Family policy and after-birth employment among new mothers: A comparison of Finland, Norway and Sweden. *European Journal of Population, 18*, 121–152.

Salmi, M., Närvi, J., & Lammi-Taskula, J. (2018). Finland country note. In S. Blum, A. Koslowski, A. Macht, & P. Moss (Eds.), *International review of leave policies and research 2018*. Retrieved from www.leavenetwork.org/lp_and_r_reports/

Seierstad, C., & Kirton, G. (2015). Having it all? Women in high commitment careers and work-life balance in Norway. *Gender, Work & Organization, 22*, 390–404.

Sigurdardottir, H. M., & Garðarsdóttir, O. (2018). Backlash in gender equality? Fathers' parental leave during a time of economic crisis. *Journal of European Social Policy, 28*, 342–356.

Van de Velde, S., Huijts, T., Bracke, P., & Bambra, C. (2013). Macro-level gender equality and depression in men and women in Europe. *Sociology of Health & Illness, 35*, 682–698.

Zalis, S. (2018, October 30). Lessons from the world's most gender-equal countries. *Forbes*. Retrieved from www.forbes.com/sites/shelleyzalis/2018/10/30/lessons-from-the-worlds-most-gender-equal-countries/#4a92729a7dd8

8 Career progression

Left out of the game?

*Nina M. Junker, Alina S. Hernandez Bark,
and Jamie L. Gloor*

Perceptions of parents at the workplace

Stereotypes refer to the widely held, oversimplified and overgeneralized ideas about people. For parents, gender and the presence of children are arguably the two most relevant characteristics to define other people's stereotypes about them. Specifically, people who have children are generally viewed as warmer, more communal, less competent, and less agentic than their childfree counterparts, particularly mothers (Cuddy, Fiske, & Glick, 2004; Heilman & Okimoto, 2007, 2008). Beyond the basic dimensions of person-perception, stereotypes of parents also often include commitment and dependability, such that mothers are rated as less committed and dependable than their male and childfree counterparts (Heilman & Okimoto, 2008; King, 2008). Of note, these parenthood stereotypes are more pronounced for women, because relative to men, their non-work demands are more salient to others at work (Eagly, 1987; Hoobler, Wayne, & Lemmon, 2009).

Although stereotypes are largely thought to be descriptive, the qualities ascribed to men and women also tend to be the same ones that are required of them (March, van Dick, & Hernandez Bark, 2016; Prentice & Carranza, 2002). In this way, parenthood stereotypes extend across work- and non-work domains to influence a range of employment-related interactions and decisions. For example, stereotype-based assumptions that women are – and should be – warm, communal, primary caregivers, but are not – and should not be – competent, agentic professionals, affect evaluations of working parents' effectiveness, interpersonal appeal, and suitability for leadership roles, predicting others' willingness to work with and promote fathers, but not mothers (Heilman & Okimoto, 2008; Okimoto & Heilman, 2012). Thus, stereotypes of gender and parenthood can restrict professional advancement particularly for mothers, as these stereotypes conflict with "ideal worker" norms and work devotion schemas that dictate unwavering dedication to work despite all other commitments – including family (see Acker, 1990; Blair-Loy, 2003).

Yet, the negative effects of parental stereotypes are not only restricted to women. Indeed, when the father role becomes salient by being an active caregiver (Berdahl & Moon, 2013) or by taking parental leave, this also influences warmth and competence attributions: fathers taking parental leave experience the same negative consequences on competence-related attributes such as job commitment, but in contrast to mothers, they experience a boost in warmth (Hernandez Bark, Junker, Morgenroth, & Heilman, 2019).

Of note, these stereotypes are somewhat dynamic and context dependent. For example, many of the aforementioned stereotypes are more prominent in male-dominated positions and fields (e.g., leadership roles; Heilman & Okimoto, 2008; Okimoto & Heilman, 2012). Especially female leaders are prone to a "double bind", namely, pressures to fulfil contradicting role expectations to be both tough and nice at the same time, and a "double standard", namely, to perform better than their male counterparts to be granted the same level of competence (Eagly & Karau, 2002; Hernandez Bark, Escartin, & van Dick, 2014). Thus, people, in general and parents, in particular, are evaluated by others based on their (in)congruence with their respective gender stereotypes (e.g., Cialdini & Trost, 1998).

Additionally, people may also internalize these stereotypes (Guerrero Witt & Wood, 2010). That is, because congruent behaviour and characteristics predict positive reactions from interaction partners whereas incongruent behaviour and characteristics predict social disapproval, women in particular tend to fulfil stereotypical expectations, often at an unconscious level (Eagly, Wood, & Diekman, 2000; Evans & Diekman, 2009; Guerrero Witt & Wood, 2010). This is reflected in the fact that women still assume more household and childcare responsibilities (European Commission, 2018) and are more likely to work part time compared with men (European Commission, 2018; OECD, 2018). Unfortunately, part-time work is often a career killer (Ng, Eby, Sorensen, & Feldman, 2005), predicting career stagnation and wage penalties for women with children (Gangl & Ziefle, 2009). Compared with their childfree counterparts, fathers earn the highest salaries (i.e., fatherhood bonuses for "breadwinners"), whereas mothers earn the lowest salaries (i.e., motherhood penalties; Kmec, 2011). When women have three or more children, evidence indicates that the motherhood penalty may persist over the whole lifespan (Kahn, García-Manglano, & Bianchi, 2014). One rationale for this is that men with family responsibilities are expected to be especially committed to their job, but the opposite is true for women, who are expected to value family over career, and thus, be less committed to their jobs. Importantly, effects of these expectations persist even if women and men do not act accordingly (Kmec, 2011). Yet, abstaining from children also does not seem to be a viable option to avoid social and work-related penalties, because even women of childbearing age may experience bias and discrimination based on expectations of impending pregnancy, which has been coined the "maybe baby" effect (Gloor, Li, Lim, & Feierabend, 2018; Gloor, Okimoto, Feierabend, & Staffelbach, 2015).

In summary, the boundaries between the seemingly discrete categories of "parents" and "non-parents" may be blurring, particularly for women and between ages 30 and 40 (Gloor et al., 2015, 2018). Parental stereotypes – and thus, also their consequences (if any) – may also differ according to employee race/ethnicity (Rosette, Ponce de Leon, Koval, & Harrison, 2018). For example, in contrast to white mothers who should stay at home and care for the children, black mothers are expected to work (Cuddy & Wolf, 2013). Thus, white mothers experience more backlash if they work compared with not working, and vice versa for black mothers (Cuddy & Wolf, 2013). Other scholars have also suggested that gendered stereotypes of parenthood and caregiving may be more relaxed in non-U.S. countries and cultures (e.g., Germany; Fleischman & Sieverding, 2015); yet, to our knowledge, this claim has not been explicitly tested. For these reasons, it is important to consider intersectionality (i.e., simultaneously acknowledge multiple axes of identity) as well as the relevant organizational and cultural contexts to better understand the stereotypes, expectations, and experiences of working parents, as well as how they might influence parents' career progressions.

Contrasting stereotypes and reality

Until now, we have focused on stereotypes about working parents. Oftentimes, people assume that there is a "kernel of truth" in such stereotypes (cf. LeVine & Campbell, 1972), meaning that if there would not be some real differences between parents and non-parents, such stereotypes could not persist. Thus, in the following, we review if there is the possibility of some truth in these mostly negative perceptions of working parents, in general, and of working mothers, in particular.

In brief, evidence for a kernel of truth in stereotypes about working parents is scarce at best. A recent quantitative study by Dumas and Perry-Smith (2018) showed that family ties such as having a spouse and/or children helped employees to focus on their tasks while at work. The authors argued that employees, who live together with a spouse and/or children, are more likely to have plans after work, such as picking a child up from kindergarten or attending a soccer game. Such anticipated activities helped employees to focus on their work, increasing their efficiency and performance. In other words, single, childfree employees may spend longer hours at work – a fact that is recognized by their supervisors – yet this does not mean they produce more or better output.

Increased efficiency and better time management are themes that have also emerged in various qualitative studies. For example, in a study of female managers, Ruderman, Ohlott, Panzer, and King (2002) found that motherhood represented – most of all – an opportunity to enrich interpersonal skills. These skills include, but are not limited to, developing, motivating, respecting, or understanding employees and to thrive psychologically. Mastering challenges at home increased these women's confidence and self-esteem, encouraging them to behave similarly at work. Moreover, they showed that being a parent and an employee were positively related to, amongst others, more life satisfaction, more self-acceptance, and more self-esteem. Although their sample comprised only women, other research suggests that men similarly benefit from their parenting experiences (Lapierre et al., 2018). Taken together, these findings suggest that instead of disqualifying parents from being good employees, having children may provide individuals with the potential to become better employees (see also Chapter 10 for more evidence on the enriching nature of parenthood).

Although working parents are not necessarily less motivated or ambitious than their childfree counterparts, the presence of negative stereotypes has negative effects for these individuals. For example, recent research by the first author found evidence for this proposition in a study of 120 working parents (Junker, 2019). Working parents who perceived others' stereotypes and expected that they would be deemed less desired employees because they had children reported lower well-being and less productivity compared with working parents who did not perceive such stereotypes. Specifically, they reported being in a worse mood and having more chronic stress, as well as being lower in self-efficacy. They were also less engaged and less likely to recommend their current employer to others. These effects were independent of participants' gender, although men were generally less likely to report that they perceived these negative stereotypes. Although these findings are only correlational and not causal, they illustrate the importance of reducing negative stereotypes about working parents and implementing interventions that prevent working parents from such negative perceptions. This is because, as outlined in the previous section, traditional gender stereotypes hinder the career progression of working women and family-oriented men.

One such intervention was recently proposed and tested by Kinias and Sim (2016), who used the following self-affirmation intervention to reduce the impact of stereotypes about women in business on their future success. In a first step, participants were asked to select the two or three values from a list of ten values, which were most important for them (such as protecting the environment/issues of sustainability or helping people in need/participating in charitable organizations). Then, they were asked to reflect upon these values for about 15 minutes. Doing so, they should answer why these were important for them and how they lived these values in their lives.

Upon first glance, this intervention may not seem directly relevant to parenthood or stereotypes about parents. However, the basic premise is that negative stereotypes pose a threat to the self (e.g., "Am I worthy?"). This means that using a self-affirmation intervention re-activates resources (e.g., "I am worthy"), thereby increasing employees' resilience against potential threats, including negative gender- or parenthood-related stereotypes. Self-affirmation may also be helpful when applying for a new position, a situation that often poses threats to the self. Thus, in the following, we outline more recommendations on how to deal with stereotypes in this specific context.

Applying for a new position

Becoming a parent is often a time wherein one reconsiders their core goals in life (see also Chapter 9). As we have seen at the beginning of this chapter, working parents – especially working mothers – may face negative career consequences because they have children, including lower chances of promotion, interview, and job offers. Thus, the question arises about how to reduce or even prevent these consequences. For example, should parents not mention their children in their curriculum vitae (CV)? Should parents disclose their work-life balance preferences to recruiters? Or should parents explicitly emphasize their parenthood-related skills and experiences in the recruiting process as relevant training and experience?

Research by Proost and Verhaest (2018) suggests that women should not mention their preferences for work-life balance as doing so resulted in ratings of lower work ethic (i.e., less respect for hard work and working less hard; Blau & Ryan, 1997) compared with women who did not mention such preferences in their CV. This, in turn, decreased positive ratings and hireability of these women. The authors did not find either positive or negative effects for men. Although this is not directly related to parenthood, work-life balance often triggers ideas of balancing work and family duties. It seems that if women state that they value work-life-balance, the traditional female gender role is activated and others interpret this preference as if these women would value family higher than work. As a result, all the negative consequences for women's career progression explained in the previous section are likely to occur.

However, relating parenting to work skills which employers desire may increase women's chances of being invited for a personal interview. In a recent experiment, 128 participants were asked to adopt the perspective of a recruiter in a scenario study (Junker, Hernandez Bark, Aydin, & Gloor, 2019). Participants read a vignette of a potential applicant, who was described either as a woman with children or without. In instances which described the female applicant with child, we further manipulated her answers to the question, "You wrote that you are a mother. How do your previous experiences influence you personally and/or your role as employee?" Building on the work-family enrichment perspective (Greenhaus & Powell, 2006), we were interested in whether women would benefit from naming competences they had acquired in their role as mothers or whether it would be more beneficial to explicitly state that one's family role did not affect one's work role. Next, they rated this applicant on several attributes (e.g., competence, loyalty, intelligence, sympathy, or resilience) and indicated, amongst others, the degree to which he/she would invite the applicant for a personal interview. Moreover, we asked them to indicate how much they were willing to pay the applicant. Results from this study indicate that it depends on which impression working mothers may want to make: If they want to be perceived as communal, which may be helpful in primarily female-dominated occupations, they should emphasize their family role and highlight how their maternal role helps them in being better employees. Alternatively, if they want to be perceived as resilient or capable of multi-tasking, they can also mention their family role. But, if they want to be recognized as agentic (e.g., when applying for a supervisory position), they may be better advised to say that their family does not impact their work role (neither positively nor negatively).

Conclusions

In this chapter, we highlighted that working mothers experience primarily negative career-related consequences because of working *and* being mothers (such as worse promotion prospects), whereas the consequences for fathers may often be more beneficial as fatherhood can further advance men's careers. Also, we established that stereotypes are not the same as the actual consequences of being parents. Mothers and fathers do not report being less motivated or less ambitious than their childfree counterparts, but the presence of negative perceptions about them (i.e., stereotype threat) may deteriorate their motivation and well-being. We concluded with recommendations about how to deal with and even prevent some of these negative perceptions and their consequences, so that rather than being "left out of the game", regardless of having children (or not), employees' career progressions can remain the same.

Key learnings from research	*Practical recommendations*
• Stereotypes about working mothers are primarily negative and contribute to the motherhood penalty; those about working fathers are primarily positive and contribute to the fatherhood bonus. • Importantly, the negative stereotypes do not adequately reflect reality. • Although stereotypes are key drivers for unconscious discrimination, there might be changes in the future because of societal changes.	• Working parents (and mothers, in particular) can buffer some of the negative effects of stereotypes by remembering their value (as employees and as parents). • When applying for a new job, working mothers can increase perceptions of competence by communicating their work-relevant parenting-related skills.

References

Acker, J. (1990). Hierarchies, jobs, bodies: A theory of gendered organizations. *Gender & Society, 4*, 139–158.

Berdahl, J. L., & Moon, S. H. (2013). Workplace mistreatment of middle-class workers based on sex, parenthood, and caregiving. *Journal of Social Issues, 69*, 341–366.

Blair-Loy, M. (2003). *Competing devotions: Career and family among women executives.* Cambridge, MA: Harvard University Press.

Blau, G., & Ryan, J. (1997). On measuring work ethic: A neglected work commitment facet. *Journal of Vocational Behavior, 51*, 435–448.

Cialdini, R. B., & Trost, M. R. (1998). Social influence: Social norms, conformity, and compliance. In D. T. Gilbert & S. T. Fiske (Eds.), *The handbook of social psychology: Volume 2* (4th ed., pp. 151–192). Boston, MA: McGraw-Hill.

Cuddy, A. J. C., Fiske, S. T., & Glick, P. (2004). When professionals become mothers, warmth doesn't cut the ice. *Journal of Social Issues, 60*, 701–718.

Cuddy, A. J. C., & Wolf, E. B. (2013). Prescriptions and punishments for working moms: How race and work status affect judgments of mothers. In R. Ely & A. Cuddy (Eds.), *Gender & work: Challenging conventional wisdom* (pp. 35–42). Cambridge, MA: Harvard Business School.

Dumas, T. L., & Perry-Smith, J. (2018). The paradox of family structure and plans after work: Why single childless employees may be the least absorbed at work. *Academy of Management Journal, 61*, 1231–1252.

Eagly, A. H. (1987). *Sex differences in social behaviour: A social role interpretation.* Hillsdale, NJ: Earlbaum.

Eagly, A. H., & Karau, S. J. (2002). Role congruity theory of prejudice toward female leaders. *Psychological Review, 109*, 573–598.

Eagly, A. H., Wood, W., & Diekman, A. B. (2000). Social role theory of sex differences and similarities: A current appraisal. In T. Eckes & H. M. Trautner (Eds.), *The developmental social psychology of gender* (pp. 123–174). Mahwah, NJ: Erlbaum.

European Commission. (2018). *2018 report on equality between women and men in the EU.* Retrieved 13 February 2019 from https://publications.europa.eu/en/publication-detail/-/publication/950dce57-6222-11e8-ab9c-01aa75ed71a1

Evans, C. D., & Diekman, A. B. (2009). On motivated role selection: Gender beliefs, distant goals, and career interest. *Psychology of Women Quarterly, 33*, 235–249.

Fleischmann, A., & Sieverding, M. (2015). Reactions towards men who have taken parental leave: Does the length of parental leave matter? *Sex Roles, 72*, 462–476.

Gangl, M., & Ziefle, A. (2009). Motherhood, labor force behavior, and women's careers: An empirical assessment of the wage penalty for motherhood in Britain, Germany, and the United States. *Demography, 46*, 341–369.

Gloor, J. L., Li, X., Lim, S., & Feierabend, A. (2018). An inconvenient truth? Interpersonal and career consequences of "maybe baby" expectations. *Journal of Vocational Behavior, 104*, 44–58.

Gloor, J. L., Okimoto, T. G., Feierabend, A., & Staffelbach, B. (2015). Young women are risky business? The "maybe baby" effect in employment decisions. *Academy of Management Proceedings, 1*, 11858.

Greenhaus, J. H., & Powell, G. N. (2006). When work and family are allies: A theory of work-family enrichment. *Academy of Management Review, 31*, 72–92.

Guerrero Witt, M., & Wood, W. (2010). Self-regulation of gendered behavior in everyday life. *Sex Roles, 62*, 635–646.

Heilman, M. E., & Okimoto, T. G. (2007). Why are women penalized for success at male tasks?: The implied communality deficit. *Journal of Applied Psychology, 92*, 81–92.

Heilman, M. E., & Okimoto, T. G. (2008). Motherhood: A potential source of bias in employment decisions. *Journal of Applied Psychology, 93*, 189–198.

Hernandez Bark, A. S., Escartin, J., & van Dick, R. (2014). Gender and leadership in Spain: A systematic review of some key aspects. *Sex Roles, 70*, 522–537.

Hernandez Bark, A. S., Junker, N. M., Morgenroth, T., & Heilman, M. (2019). I'll be back. Consequences of taking parental leave for mothers and fathers. Manuscript in preparation.

Hoobler, J. M., Wayne, S. J., & Lemmon, G. (2009). Bosses' perceptions of family-work conflict and women's promotability: Glass ceiling effects. *Academy of Management Journal, 52*, 939–957.

Junker, N. M. (2019). Attitudinal consequences of stereotype threat for working parents. Manuscript in preparation.

Junker, N. M., Hernandez Bark, A. S., Aydin, A. L., & Gloor, J. L. (2019). Integrate on re-entry? Navigating the motherhood impression management paradox. Manuscript in preparation.

Kahn, J. R., García-Manglano, J., & Bianchi, S. M. (2014). The motherhood penalty at midlife: Long-term effects of children on women's careers. *Journal of Marriage and Family, 76*, 56–72.

King, E. (2008). The effect of bias on the advancement of working mothers: Disentangling legitimate concerns from inaccurate stereotypes as predictors of advancement in academe. *Human Relations, 61*, 1677–1711.

Kinias, Z., & Sim, J. (2016). Facilitating women's success in business: Interrupting the process of stereotype threat through affirmation of personal values. *Journal of Applied Psychology, 101*, 1585–1597.

Kmec, J. A. (2011). Are motherhood penalties and fatherhood bonuses warranted? Comparing pro-work behaviors and conditions of mothers, fathers, and non-parents. *Social Science Research, 40*, 444–459.

Lapierre, L. M., Li, Y., Kwan, H. K., Greenhaus, J. H., DiRenzo, M. S., & Shao, P. (2018). A meta-analysis of the antecedents of work-family enrichment. *Journal of Organizational Behavior, 39*, 385–401.

LeVine, R. A., & Campbell, D. T. (1972). *Ethnocentrism*. New York: Wiley.

March, E., van Dick, R., & Hernandez Bark, A. S. (2016). Current prescriptions of men and women in differing occupational gender roles. *Journal of Gender Studies, 25*, 681–692.

Ng, T. W., Eby, L. T., Sorensen, K. L., & Feldman, D. C. (2005). Predictors of objective and subjective career success: A meta-analysis. *Personnel Psychology, 58*, 367–408.

OECD. (2018). *Part-time employment rate*. Retrieved 13 February 2019 from www.oecd-ilibrary.org/employment/part-time-employment-rate/indicator/english_f2ad596c-en

Okimoto, T. G., & Heilman, M. E. (2012). The "bad parent" assumption: How gender stereotypes affect reactions to working mothers. *Journal of Social Issues, 68*, 704–724.

Prentice, D. A., & Carranza, E. (2002). What women and men should be, shouldn't be, are allowed to be, and don't have to be: The contents of prescriptive gender stereotypes. *Psychology of Women Quarterly, 26*, 269–281.

Proost, K., & Verhaest, D. (2018). Should we tell the recruiter that we value a good work-life balance? *Journal of Personnel Psychology, 17*, 120–130.

Rosette, A. S., Ponce de Leon, R., Koval, C. Z., & Harrison, D. A. (2018). Intersectionality: Connecting experiences of gender with race at work. *Research in Organizational Behavior, 38*, 1–22.

Ruderman, M. N., Ohlott, P. J., Panzer, K., & King, S. N. (2002). Benefits from multiple roles for managerial women. *Academy of Management Journal, 45*, 369–386.

9 Career development after parenthood

Choices, challenges and opportunities

Julia Yates

Introduction

Changes in policy and legislation promoting family flexible working have brought new opportunities to those wanting to combine parenthood with paid work, but the cultural shift needed to allow these policy changes to have a real impact is lagging behind (Haas & Hwang, 2009). Working parents rarely feel that the perfect option is on the table, and each set of choices comes with a certain degree of compromise (Kanji & Cahusac, 2015).

The proportion of mothers working has increased over the past 20 years, and looking at the careers of women who have dependent-aged children in the UK, we see that it splits fairly neatly into three equal groups, with a third of mothers working full time, a third working part time, and a third not engaged in paid work outside the home (ONS, 2017). In contrast, the proportion of fathers in work has been relatively stable over the past 20 years, with about 93% of fathers of dependent-aged children in the UK working full time. But whilst fathers are much less likely than mothers to opt for part-time work after the birth of a child, they do often take advantage of flexible working practices, for example starting their working day later, to enable them to drop the children at childcare.

The figures for the UK are fairly close to the overall EU average (OECD, 2017), but the picture varies considerably from one country to another, and the availability of public childcare, family friendly policies and the prevalent social norms all affect the options that mothers choose. In Italy, for example, a social family bias and a rigid labour market has led to a smaller proportion, around half, of mothers working full or part time, whereas the Swedish commitment to egalitarian ideals, high-quality childcare provision and their political goal of full employment mean that more than 80% of mothers work outside the home (Anxo et al., 2007; OECD, 2017). In contrast to this variation in the employment status for mothers across the developed world, the picture for fathers is fairly consistent, with the vast majority of fathers of dependent-aged children working full time across all European countries, North America and Australia and New Zealand (Lewis, Campbell, & Huerta, 2008).

What are the options?

After parental leave or a career break, decisions need to be made. Parents can choose whether to continue in the same job and whether to stick with a full-time schedule, or to return to work on reduced or more flexible hours. These two decisions lead to four options: same role and same conditions; same role but different conditions; new career – a wholesale reinvention; or a new family-friendly job.

Same role, same conditions

Work offers a range of practical and psychological benefits, bringing purpose, identity, social connections and, of course, the joys of a regular salary. Continuing in your previous role, just as before, is the most straightforward way to ensure that becoming a parent has a minimal impact on your career path, earnings potential and professional identity. Evidence indicates too that full-time working parents have greater life satisfaction than part-time workers or stay-at-home parents, so it seems that the social networks, salary and status associated with a full-time role make a difference (Berger, 2013).

Alongside these positive reasons, some parents return to their roles full time because they have to, finding that their hands are tied as a consequence of the type of role or organisation they are working in. The economic imperative in some families too will mean that a return to work is inevitable as family finances depend on a full-time salary.

One final reason to opt to carry on as before is that you can. As we will see later on, finding a new job after a career break can be challenging. If you know that you want to go back to the same kind of position, then long term it can make sense to stick with it from the start.

For those who return to their role full time, there are, of course, practical challenges to deal with. For some, the financial benefits of full-time work make the logistics more straightforward, but for most, coping with a full-time job and taking care of one child or more will require military precision, creative problem solving and some self-compassion, to be administered liberally when things don't quite go to plan.

Johnston and Swanson (2006) explored the experiences of a range of mothers, asking them about their working patterns and how they felt about their choices. The full-time working mothers in their study felt that their children were happier because they, as mothers, felt fulfilled in their work, observing that a happy mother leads to a happy child. But whilst they were generally very positive about the choices they had made, they did regret not being more physically available to their children.

Case study: Sarah, full-time production manager

Sarah had worked in advertising since she left university. She had put her heart and soul into her career and for ten years lived and breathed the advertising industry, working long hours and socialising every evening. Sarah had always known that she would have to go back to work full time after she had children. Her job was better paid than her husband's so it made economic sense for her to be the main breadwinner, and this had never troubled her because she enjoyed her work.

When Sarah returned to work after nine months on maternity leave, she was delighted to be back. She had missed the routine of a regular job, felt that her world had narrowed too much whilst she had been at home, and enjoyed having her own professional identity back. She was, however, surprised to find that her attitude to work had shifted: her priority was now to her family and whilst work was still important to her, her life no longer revolved around it. Paradoxically, she found that this actually made her better at her job. She was no longer as anxious about her work projects as she used to be, and this new laid-back attitude seemed to make things run more smoothly at work. Sarah felt that she was just as productive as she had been before children. She worked shorter hours – now tearing out at 5pm on the dot to get home to her children but found that this made her more productive whilst was in the office. One big change was the amount of socialising that she did with work. In her pre-children days, Sarah had partied hard, going out with colleagues and clients in Soho most evenings, but now work outings are restricted to the occasional leaving-do and the Christmas party. But Sarah doesn't mind – she is keen to rush back from work to see her children and doesn't resent the new regime at all.

Looking back she has no regrets. Sarah continues to enjoy the role and loves the organisation she works for. In an ideal world she thinks that she might have reduced her hours to perhaps four days a week. She wonders what life would be like if she were a bit more involved with her daughters' school – dropping off and picking up every day, getting involved in the PTFA and developing closer relationships with the other mothers. But she is clear that whilst these things might have made her feel more involved with her children, they would have made only a minimal difference to her children.

Same role, different conditions

Working part time is a popular choice amongst mothers (Lovejoy & Stone, 2012), and the benefits are apparent to a number of fathers too. For many, it seems to strike the ideal balance, in which people feel that they can be the involved parent they want to be, without losing the benefits that work brings.

Some employers are enormously supportive when it comes to accommodating a request for a change in conditions, helping employees work from home, offering condensed hours or even trying to find some extra support staff to accommodate the parent's new circumstances. Part-time workers can be a great asset to employers, as they can be keen to prove that their part-time status does not come with a loss of commitment or a reduction in standards. But employers are not always aware of the benefits of the opportunity they are being offered and sometimes, however compelling the case is, the employer just can't see how it could work and is not prepared to take the risk. One option that can appeal to parents who are looking for more control over their work schedule is working freelance. Employers who are against a part-time contract are sometimes happy to re-employ staff as freelancers or associates, doing more or less the same work, but with more built-in flexibility for both parties.

Many part-time working parents struggle on a personal level with the sense that they are not fulfilling either role well enough. They are trying to be the ideal, available and committed worker and the ideal, available and committed parent, and these two things can be difficult to squeeze into the same day. On balance though, part-time working mothers tend to feel satisfied with their choices, finding that time away from their child is valuable for both child and mother, and reporting higher levels of job satisfaction than full-time working mothers (Gregory & Connolly, 2008; Zou, 2015).

Case study: Duncan, freelance sports consultant

At the age of 30, before children were even on the horizon, Duncan took the unusual step of getting a job that would allow him to work from home. He applied to head up the London office of a national sports association, and it turned out that that office was to be his living room and he was to be the sole employee. This suited him well. He was perfectly happy to be away from office politics and free from the daily commute; he liked the peace and convenience of working in his own flat and felt that he had plenty of contact with colleagues at the head office in Birmingham and with clients all over the country, if he needed company. Seven years on, the chief executive of the organisation told Duncan that he was planning to leave and set up a consultancy of his own, and offered Duncan the chance to join him. The two of them had talked about this possibility off and on over the years, and Duncan had always been drawn to the idea of working more independently. But now it was crunch time. Two other factors affected his decision. His first child was due to be born just a few months down the line, and Duncan's wife was a high-flying commercial solicitor. She loved her job and knew that it wasn't going to be possible to cut down her hours, or work more flexibly: if one of them was going to be available to attend school nativity productions or look after a sick child, she couldn't, hand on heart, promise that it would be her. So Duncan seized the day and decided to go freelance.

The new set up worked well. It was the run up to the London Olympics, 2012, and there was plenty of work for two well-networked and experienced sports consultants. Their business thrived. Duncan worked hard, but the work was flexible. His daughter, and then his two sons when they came along, were enrolled at a local nursery, so Duncan could usually work his full complement of hours, but when he needed to, he could make different arrangements. He could take the afternoon off and work till late at night, and could make up at the weekends what he missed during the week.

Duncan is happy with how things have worked for him. He doesn't feel that his career has suffered – he has worked more flexibly, but no less hard, and his consultancy has been successful. He wonders where his career would be now, had he made different choices. He would certainly have had more opportunities to gain promotions and pay raises (he notes that since the heady days of the Olympics, his salary hasn't increased at all), but would he have had a more fulfilling journey? He doubts it. His career has been full of great collaborators and interesting and varied projects; he has had a lot of fun, and he is not at all sure that a more conventional path would have offered him as much. Added to that, he thinks he has been a better and more fulfilled father as a result of his choices. He sees that he has been able to be more present and more involved than many of his peers, and he feels that this has been of benefit to everyone in the family.

A new career

We have traditionally thought of career paths as being linear (onwards and upwards) and have judged career success by external factors such as pay and promotion, but it is becoming more common to think about careers in terms of subjective constructs such as job satisfaction and fulfilment (Ng & Feldman, 2014). Parental leave or a longer career break can provide some time to reflect on life and career ambitious, and this leads many people to consider new career avenues.

For some parents (particularly women), this opportunity to reinvent themselves steers them towards a more values-driven career (Hewlett & Luce, 2005). Women sometimes find that their time away from the workplace can lead them to reassess their career goals, as they look up the career ladder and decide that they don't like what they see. Combining re-training with caring responsibilities can work well for parents, as universities and other training providers often offer flexible learning options, with classes in the evening and at weekends, and options for on-line learning. With a bit of forward planning, an individual can emerge from a career break well-equipped to start something new.

Whilst it can be fairly obvious that your old job didn't make you happy, working out what to do next can be more challenging. The first hurdle is identifying the range of possible options, and the second is trying to narrow the possibilities down to a shortlist of viable options, which might suit your skills, values and lifestyle. A career change in mid-life can feel particularly pressured as it involves giving something up as well as starting something new. Evidence suggests that it takes on average two years to make a career decision (Murtagh, Lopes, & Lyons, 2011), so it is important not to put pressure on yourself to make a quick decision. A career change is always going to involve some element of risk, and it is a good idea both to give yourself some time to make sure you are ready and to start laying the groundwork – perhaps developing a local network, taking a few relevant training courses, or offering some work for free, both to build your confidence and your credibility.

There are plenty of self-help books and websites which can give you a starting point, and evidence suggests that talking your ideas through with family and friends can help you to clarify your thoughts (Amundson et al., 2010). Professional career coaches too can offer some valuable support; have a look at the professional registers of career coaches on professional body websites (such as the Career Development Institute) to ensure that you are getting someone suitably qualified.

Re-thinking your career altogether can often mean going back in at the bottom of the career ladder. This can be frustrating for experienced and successful professionals who have already proved themselves in one field, and it can be galling to find that your previous experience and achievements are not valued in the way they perhaps should be. Starting back at the bottom can be difficult from a financial perspective too, but long term, prospects can be more encouraging – mature entrants into a new career are often able to progress unusually quickly through the ranks of their new field, as their more transferable professional or managerial skills come into their own, and evidence supports the idea that career changers end up more satisfied with their jobs than those who stayed put (Carless & Arnup, 2011).

Case study: Ranj, full-time park ranger

Ranj graduated with a degree in politics, and after a few years of trying various different options, she found her way into marketing. She was a creative thinker and working in the health sector; she felt that she might be able to provide an important service to the public. Ranj worked in this field for ten years, rose up the ranks but became jaded about the industry and questioned the real value of the work she did.

The birth of her first child coincided with a move to the midlands to be nearer to her parents. Ranj resigned from her job and embraced the life of a full-time mother, sorting out their new house and developing a new life for the family. Seven years later, when her younger child started school, Ranj decided that she needed to re-engage with her career. She had toyed with a number of alternative careers since over the years, but the one she kept coming back to was working in conservation. It was a completely new field for her, but Ranj found that she would be able to do a masters course in conservation at a local university, part distance learning and part weekend lectures. It would take some years to qualify, but Ranj was in no hurry – she wasn't quite ready to embrace a full-time role and she still wanted to be very available for her children. Still, the logistics of managing the course were difficult for the family. Ranj's partner was very supportive but found the additional childcare he needed to do at the weekends draining, on top of his full-time job, and the whole family found that they missed out on the family time that had been so precious to them.

But Ranj persevered. She enjoyed the course itself, and if the truth be told, liked having some time away from the family, where she could find her own identity again and gradually re-build her confidence.

Finding a job in this new field was more tricky than Ranj had expected, and it became clear that she would need to start at the bottom again, working for free. This was a blow. They had just about managed living on one salary for the past few years, but with the debt from her MSc now to re-pay, their family finances were tight. She found herself a part-time voluntary job with the national parks, and the family muddled along. Ranj loved the work, enjoyed being part of a team and appreciated being able to put her new-found knowledge to good use, but it wasn't easy for the family and she kept wondering whether she should just go back to her old field of marketing. After six months working without a salary, her department was awarded a grant, and as part of that, they were able to hire Ranj to work part time for six months. The money wasn't great, but at least she was finally earning. And more than that, she felt that she was now on the right track. When the contract finished, the organisation found a way to keep her salary going, and her hours gradually inched their way up. Three years down the line, Ranj applied for a more senior ranger's job and was offered the role full time and permanently.

For Ranj it has all worked out well, but there were moments when she felt that she had let everyone down, and feared that she would never make it. She is earning less now than she was when she gave up her marketing role, but in terms of job satisfaction, it is incomparable.

New family-friendly job

In many cases, the primary requirement of a new career after parenthood is one that fits in with the new family. There are some career areas which are not readily compatible with hands-on parenting, and the impetus to find a new career can be driven largely by the need to find something flexible. One sector which is appealing to many parents looking for a family-friendly option is education. The school hours and holidays are attractive to parents of school-age children, and it is a field which offers a range of different roles and is used to accommodating part-time hours. Other industries too are increasingly seeing the benefits of offering flexible working. The NHS has a great tradition of even very senior roles being available part time, and within the technology sector, employers are actively campaigning for mothers to re-train as coders, promising flexible hours and the chance to work from home.

Freelance roles can come into their own too in this category, as parents can take their existing interests or talents and work out ways to use them to make money. Parents make a living through applying a vast range of skills from admin to yoga teaching, but making a living as a freelancer is not an easy option. Many successful parent-freelancers make it work through a lot of hard graft, and some find that their success comes at too high a price. But if you are looking for an option where you can be in control, this might be worth considering.

One big drawback with part-time, family-friendly roles is that they tend to be more likely to be low skilled and low status. There are, of course, exceptions, but it is certainly true that primary schools are filled with over-qualified teaching assistants, office staff and exam invigilators as mothers (and it does tend to be mothers) are prioritising the part-time nature of the work over personal challenge, salary and status. Overall, there is a significant mismatch between the number of interesting, challenging part-time jobs and the number of highly skilled parents looking for part-time work. It is frustrating that organisations are so reluctant to organise their work so that employees could work from 10am–2pm, term time only, reserving this kind of working pattern almost exclusively for low-level jobs. Some organisations are trying to promote a more flexible culture in the labour market (such as the employment agencies *2 to 3 Days* and *Women Like Us*), and some larger organisations are now focusing on offering flexible work or additional support for returning parents. The culture is changing, but more needs to be done to allow the economy to take advantage of this pool of talent, and to allow parents to put their skills to good use without sacrificing their family time.

Case study: Juley, part-time teaching assistant

Juley trained as a graphic designer and worked for 14 years in a publishing company, designing and producing corporate brochures. She had significant responsibility, dealing with a substantial budget and managing complex projects and teams. For the first ten years or so, she loved it – the fast pace, the chance to use her creative skills and her like-minded colleagues. Over the years, Juley's enthusiasm for her job waned a little, but after the birth of her first child, she decided to go back to her job part-time. She appreciated the flexibility her employer offered her and felt that she had built up some trust over the years which could prove particularly useful now. It was also great being in a job that she knew well, so that any spare energy could be channelled towards her family. But with the birth of her second child, and her son's move to the shorter days of nursery school, Juley felt that it was time to leave, seeing her more complicated family life as an excuse to pull the plug on the career that no longer captured her imagination.

Juley spent a few happy years as a stay-at-home mum, but once her daughter was settled at school, she started to think about going back to work. She had no interest in returning to her former role, and she needed something part time and local – her first priority was to her family. Casting around to see what options might be open to her, she first applied for a job working in the office at her children's primary school but was told that the job was only possible on a full-time basis. The office manager at the school hinted that there would be a vacancy coming up soon as a part-time teaching assistant and wondered if that might suit Juley better. Teaching had been an idea Juley had toyed with years ago and decided now that this role was worth a shot. She had not worked in the field before, but over the past few years had been very involved in the school as a mother, helping in the classrooms one morning each week, and chairing the PTFA for a year. The selection process was more gruelling than she imagined, but Juley was delighted to be offered a job, two days a week.

Three years on, it is working out well. She enjoys being around the children and loves the fact that the school hours and holidays allow her to be the mother she wants to be. She wonders what her life would have been like had she been more enthusiastic about her previous job and had she made the decision to stick with it. She worries that her world has shrunk down to her narrow local community in and around the school, and occasionally reflects on her husband's life, wondering if she would have liked a bit more of his identity and status. And she thinks about the future. She worries about what kind of role model she is for her daughter and whether she will be a teaching assistant until retirement. But if she had her time again she wouldn't change anything. She feels enormously privileged to have been able to make the choices that she made. She has been the mother she wanted to be, and doing that job well seems much more important than any status or salary that a glitzy job in the city could have given her.

Making it work

Each of the options outlined herein has its plus points, but many parents find that their situation is not perfect, as they struggle to be both the worker they want to be and the parent they feel their child deserves (Kanji & Cahusac, 2015). A successful new arrangement relies on three key factors: a supportive employer, a supportive family and available childcare provision (Woolnough & Redshaw, 2016). The employer needs to understand the new parents' constraints, and there is a need for an organisational culture in which there is no stigma attached to flexible working; a partner needs to share the domestic responsibilities, and together the parents need to ensure that both careers are valued at home; and childcare needs to be high-quality, affordable and accessible.

One of the biggest challenges that parents face as they return to work after a career break is a reduced level of confidence. Work confers identity, status and financial independence, all of which can dissipate swiftly as soon as you give up your full-time role. Add to that, the simple fact that being out of the workplace, even for a relatively short spell, will mean that you are not up to speed on the most recent developments and trends, and that some of your skills might be a little rusty, and it is no wonder that parents returning to work after parental leave or a career break can feel a little unsure of themselves (Stout & Chaker, 2004).

But the evidence is clear. Time away from the workplace in caring roles enhances your professional skills (Ruderman, Ohlott, Panzer, & King, 2002). When you return to the workplace after a year or more of looking after your children, you will have improved your interpersonal skills, you will have developed your psychological resources and you will have further honed your time management skills. Sadly, it is also clear that hiring managers do not tend to understand the value of this year-long immersive training programme (Woolnough & Redshaw, 2016), but it is important that you know it yourself and can sell your newly developed skills with confidence. Time spent reflecting on your skills, either on your own, or with a coach, can help you to prepare for a conversation with a future employer (see also Chapter 4).

A second challenge new parents face is the influence of gender norms. Across most of Europe (except for the Nordic countries), North America and Australia and New Zealand, society generally assumes that fathers will continue with their full-time jobs and focus on their careers as a way to best provide for their families. It is then assumed that mothers' careers will take a back seat as their priority becomes caring for their children. These women may go back to work part time, as long as their part-time hours allow them to be the primary carer for the children and don't jeopardise their partner's career.

In reality, many, many families do things differently, but these gender norms are powerful and significantly impact the decisions that parents make, their subsequent experiences and how they view their own choices. Flouting gender norms comes at a price. It can be harder for fathers to become integrated with the local community, and some men report social isolation, mixed reactions from family and friends, and instances of feeling stigmatised (Lee & Lee, 2018). Mothers who return to work full time may find it easy to be self-critical of their behaviour as a mother, questioning their own maternal instincts or being concerned that others will judge them for their choices. But recent evidence brings hope to families making non-traditional choices. Rushing and Powell's study of working mothers and stay-at-home fathers (2015) suggested that this arrangement worked very well for these families, with parents both reporting great relationships with their children and with each other.

Conclusion

Bringing a child into the world and raising it to independence is quite a task in itself, and managing this on top of the increasing demands of the workplace, and the societal requirements to be the ideal mother, father and worker, is a tall order. If you are a working parent and you are finding your situation challenging, that's because it is. If you are wondering whether there is a better or easier option out there, well, there may be; but it is possible that there is not. Being a working parent is always a process of compromise and trade-offs. Families make all manner of career solutions work for them, and whilst there is rarely a right answer, there is also rarely a wrong answer. Working parents are resourceful, hard-working and creative – they have to be. But they can also be satisfied and fulfilled, both at home and at work, and whilst this generation is having to fight, negotiate and compromise, these efforts are making a difference and the cultural norms are slowly shifting.

Key learnings from research	*Practical recommendations*
• Although policy and legislation now offer more family-friendly options for working parents, the cultural shift is lagging behind, and whilst most fathers continue in work full time, mothers are still likely to take a career break, return to work part time or in a lower-level job. • Taking time out to look after children is detrimental for parents' careers, and the parenting pay gap never goes away. • Women are often surprised by the barriers they face when returning to the workplace after a career break, finding that employers are not always very flexible, suitable childcare is difficult to come by and their work confidence is significantly diminished. • Yet, despite these challenges, it seems that whatever decisions they make, parents in general end up being happy about their choices.	• Employers need to be educated to understand the real value of part-time staff and working mothers, and should be incentivised to be more creative in their approach to flexible work for parents. • Investing in coaching could help those returning from parental leave or a longer career break to identify and evidence the work-relevant transferable skills that they have developed. • The government needs to support the provision of more high-quality, affordable childcare. • Society as a whole needs to be less rigid in its social norms, acknowledging that successful mothers, fathers and workers can come in all shapes and sizes.

References

Amundson, N. E., Borgen, W. A., Iaquinta, M., Butterfield, L. D., & Koert, E. (2010). Career decisions from the decider's perspective. *The Career Development Quarterly*, *58*(4), 336–351.

Anxo, D., Flood, L., Mencarini, L., Pailhé, A., Solaz, A., & Tanturri, M. L. (2007). *Time allocation between work and family over the life-cycle: A comparative gender analysis of Italy, France, Sweden and the United States*. IZA Discussion Papers, 3193. Institute for the Study of Labor, Bonn.

Berger, E. M. (2013). Happy working mothers? Investigating the effect of maternal employment on life satisfaction. *Economica*, *80*(317), 23–43.

Carless, S. A., & Arnup, J. L. (2011). A longitudinal study of the determinants and outcomes of career change. *Journal of Vocational Behavior*, *78*(1), 80–91.

Gregory, M., & Connolly, S. (2008). Feature: The price of reconciliation: Part-time work, families and women's satisfaction. *The Economic Journal*, *118*(526), F1–F7.

Haas, L., & Hwang, C. P. (2009). Is fatherhood becoming more visible at work? Trends in corporate support for fathers taking parental leave in Sweden. *Fathering*, *7*(3), 303–322.

Hewlett, S. A., & Luce, C. B. (2005). Off-ramps and on-ramps: Keeping talented women on the road to success. *Harvard Business Review*, *83*, 43–54.

Johnston, D. D., & Swanson, D. H. (2006). Constructing the "good mother": The experience of mothering ideologies by work status. *Sex Roles*, *54*(7–8), 509–519.

Kanji, S., & Cahusac, E. (2015). Who am I? mothers' shifting identities, loss and sensemaking after workplace exit. *Human Relations*, *68*(9), 1415–1436.

Lee, J. Y., & Lee, S. J. (2018). Caring is masculine: Stay-at-home fathers and masculine identity. *Psychology of Men & Masculinity*, *19*(1), 47.

Lewis, J., Campbell, M., & Huerta, C. (2008). Patterns of paid and unpaid work in Western Europe: Gender, commodification, preferences and the implications for policy. *Journal of European Social Policy*, *18*(1), 21–37.

Lovejoy, M., & Stone, P. (2012). Opting back in: The influence of time at home on professional women's career redirection after opting out. *Gender, Work & Organization, 19*(6), 631–653.

Murtagh, N., Lopes, P. N., & Lyons, E. (2011). Decision making in voluntary career change: An other-than-rational perspective. *The Career Development Quarterly, 59*(3), 249–263.

Ng, T. W. H., & Feldman, D. C. (2014). Subjective career success: A meta-analytic review *Journal of Vocational Behavior, 85*, 169–179.

OECD. (2017). *OECD family database.* Retrieved from www.oecd.org/social/family/database. htm

ONS. (2017). *Families and the labour market.* London: Office for National Statistics.

Ruderman, M. N., Ohlott, P. J., Panzer, K., & King, S. N. (2002). Benefits of multiple roles for managerial women. *Academy of Management journal, 45*(2), 369–386.

Rushing, C., & Powell, L. (2015). Family dynamics of the stay-at-home father and working mother relationship. *American Journal of Men's Health, 9*(5), 410–420.

Stout, H., & Chaker, A. M. (2004). Second chances: After years off, women struggle to revive careers. *The Wall Street Journal, 243*(89), A1.

Woolnough, H., & Redshaw, J. (2016). The career decisions of professional women with dependent children: What's changed? *Gender in Management: An International Journal, 31*(4), 297–311.

Zou, M. (2015). Gender, work orientations and job satisfaction. *Work, Employment and Society, 29*(1), 3–22.

10 Training and development for employees returning to work after parental leave

Joanna B. Yarker, Hans-Joachim Wolfram, and Nina M. Junker

Overview of the field

Formal training and development for employees returning to work after parental leave appears varied in content and delivery. Despite such large numbers of parents returning to work following parental leave every day (Office for National Statistics, 2018), evidence on the prevalence and impact of practices employed by organisations is sparse. Support for returning parents often places a focus on the practicalities of return. A recent report by the Chartered Institute of Personnel Development UK (CIPD, 2016) noted that organisations primarily focus on flexible working provision (offered by 30% of organisations), flexible working to support drop-offs/pickups (25%), mentoring or counselling (20%), and other practical supports such as childcare support. While guidance in the form of online fact sheets, webinars, podcasts, and discussion groups is plentiful (e.g., Working Families), and training is available for those who are overseeing parental leave (e.g., HR, management, or administration) to better understand the largely legal obligations of employers (e.g., CIPD Maternity and Parental Leave Short Course), training for returning employees appears to be largely focused on the process of return (e.g., keep-in-touch days, access to flexible working) and on career coaching or mentoring.

Business in the Community (2019), a UK business network, synthesised ideals for best practice in return-to-work. Their report calls for organisations to offer development for managers to help them better understand the psychological and emotional changes during parental leave and tailored induction programmes for returners. Employers are also encouraged to consider the location, timing, and delivery mode of the training to ease additional childcare demands. Recommended learning modules focus on confidence building, team building, communication, work-life balance, and stereotyping in the workplace. The extent to which organisations offer or employees take up the opportunities to engage in these practices is unknown. Furthermore, there is little mention of factors within the home, which considering the wealth of research relating to identity and spillover between family and work noted later in this chapter, may present an important gap in current provisions for returning parents.

Returnship programmes developed for those who have been out of the workforce for an extended period of time are increasingly popular among organisations and returning employees alike, and place a focus on building confidence and technical skills (Gicheva & Keohane, 2018). Again, little systematic research is available to guide our understanding of what works; however, the research that does exist provides useful learnings. For instance, a recent study by Herman, Gracia, Macniven, Clark, and Doyle (2018) noted that a blended learning approach to return, including networking, webinars, and career coaching, enabled women to successful return to a range of STEM roles. Importantly, they call for an integrated approach that incorporates different life course stages. This is echoed in a report by Rieger, Bird, and Farrer (2018), who interviewed professionals leading the schemes and found that line manager buy-in and support, flexibility of support, involving successful returners, and striking a balance between specific and general skills were important components of returnship programmes. A comprehensive programme of evaluation of returnship programmes is required to identify the key ingredients that promote successful and sustainable returns.

It is important to note that men and women across the globe have different experiences of returning to work driven by variations in parental leave systems (OECD, 2017) and individual differences (Feldman, Sussman, & Zigler, 2004) that require consideration in any training and development programme. Policy contexts drive decisions made by parents and have implications for training and development needs, specifically around technical skills. For example, the duration of paid leave varies widely and for many the month of return is determined by financial drivers. Furthermore, there is a disconnect between policy and practice (ILO, 2014). The Institute of Leadership and Management (2014) noted that fewer than 10% of UK fathers took two weeks of parental leave available to them, while a quarter of new fathers take no parental leave at all, often for fear of reprisal or because of workload demands. Interestingly, a report by Bright Horizons and Working Families (2017) describes how men are less likely to disclose their family issues at work and are afraid to request flexible working. These findings have important implications for the content of future training and development offered to new fathers and those who are working with them.

In the following, we discuss two relevant aspects in research and practice to highlight what training to assist returning parents should focus on. These involve changes in behaviour, attitudes, and identity as a result of becoming a parent as well as spillover experiences between family and work. Then, we turn to the literature on sickness absence to see how models developed to support employees after long-term sickness absence may be helpful in guiding return-to-work programmes after parental leave. We conclude with practical recommendations and lay out a journey to navigate employees' training and development before, during, and after parental leave.

Key debates in research and practice

Changes in gender-typical behaviours, gender role attitudes, and gendered identity facets

Research about changes in individual attributes examined gender-typical behaviours (stereotypically feminine and stereotypically masculine, e.g., Endendijk, Derks, &

Mesman, 2018), gender role attitudes (endorsement of traditional gender roles, e.g., Katz-Wise, Priess, & Hyde, 2010) as well as gendered identity facets (parent role and professional role, e.g., Hodges & Park, 2013). Two main mechanisms have been suggested to explain such changes: the balance of demands and resources and the recalibration of role attitudes and identity. Changes in gender-typical behaviours may be seen as a response to demands associated with the new parent role (e.g., Katz-Wise et al., 2010). Resources, such as time, energy, and money (Hobfoll, 1989), might be shifted between life domains, in an attempt to reinstate a balance between demands and resources needed to cope with these demands (Thoits, 1992). For example, a fairly gender-egalitarian couple transitioning to parenthood may decide that both should engage equally in childcare. Accordingly, both parents would be likely to engage more in stereotypically feminine behaviours after becoming parents, indicating a shift of resources to the parent role.

A second mechanism describes recalibration after transitioning to parenthood, and here the focus is on changes in gender role attitudes and gendered identity facets, in order to reconcile changed behaviours with attitudes and identity, thereby reducing cognitive dissonance (e.g., Schober & Scott, 2012), and reorganising identity (e.g., Kaźmierczak & Karasiewicz, 2018). For example, another fairly gender-egalitarian couple may decide that, because of economic pressures, the mother should focus on childcare, whereas the father should engage more with paid labour outside the home. Under these circumstances, both parents engage more in traditionally gender-typed behaviours, which is likely to be perceived as inconsistent with their egalitarian-gender role attitudes. In an attempt to restore consistency between behaviour and attitudes, these parents may then develop more traditional attitudes (e.g., Endendijk et al., 2018). The latter process may also apply to gendered identity facets, in that these parents might attach increased importance to life roles that are consistent with stereotypical expectations about mothers and fathers (e.g., Kaźmierczak & Karasiewicz, 2018).

Research findings suggest that after becoming parents, women engage more in stereotypically feminine behaviours (i.e., caring), whereas men demonstrate more stereotypically masculine behaviours (i.e., assertiveness). This pattern emerged examining parents from the USA (e.g., Katz-Wise et al., 2010), but also with parents from the Netherlands – a country generally seen as relatively gender egalitarian (Endendijk et al., 2018). These changes in gender-typical behaviours go along with corresponding changes in gender role attitudes as well as gendered identity facets. After transitioning to parenthood, people reported more traditional gender role attitudes (e.g., Baxter, Buchler, Perales, & Western, 2015). Gender role attitudes, however, may also shift in the opposite direction after the transition to parenthood (Schober & Scott, 2012) or may remain unchanged (Endendijk et al., 2018), depending on the extent of mothers' labour market participation, formal childcare arrangements, and egalitarian task division at home.

With regards to gendered identity facets, on the other hand, research findings indicate that the importance of the parent role increased in both women and men after transitioning to parenthood. However, parent role importance was higher in mothers than in fathers, whereas professional role importance was higher in fathers than in mothers (Kaźmierczak & Karasiewicz, 2018), especially when comparing stay-at-home mothers with breadwinning fathers (Gaunt & Scott, 2016). Slightly, and temporarily, reduced professional role importance was also found in a sample of mothers from Sweden – a country that is not only considered as rather gender egalitarian, but also as "the archetype of the women-friendly welfare state" (Evertsson, 2013, p. 143). Importantly, working mothers may "assume the bigger share of family duties" (Mayrhofer, Meyer, Schiffinger, & Schmidt, 2008, p. 312) voluntarily, or as a result of not successfully negotiating greater father involvement with family responsibilities (Bulanda, 2004). Therefore, we recommend that the need for change is highlighted to "parents to be", and that they are conscious of the practicalities of combining work and parenting and the options available to them. Furthermore, they should openly discuss with their partner how much they would like to take on and what they expect from their partner to contribute and to come to an agreement on each other's responsibilities.

Further empirical evidence suggests that mothers, but not fathers, changed the importance attached to professional roles and parent roles, depending on situational context (Hodges & Park, 2013). This finding may indicate that women are still expected to make themselves more available to their families than men (e.g., Greenhaus & Parasuraman, 1999), and that they experience these two roles and associated expectations not to easily match together (Özbiler & Beidoğlu, 2018). Working fathers may not experience similar conflicting expectations but can focus on their professional role (for a discussion of an emerging folk model of parenthood as "gender-neutral engineering", on the other hand, see Kaplan & Knoll, 2018). Working mothers' identity shifts between professional role and parent role may lead to negative mental health outcomes (e.g., fragmented sense of the self, lower self-esteem, greater depression: Hodges & Park, 2013). Furthermore, family responsibilities are associated with fewer applications for career advancement (Luekemann & Abendroth, 2018), which can negatively affect women's career success. Implications for career progression are more fully discussed in Chapter 5.

There is need to raise awareness of likely changes in demands and resources, and attitudes and identity, and to equip returning parents with the knowledge and skills to both reflect on these changes and to hold open dialogues about how these changes affect their home and working lives. Such training and development may help returning parents reach more effective solutions for reconciling their new home and work lives.

Spillover between life domains and informal training

Changes in behaviour, attitudes, and work and family role importance typically occur at the transition to parenthood. Role importance, again, changes once employees return to work. Moreover, a major concern of many employees returning to work after parental leave is the presumed inability of balancing their work and family demands (e.g., Buzzanell & Liu, 2007; see also Chapter 4). From a training and development perspective, however, the new role as mothers and fathers can also be understood as continuous informal training. As such, parenthood offers opportunities to learn and develop skills, which are desired by employers (Greenhaus & Powell, 2006). These skills include conflict management, communication, and multi-tasking, but also leadership skills, such as strategic planning or achieving goals through others (e.g., Ruderman, Ohlott, Panzer, & King, 2002). Moreover, parents are more patient and more resilient than child-free employees. Parents more often have plans after work (such as to pick up their child at a specific time), which helps them be more absorbed at work (Dumas & Perry-Smith, 2018). Being absorbed at work means to be fully immersed in one's job and to experience that time flies while at work. To fully concentrate on one's work tasks is particularly important when working on complex issues (Quinn, 2005).

Some employers have recognised the potential of their employees' parental role to positively affect their work role and use this potential in training and developing their employees (Fortune, 2018). As a starting point, these organisations may map the skills their employees learn in their parental role to the skills they desire in these employees' work role. Doing so, some working parents may particularly benefit from their social skills, whereas others may find their leadership skills more beneficial for their jobs. In a next step, employers may recognise these additional skills because of one's parental role, alongside work-specific skills, in decision-making processes (e.g., concerning promotion). Some organisations have, for instance, implemented relevant parental experiences as a module in their leadership development programmes. Employees with parental obligations may use these instead of attending a formal training on the respective topic.

From a training and development perspective, the most efficient trainings are informal rather than formal (Cerasoli et al., 2018; OECD, 2019). Informal training happens without a specific curriculum, without a formal trainer, and typically in such a way that individuals are not really aware that they are in a training situation. An example for an informal training situation would be a parent who wants his or her child to get dressed in the morning and who has to decide on the most promising way to achieve this. Through trial and error, the parent develops this way but would typically not refer to this situation as a training. At work, a discussion about a specific issue would be an example of informal learning. Through the discussion, every member learns new aspects, arguments, and perspectives to approach the problem, which help them in developing their view on the issue. To increase the efficiency of such informal training situations, it is important that employees reflect on their experiences (e.g., Boyd & Fales, 1983): What did I learn in this situation? How can I use these learning experiences? Where could this be helpful? Accordingly, employees and employers should raise awareness of these training situations. One way to do so could be an App (such as the be:able App: Work-Family Institute, 2018), which supports employees in describing their informal training situations at home and to map them onto specific skills, which can be transferred to the workplace (in the foregoing example, these could be remaining patient in the situation and understanding the child's needs, to come up with a good solution).

Thus far, we have focused our discussion in this chapter on the individual working parent and highlighted changes in behaviour, attitudes, and identity because of parenthood as well as positive spillover experiences from family to work as relevant training and development aspects. Next, we turn to how employers manage the return-to-work of employees after long-term sickness absence to relate the processes typically used to re-board these employees to their potential usage to manage the return-to-work after parental leave.

Lessons to consider from research on return-to-work experiences following sickness absence

Research within the field of return-to-work following sickness absence has aimed to elucidate the contributors to successful returns. Moving beyond policies, the consideration of contextual and process factors has been found to be pivotal in the returning employee's journey. These include the importance of maintaining contact during sickness absence and the value of line manager communications (Munir, Yarker, Hicks, & Donaldson-Feilder, 2012), implementing work adjustments such as job re-design (Williams-Whitt et al., 2016), and considering integrated systemic approaches (e.g., IGLOO: Nielsen, Yarker, Munir, & Bültmann, 2018).

Developing an integrated framework, considering resources available to the individual within the workplace and at home, Nielsen et al. (2018) introduced the IGLOO model and proposed that **I**ndividual, **G**roup, **L**eader, **O**rganisational, and **O**verarching resources work together to promote sustainable return-to-work following sickness absence. This framework is readily transferable to the context of returning to work after parental leave. In a practical sense, at the **I**ndividual level, a returning mother may have more or less confidence in her ability to do the job on her return, or may be struggling to reconcile her new identity as a working parent. The benefits of **G**roup-level social support at work and home are well established (Pluut, Ilies, Curşeu, & Liu, 2018) and examined further in Chapter 2, while comments from colleagues such as 'Thank you for coming' or 'Oh, you are only working part time today?', when a returning father leaves at 4.30 pm to pick his child up from nursery, present a group-level barrier. At the **L**eader level, a manager who has been trained to confidently hold challenging conversations and manage flexible teams may be better able to support a returning father hoping to work flexibly to enable him to return home for bath time. At the **O**rganisational level, clear policies and procedures to obtain flexible working practices are important, while **O**verarching resources will differ between organisations and countries, such as childcare provisions and benefits.

Drawing from the diverse research and practice presented in this chapter, a framework for future practices in training and development following parental leave is presented in Figure 10.1.

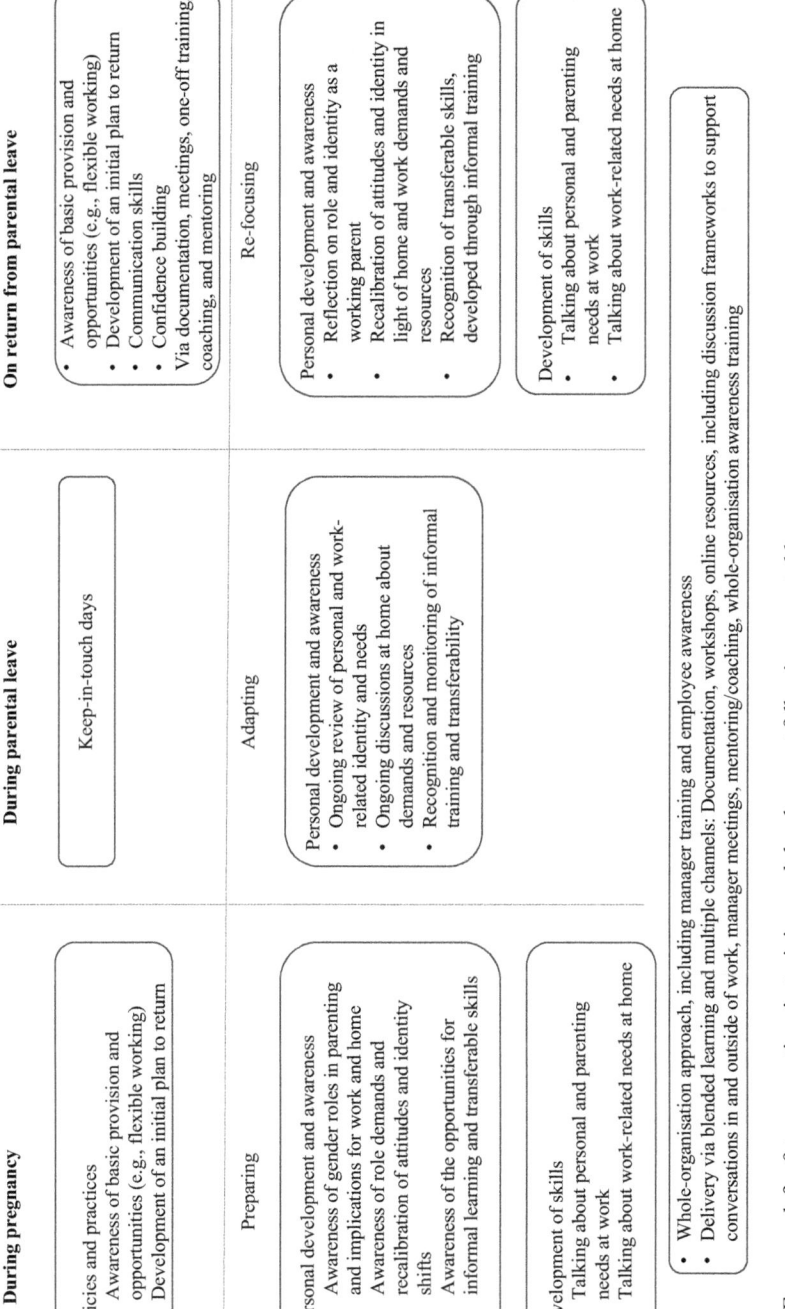

During pregnancy

Policies and practices
- Awareness of basic provision and opportunities (e.g., flexible working)
- Development of an initial plan to return

Preparing

Personal development and awareness
- Awareness of gender roles in parenting and implications for work and home
- Awareness of role demands and recalibration of attitudes and identity shifts
- Awareness of the opportunities for informal learning and transferable skills

Development of skills
- Talking about personal and parenting needs at work
- Talking about work-related needs at home

During parental leave

Keep-in-touch days

Adapting

Personal development and awareness
- Ongoing review of personal and work-related identity and needs
- Ongoing discussions at home about demands and resources
- Recognition and monitoring of informal training and transferability

On return from parental leave

- Awareness of basic provision and opportunities (e.g., flexible working)
- Development of an initial plan to return
- Communication skills
- Confidence building
Via documentation, meetings, one-off training, coaching, and mentoring

Re-focusing

Personal development and awareness
- Reflection on role and identity as a working parent
- Recalibration of attitudes and identity in light of home and work demands and resources
- Recognition of transferable skills, developed through informal training

Development of skills
- Talking about personal and parenting needs at work
- Talking about work-related needs at home

- Whole-organisation approach, including manager training and employee awareness
- Delivery via blended learning and multiple channels: Documentation, workshops, online resources, including discussion frameworks to support conversations in and outside of work, manager meetings, mentoring/coaching, whole-organisation awareness training

Current practices

Additional recommended practices

Figure 10.1 Framework for future practices in training and development following parental leave

Practical recommendations

Extrapolating learnings from the fields of gendered attributes, spillover between life domains, and sickness absence, we propose that future training and development programmes to support parents returning to work consider the following content and contextual features:

Content considerations

- Awareness of policies and practices such as flexible working, breastfeeding, and childcare support.
- Development of essential skills, such as confidence building and communication skills, to enable returnees to hold potentially challenging conversations with managers and peers.
- Development of personal awareness in relation to gender-typical behaviour and identity, supported by frameworks to explore the impact of the changing demands and changing identity at home and work, and the tools to engage in conversations about demands, resources, and identity at work and at home.
- Encouragement of mapping and recognition of informal learning and development, both in and outside of the work environment.
- Tailor content for non-parents by adopting an inclusive approach to include all employees with changing individual circumstances or caring responsibilities (e.g., illness or caring for older relatives).

Contextual considerations

- Early intervention: Equipping employees with the skills and knowledge to navigate the return process is essential, preferably starting before the employee exits the workplace.
- Move beyond awareness and knowledge: Awareness and knowledge of policies and practices are important; however, awareness does not suffice. To fully realise the benefits of these policies, there is a need to move beyond *what* to do and also provide guidance on *how* to do it.
- Move beyond one-off training events towards an ongoing programme of continuous development throughout the stages of preparation before, adaption during, and re-focusing following parental leave.
- Develop line manager skills: Line managers play a pivotal role in the returning employee's re-integration into the workplace. There is need to extend training and development to equip those who manage returning employees, to provide effective support.
- Adopt a whole-systems approach: Parents return to work into a complex social system, where colleagues can provide an important source of support but may also, perhaps unintentionally, impose barriers to successful returns. We propose that a whole-organisation approach to training and development is adopted, whereby colleagues and managers are equipped with an understanding of policies and practices, as well as an understanding of the likely

experiences of parents returning to work, and the skills and know-how to support the return.

- Evaluate to inform practice: We would encourage employers to partner with academics to develop the evidence base in this important area. Longitudinal studies examining the impact of specific activities over time, fine-grained analyses of identity facets, and life roles, and their intersections, as well as examining the implications for non-traditional parents (e.g., single parents, caring fathers) are all areas that require further exploration.

Conclusions

Despite the significant numbers of parents returning to work each week following parental leave, there is a dearth of evidence to guide practice. In this chapter, we have brought together research that could usefully inform the content and design of training programmes to support those returning to work following parental leave, and those who work alongside them. There is need for periodic evaluations of the return process and the benefits that different training and development interventions afford the individual and organisation. This is an area that requires urgent attention, if we are to support returning parents to achieve a successful balance between work and life, as they navigate their new journey. Importantly, according to a report by the UK's Equality and Human Rights Commission (2018), three quarters of working mothers experience a negative or discriminatory experience during pregnancy, maternity leave, and/or on their return form maternity leave. This points to the need for a whole-organisation approach to training and development to support returning parents.

Key learnings from research	*Practical recommendations*
• Traditional gender roles are often endorsed following parenthood, as a response to new demands. • The parenting role offers many unrecognised informal training opportunities. • The experience of returning to work after parental leave is likely to be influenced by the behaviour and support received by their team, line manager, and organisation. • Evidence suggests that training and development following parenthood is typically one-off training, or ongoing mentoring; however, experiences and needs are continually changing.	• New parents need to be conscious of the practicalities of balancing work and parenting and review their available demands and resources. • New parents could be encouraged to map out informal training opportunities and newly developed skills, while organisations should be encouraged to recognise these skills gained outside the workplace. • A whole-organisation approach to training and development is recommended, whereby colleagues and managers are equipped with an understanding of policies and practices, as well as an understanding of the likely experiences of parents returning to work. • Training and development throughout pregnancy and beyond could be provided to help new parents prepare, adapt, and refocus.

References

Baxter, J., Buchler, S., Perales, F., & Western, M. (2015). A life-changing event: First births and men's and women's attitudes to mothering and gender divisions of labor. *Social Forces, 93*(3), 989–1014. http://doi.org/10.1093/sf/sou103

Boyd, E. M., & Fales, A. W. (1983). Reflective learning: Key to learning from experience. *Journal of Humanistic Psychology, 23*(2), 99–117. http://doi.org/10.1177/0022167883232011

Bright Horizons and Working Families. (2017). *The 2017 modern families index*. Retrieved from www.workingfamilies.org.uk/wp-content/uploads/2017/01/MFI_2017_Report_UK_FINAL_web-1.pdf

Bulanda, R. E. (2004). Paternal involvement with children: The influence of gender ideologies. *Journal of Marriage and Family, 66*(1), 40–45. http://doi.org/10.1111/j.0022-2455.2004.00003.x

Business in the Community. (2019). *Exemplar employers best practice recommendations women returners*. Retrieved 05 March 2019 from https://workplace.bitc.org.uk/node/27523

Buzzanell, P., & Liu, M. (2007). It's "give and take": Maternity leave as a conflict management process. *Human Relations, 60*(3), 463–495. http://doi.org/10.1177/0018726707076688

Cerasoli, C. P., Alliger, G. M., Donsbach, J. S., Mathieu, J. E., Tannenbaum, S. I., & Orvis, K. A. (2018). Antecedents and outcomes of informal learning behaviors: A meta-analysis. *Journal of Business and Psychology, 33*(2), 203–230. http://doi.org/10.1007/s10869-017-9492-y

CIPD. (2016). *Labour market outlook: Views from employers – focus on working parents*. Retrieved 05 March 2019 from www.cipd.co.uk/Images/labour-market-outlook-focus-on-working-parents_tcm18-17048.pdf

Dumas, T. L., & Perry-Smith, J. (2018). The paradox of family structure and plans after work: Why single childless employees may be the least absorbed at work. *Academy of Management Journal, 61*, 1231–1252. http://doi.org/10.5465/amj.2016.0086

Endendijk, J. J., Derks, B., & Mesman, J. (2018). Does parenthood change implicit gender-role stereotypes and behaviors? *Journal of Marriage and Family, 80*(1), 61–79. http://doi.org/10.1111/jomf.12451

Equality and Human Rights Commission. (2018). *Is Britain fairer? The state of equality and human rights 2018*. Retrieved 22 March 2019 from www.equalityhumanrights.com/britain-fairer

Evertsson, M. (2013). The importance of work: Changing work commitment following the transition to motherhood. *Acta Sociologica, 56*(2), 139–153. http://doi.org/10.1177/0001699312466177

Feldman, R., Sussman, A. L., & Zigler, E. (2004). Parental leave and work adaptation at the transition to parenthood: Individual, marital, and social correlates. *Journal of Applied Developmental Psychology, 25*(4), 459–479.

Fortune. (2018, November 29). *The best workplaces for parents maximize the full human potential of their employees*. Retrieved from http://fortune.com/2018/11/29/best-workplaces-parents-2018-human-potential/

Gaunt, R., & Scott, J. (2016). Gender differences in identities and their sociostructural correlates: How gendered lives shape parental and work identities. *Journal of Family Issues, 38*(13), 1852–1877. http://doi.org/10.1177/0192513X16629182

Gicheva, N., & Keohane, N. (2018). *Back on track*. London: Social Market Foundation.

Greenhaus, J. H., & Parasuraman, S. (1999). Research on work, family, and gender: Current status and future directions. In G. N. Powell (Ed.), *Handbook of gender and work*. (pp. 391–412). https://doi.org/10.4135/9781452231365.n20

Greenhaus, J. H., & Powell, G. N. (2006). When work and family are allies: A theory of work-family enrichment. *Academy of Management Review*, *31*(1), 72–92. https://doi.org/10.5465/amr.2006.19379625

Herman, C., Gracia, R., Macniven, L., Clark, B., & Doyle, G. (2018). Using a blended learning approach to support women returning to STEM. *Open Learning: The Journal of Open, Distance and e-Learning*, *34*(1), 40–60. https://doi.org/10.1080/02680513.2018.1554475

Hobfoll, S. E. (1989). Conservation of resources: A new attempt at conceptualizing stress. *American Psychologist*, *44*, 513–524.

Hodges, A. J., & Park, B. (2013). Oppositional identities: Dissimilarities in how women and men experience parent versus professional roles. *Journal of Personality and Social Psychology*, *105*(2), 193–216. http://doi.org/10.1037/a0032681

ILO. (2014). *Maternity and paternity at work: Law and practice across the world*. Retrieved from www.ilo.org/global/topics/equality-and-discrimination/maternity-protection/publications/maternity-paternity-at-work-2014/lang – en/index.htm

Institute of Leadership and Management. (2014). *Shared opportunity: Parental leave in UK business*. ILM. Retrieved from www.institutelm.com/asset/EFC9319D-59AF-4E17-BCF9C3EED8EBFBEA/

Kaplan, D., & Knoll, E. (2018). A cultural model of parenthood as engineering: How care-giving fathers construct a gender-neutral view of the parent role. *Journal of Family Issues*, *40*(3), 363–389. https://doi.org/10.1177/0192513X18811387

Katz-Wise, S. L., Priess, H. A., & Hyde, J. S. (2010). Gender-role attitudes and behaviour across the transition to parenthood. *Developmental Psychology*, *46*, 18–28. https://doi.org/10.1037/a0017820

Kaźmierczak, M., & Karasiewicz, K. (2018). Making space for a new role: Gender differences in identity changes in couples transitioning to parenthood. *Journal of Gender Studies*, *28*(3), 271–287. https://doi.org/10.1080/09589236.2018.1441015

Luekemann, L., & Abendroth, A.-K. (2018). Women in the German workplace: What facilitates or constrains their claims-making for career advancement? *Social Sciences*, *7*(11), 214. https://doi.org/10.3390/socsci7110214

Mayrhofer, W., Meyer, M., Schiffinger, M., & Schmidt, A. (2008). The influence of family responsibilities, career fields and gender on career success. *Journal of Managerial Psychology*, *23*(3), 292–323. https://doi.org/10.1108/02683940810861392

Munir, F., Yarker, J., Hicks, B., & Donaldson-Feilder, E. (2012). Returning employees back to work: Developing a measure for Supervisors to Support Return to Work (SSRW). *Journal of Occupational Rehabilitation*, *22*(2), 196–208. https://doi.org/10.1007/s10926-011-9331-3

Nielsen, K., Yarker, J., Munir, F., & Bültmann, U. (2018). IGLOO: An integrated framework for sustainable return to work in workers with common mental disorders. *Work & Stress*, *32*(4), 400–417. https://doi.org/10.1080/02678373.2018.1438536

OECD. (2017). *Parental leave systems*. Retrieved from www.oecd.org/els/soc/PF2_1_Parental_leave_systems.pdf

OECD. (2019). *Recognition of non-formal and informal learning*. Retrieved from www.oecd.org/education/skills-beyond-school/recognitionofnon-formalandinformallearning-home.htm

Office for National Statistics. (2018). *Families and the labour market, England: 2018*. Retrieved from: www.ons.gov.uk/employmentandlabourmarket/peopleinwork/employmentandemployeetypes/articles/familiesandthelabourmarketengland/2018

Özbiler, Ş., & Beidoğlu, M. (2018). Maternal subjective well-being intervention effects: Subjective well-being and self-perception of the parental role. *Current Psychology*. https:// doi.org/10.1007/s12144-018-9818-6

Pluut, H., Ilies, R., Curşeu, P. L., & Liu, Y. (2018). Social support at work and at home: Dual-buffering effects in the work-family conflict process. *Organizational Behavior and Human Decision Processes*, *146*, 1–13. https://doi.org/10.1016/j.obhdp.2018.02.001

Quinn, R. W. (2005). Flow in knowledge work: High performance experience in the design of national security technology. *Administrative Science Quarterly*, *50*(4), 610–641. https://doi.org/10.2189/asqu.50.4.610

Rieger, P., Bird, G., & Farrer, M. (2018, March). *Employer research on returner programmes: Research report*. London: Government Social Research. Retrieved from https://assets.publishing.service.gov.uk/government/uploads/system/uploads/attachment_data/file/694479/Employer_research_on_returner_programmes.pdf

Ruderman, M. N., Ohlott, P. J., Panzer, K., & King, S. N. (2002). Benefits from multiple roles for managerial women. *Academy of Management Journal*, *45*(2), 369–386. https://doi.org/10.5465/3069352

Schober, P., & Scott, J. (2012). Maternal employment and gender role attitudes: Dissonance among British men and women in the transition to parenthood. *Work, Employment and Society*, *26*(3), 514–530. https://doi.org/10.1177/0950017012438577

Thoits, P. A. (1992). Identity structures and psychological well-being: Gender and marital status comparisons. *Social Psychology Quarterly*, *55*(3), 236–256. https://doi.org/10.2307/2786794

Williams-Whitt, K., Bültmann, U., Amick III, B., Munir, F., Tveito, T. H., Anema, J. R., & Hopkinton Conference Working Group on Workplace Disability Prevention. (2016). Workplace interventions to prevent disability from both the scientific and practice perspectives: A comparison of scientific literature, grey literature and stakeholder observations. *Journal of Occupational Rehabilitation*, *26*(4), 417–433. https://doi.org/10.1007/s10926-016-9664-z

Work-Family-Institute. (2018). Be:able (0.13.0) [mobile application software].

11 Childcare options in France

Beyond the hypothetic free choices

Danielle Boyer and Claude Martin

Introduction

In this contribution, we point out a number of relatively unknown aspects of the French situation on the issue of striking a balance between family and professional life. International comparisons on family policies generally describe France by highlighting the following two key characteristics:

- Firstly, it was probably one of the first countries to explicitly make family matters an affair of the state since the end of the nineteenth century, by developing a pro-birth family policy and then integrating progressively other targets (to recognize women's rights, combat inequalities, promote employment, and facilitate the work-life balance with an early-childcare policy, and in the last decades supporting parents in their parenting role) (Martin, 2010, 2017; Knijn et al., 2018).
- Secondly, early childcare has been the object of significant public investment, including a policy on establishing crèches and the development of places in public preschool (Le Bihan & Martin, 2008a). The various reforms since the beginning of the 1990s to facilitate work-life balance were qualified by policymakers as promoting "free choice".

Nevertheless, this longstanding and high level of public investment masks significant social and territorial disparities that we point out herein. These considerable measures disguise the extent of informal childcare provided by parents, who are the first involved in socialising and caring for their children, and the family network, starting with grandparents. Changes in the labour market resulting in the development of precarious employment contracts and an increase in non-standard working hours contribute to the growth of this informal contribution in the organisation of complex childcare arrangements.

From family to childcare policy

Starting from the 1970s, France has progressively established complex measures to support parents who work (Pailhé & Solaz, 2009). The country's family policy is explicit and highly institutionalised and has gradually integrated the "working mother" model, that is, a model where mothers who work are not stigmatised or considered as bad mothers (Morgan, 2006). Compared with most of its European neighbours, France offers a developed, diverse range of care solutions, including: places in early childcare establishments (*établissements d'accueil de jeunes enfants* – EAJE); allowances devised to reduce the cost of having children cared for by a registered childminder, or by a home-based childminder (*complément mode garde* – CMG); obligatory preschool from the age of 3 and sometimes 2 and a half in nursery schools (Box 11.1); and the possibility of taking parental leave, often compensated by shared child-rearing benefits (*prestation partagée d'éducation de l'enfant* – PreParE) (Box 11.2). A set of employment policy measures interconnect with these family policy measures. In particular, since 2004, part-time work has been encouraged in households with young children through higher remuneration of part-time parental leave.

Box 11.1   Childcare options for children under age 3[1]

Individual childcare arrangements include:

Registered childminders, who since 2009 can care for up to four children at once in their home. Approval is granted by the mother and infant welfare services (*Protection Maternelle et Infantile* – PMI (or more recently grouped together in "MAM" (*Maison d'Assistante Maternelle*))) based on a set of criteria, primarily habitat and environment, followed by the candidate's knowledge of infants' needs. Parents who employ registered childminders receive the CMG complement (*Complément de mode de garde*) of the PAJE allowance (*prestation d'accueil du jeune enfant*). The amount of the benefit varies depending on the age of the youngest child and household income. As private employers, parents also benefit from a tax reduction of 50% of the cost (capped). In the 1990s, the family branch of the social security system (Caisse nationale des allocations familiales – CNAF) developed childminder networks (*Relais Assistante Maternelle* – RAM) as part of "childhood" contracts, "leisure time" contracts, and then "children and young people" contracts. The objective is to improve the quality of childcare.

Childcare in the home: Parents can opt to employ a childminder to care for their child or children in the home. In both cases, direct employment by parents opens the right to a "freedom of choice of childcare benefit" (*Complément libre choix du mode de garde*), which is part of the early childhood allowance (*Prestation d'accueil du jeune Enfant* – PAJE). The amount of the benefit varies depending on the age of the youngest child and household income. As private employers, parents also benefit from a tax reduction of 50% of the cost (capped).

Collective childcare, which corresponds to early-childcare establishments (EAJEs) and covers different types of childcare:

- *Collective crèches* provide regular day care for the under-3s. This includes traditional neighbourhood crèches (capacity restricted to 60 places per unit, daytime opening for 8 to 12 hours, closed at night, on Sundays and public holidays), *company crèches* (capacity restricted to 60 places per unit, opening times adapted to company or administration timetable), and *parent-run crèches*, which require time input from parents (maximum capacity 20 places).
- *Drop-in childcare centres* provide occasional care for children under age 6. They include traditional neighbourhood drop-in centres (maximum 60 places per unit) and drop-in centres run by parents (maximum 20 places, 25 with special authorisation).
- *Kindergartens (jardins d'enfants)* provide regular care for children aged 2 to 6. Their capacity can reach 80 places per unit.
- Multi-childcare establishments group different forms of childcare for the under-6s within the same structure: regular or occasional care, full- or part-time care. Their capacity is 60 places if they are organized in a traditional way and 20 to 25 places when run by parents. Some establishments that provide collective and family childcare can reach a maximum overall capacity of 100 places.
- *Family crèches (services d'accueil familial)* gather registered childminders who look after children in their homes but also attend a collective establishment for various activities. They are managed in a similar way to collective crèches, and the childminders who work there are paid by the local authority or by the private organisation that employs them. The maximum capacity of these units is 150 places.

Preschools or *nursery schools* come under the ministry for education and can enroll children who are aged 2 at the start of the academic year "within the limits of available places . . . on the condition that they are physically and psychologically ready to attend" (practical guide for parents, *Votre enfant à l'école maternelle*, 2010–2011).

Box 11.2 Recent reform: the "PreParE" shared child-rearing benefit

Since 1 January 2015, for all births or adoptions, the PreParE (*prestation partagée de l'éducation de l'enfant*) shared child-rearing benefit is aimed at parents of children under age 3 who work part-time or have stopped working (provided they were previously employed) to take care of their child(ren). The benefit applies until the first birthday of a first child, or up to the third birthday of the last child when parents have several dependent children.

For a first child, this benefit is paid out per parent during a maximum period of six months up until the child's first birthday. From the second child, it is paid for a maximum of 24 months per parent up to the third birthday of the youngest child. Couples are encouraged to share this benefit. This sharing incentive consists in "reducing" the total allowance period if both parents do not individually claim a share of the benefit. Thus, for a first child, the allowance is only paid out for a maximum of six months (instead of one year) if only one parent claims it. Starting from the second child, it is paid for a maximum of 24 months if it is not alternated, and for a maximum of 36 months if shared.

These various arrangements offer families, and especially mothers, a way to balance family and work, and are usually considered as a key factor that explains France's relatively high levels of fertility (1.92 in 2017) and full-time working mothers compared with its European neighbours (Le Bihan & Martin, 2008b). An overview of coverage rates, correspondence between requests and take-up, and family satisfaction do indeed indicate that the state response to early childcare is of a high level (Boyer & Crépin, 2018).

Thus, the 2018 report by the National Observatory of Early Childcare mentions a coverage rate for children under age 3 of 58 places for 100 children in 2016, which is a high coverage rate compared with many developed countries in particular for the youngest children (from 2 months of age) (Boyer, 2019).[2] Most of this childcare is provided by registered childminders: 33.4 places. Second comes early childhood care establishments, which cover 18.5% of places for children under age 3 (Table 11.1). The availability of preschools ranks the national education system third since it provides childcare for about one in 25 under-3-year-olds (4.1%), while childminders employed in the home represent the lowest percentage (1.8%) (Boyer, 2018, p. 28).

Table 11.1 Theoretical capacity for under-3s in "formal" childcare options for 100 children aged under 3 in 2016

	Theoretical capacity	*Capacity per 100 children aged under 3 (%)*
Registered childminder directly employed by individuals	787,800	33.4
Home-based childminder	46,700	1.8
Childcare in an EAJE (collective, family, parent-run, micro-crèche)	437,600	18.5
Preschool	96,300	4.1
Theoretical capacity of total "formal" childcare options*	1,368,300	58.0

Source: ONAPE, 2018

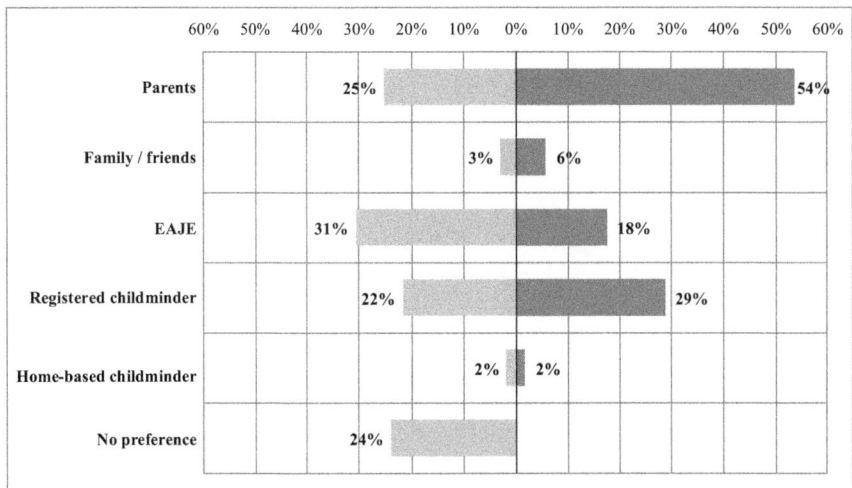

Figure 11.1 Childcare options preferred and taken up at the start of the 2017 school year[3]

Note: Preference, Take-up

Source: TMO-régions – barometer survey of early childhood, September 2017.

Field: Families with at least one child aged 6 months to 1 year.

Key: At the birth of their first child, 25% of families preferred to care for their child themselves; at the start of the 2017 academic year, 54% of families pursued this option (take up).

In addition, a recent barometer survey of early childcare completes this satisfactory overview since it indicates a 72% correspondence between families' preferences and take-up (Crépin, 2018). The same survey also reports that 92% of families say they are satisfied with their solution, even when the childcare they use is not the option that they initially sought (Figure 11.1).

Beyond the free-choice rhetoric

These observations indicate that the childcare solutions available in the French system are effective. However, data on the evolution of family take-up raises numerous questions, in particular concerning availability for those with the lowest incomes. A more careful look at the French data reveals important disparities and a growing share of informal care arrangements to compensate for the lack of access to services or more important work constraints.

The first point is that most children under age 3 (64%) are still mainly cared for by their parents (usually the mother) or a close family member, and that families do not have equal access to the various forms of childcare. The choice is highly restricted for families on the lowest incomes. In these families, the likelihood that children will be cared for by a parent is greater than in other families.

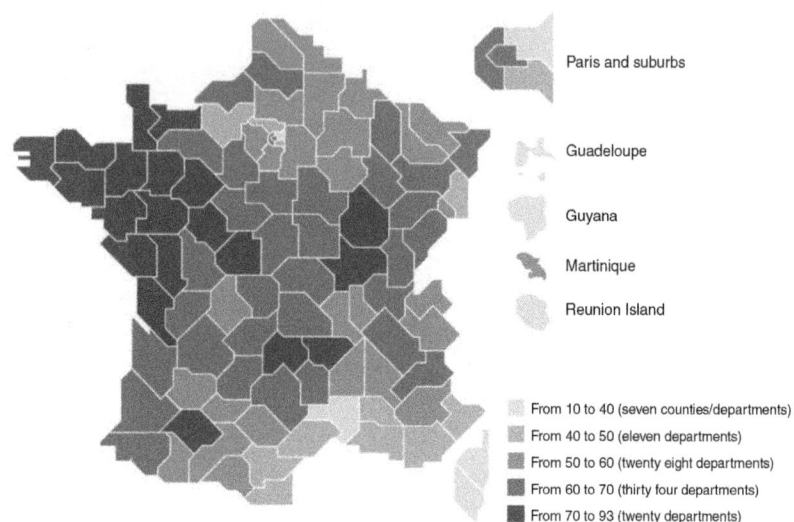

Figure 11.2 Theoretical capacity for children under age 3 by type of "formal" childcare for 100 children under age 3 (%) in 2016

Note: Formal childcare solution = collective or individual childcare establishments that are the object of legislation and generally managed by the state. They include registered childminders, home-based childminders, early childhood care establishments, and preschools.

Source: ONAPE, 2018

Geographic inequalities are also considerable (Figure 11.2). These inequalities are strongly correlated to social inequalities: the relationship between the number of childcare places available and the number of children under age 3 is thus highly variable from one administrative area, municipality, and neighbourhood to another. Availability of childcare places is much greater in "wealthy" neighbourhoods than in working-class neighbourhoods (Boyer, 2018 and caf data.fr).

Lastly, recent developments are worth noting. For example, while parental childcare is the most common option, the take-up of benefits aimed at compensating the total or partial stopping of work has dropped considerably. From 2006 to 2017, the number of beneficiaries of paid parental leave dropped by 64.3%, from around 600,000 to 279,000 (−292 400) (Figure 11.3). These results can partly be explained by the low financial appeal of the allowance (€396 per month for completely stopping work) and the low level of sharing between both parents, which has been obligatory since 2015. It is worth noting that fathers still participate very little in this area (6% of PrePareE benefits.ere paid out to men).

In addition to these financial explanations and the continued gender-based division of parental roles in couples, other studies (Boyer, 2018, p. 76 and following) also suggest that, the relationship mirrored between men and women in the workplace and the high pressure for parental success have the effect that women

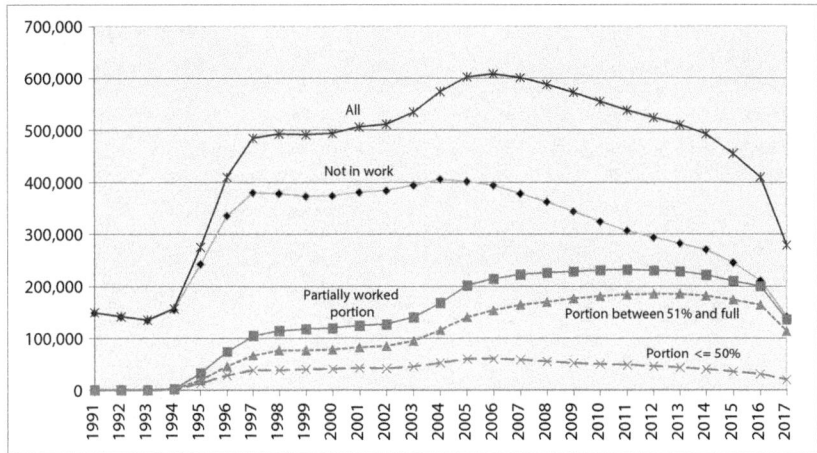

Figure 11.3 Evolution of the number of families receiving benefits to compensate for total or partial interruption of employment

Source: ONAPE, 2018

Legend: All: All family beneficiaries

Not in work: Family beneficiaries without activity

Partially worked portion: Family beneficiaries working part time

Portion between 51% and full: Family beneficiaries who work between 51% and 80% of full time (35 hours)

Portion ≤ 50%: Family beneficiaries who work less than 50% of full time

Field: Total France, families with at least one child under 3 years old, who receive allowances to support total or partial interruption of activity.

do not want to stop working because parental responsibility could concentrate too much on only their shoulders as if they must "raise their children alone".

Also worth noting is the drop in the number of families employing registered childminders. From 2012 to 2017, the number of families who received "freedom of choice" of childcare (CMG) benefits for a registered childminder went down by 5.5%, or about 43,000 beneficiaries. Moreover, the number of places in collective childcare establishments rose slightly (+1.8%, from 428,500 places in 2015 to 436,300 places in 2016) (Figure 11.4) – a very low level compared with the promises of the governments, the needs and demands. A qualitative examination of the way that parents perceive these two types of childcare reveals that they rank crèches much more highly than childminders (Collet, Cartier, Czerny, Gilbert, & Lechien, 2016).

Lastly, the rate of working mothers decreases with the number of dependent children, in particular when one of them is an infant. While 71% of women living in a couple with one child aged under 3 are in work, only 38% of mothers of large families (three or more children) with at least one child under 3 years old continue

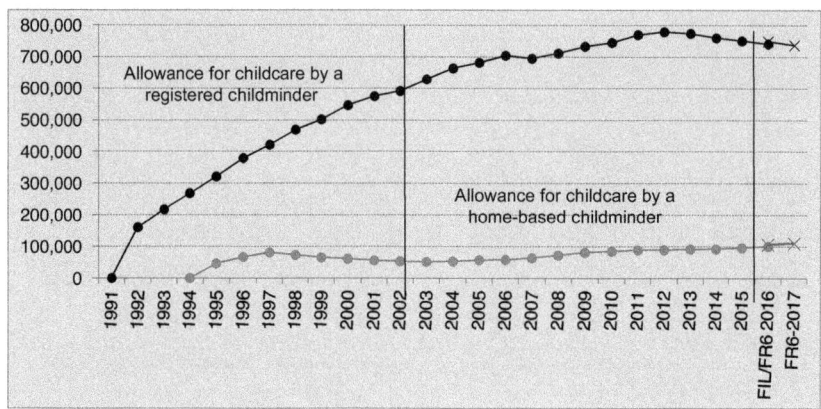

Figure 11.4 Evolution of the number of families receiving individual childcare benefits
Source: ONAPE, 2018

to pursue an employed activity. In addition, this rate is lower for single-parent families: fewer than half (44%) of single mothers of one child aged under 3 is in work, compared with 71% of those living in a couple.

Concerning the role played by family members and informal childcare to compensate for a lack of childcare solutions, grandparents make the greatest contribution. They provide alternative or complementary solutions to make up for a shortfall in regular formal care for young children. Support from grandparents takes the form of regular and occasional care and is a response to everyday constraints faced by parents (in particular, mothers' professional constraints). This partly depends on mothers' professional situation: with the same characteristics, children whose mothers are not working are less likely to be cared for by their grandparents (−7 points) than children whose mothers work regular hours. On the other hand, children are more likely to be cared for by their grandparents when their mother has a job with time constraints that can impact her availability (+3 points) (Kitzmann, 2018). Children whose mothers are not in work are in particular less likely to be cared for by their grandparents on a regular basis (−13 points), as are those, of course, whose grandparents live far away. However, children whose mothers have constrained work schedules are more frequently cared for by their grandparents on a regular basis than are children whose mothers work on less-restrictive schedules (+5 points). Grandparents are more likely to be solicited on a regular basis by single-parent households. They are then less frequently involved as a stopgap only.

In addition, the probability that a child will be cared for by his or her grandparents on a regular basis is lower in geographic areas with a higher number of available childcare places with registered childminders and in early-childcare establishments (EAJEs). Nevertheless, in situations in which the formal supply is higher, the probability is greater of being cared for by grandparents as a stopgap solution or during the holidays and weekends. The fact that a child has a place in a formal childcare establishment has the same impact. Grandparents could therefore, when they are available, provide alternative or complementary solutions to make up for the shortage of regular, formal solutions for young children.

Atypical work timetables and new demands

Some other trends are at stake to figure the way parents try to balance work and care. With regard to the evolution of the labour market, the Fordist standard still represents a main reference in the aftermath of the Second World War: that is, a situation marked by full-time work with relatively homogenous, regular hours, synchronised with other social hours (stores and services hours of operation). Previously considered as the pivot of our social organisation, this standard has, for about 30 years, tended to shatter in favour of an increasingly sustained recourse to flexibility (Knijn, Le Bihan, & Martin, 2013). However, the development of direct services to households and the precariousness of jobs in many sectors, such as retail or transport, have intensified this phenomenon over the past decade. For instance, in France, atypical working hours concern 44% of salaried people (DARES, 2018).

The development of atypical working hours and the increased number of households where two people work has considerably changed the demand for care services. A large percentage of these new requirements are regulated by the households themselves, which organise more or less stable and adequate arrangements, combining formal resources (childcare system) and informal resources (network of relations, kinship, and neighbours), which often, however, implies significant pressure and heavy mental load daily (Kröger & Sipilä, 2005; Le Bihan & Martin, 2005; DARES, 2018).

Atypical working hours correspond to very different working conditions. The common point is that these hours are staggered, which means that they are not in phase with standard working hours or with the normal opening of many public and private services (including childcare services) (8am–6pm). Two factors must be taken into account when defining atypical working hours: variability/invariability and regularity/irregularity (Le Bihan & Martin, 2005; Bressé et al., 2007). Two additional main factors affect family life and parental responsibilities: *predictability/unpredictability* of working hours and the possibility for parents to *negotiate* their work schedules. In reality, what is at stake in the irregularity of different working hours is their *predictable* or *unpredictable* nature. In fact, in a number of job sectors, employees are informed at the last moment of their work timetables for the days or weeks to come. Whilst shift work can be planned, which enables relatively stable solutions to be arranged, this is not the case for those types of jobs that have completely unpredictable work hours. From one week to the next, even from one day to the next, solutions have to be reinvented, often informally, calling on a network of relatives or neighbours.

Faced with constantly changing work-hour requirements, the responses of public authorities are still not clear cut. Some experimental services try to offer a solution to these needs: for instance, home services such as the programme *GEPETTO* can complement formal sources of childcare for time periods lacking solutions (e.g., very early in the morning or late at night) (Campéon, Le Bihan, & Martin, 2005). These services are practical solutions for parents working atypical hours, with the objective to maintain the usual rhythm of the child. These services, which are being developed throughout the country, have three main advantages: their cost, their professional dimension, and their home-based principle. Thus, children are looked after at home, in their familiar environment, by professionals. This solution is necessarily complementary to standard childcare services. The experimental phase of these services has proved the existence of a real need for care at atypical times and the importance of such services for single parents who have even greater difficulties combining work and family life. These services still require official recognition at the local and national levels before being generalised. They are also confronted with the difficulty of recruiting and maintaining professional childcarers to work non-standard hours themselves. However, the existence of these types of services is clearly a promising solution to meet the developments of the labour market. Companies can also play a key role in promoting this kind of solution (which is the case in sectors such as the airline industry; [Brochard & Letablier, 2017]).

Conclusions

This chapter aimed to present some hidden characteristics of the French configuration of services to balance work and family responsibilities. If the importance of the public offer is often mentioned in comparative studies about France (like the role of crèches and preschools), then it is important to underline some other crucial characteristics such as the role of the parents themselves who still clearly represent the main pillar of childcare arrangements or the still slow process of change to equalize respective gender contributions in a couple. But we want to insist not only on the role of other informal actors, in particular grandparents, in these childcare arrangements, but also on the impact of atypical working timetables which threaten classical childcare arrangements and oblige parents to invent alternative solutions to the formal offer. These new flexible working conditions are also challenging the quality of the childcare arrangement. France is still relatively reluctant to develop public services to face this transition in the workplace, and more research is needed to understand and compare the different solutions and their impacts.

Notes

1 www.senat.fr/rap/r14-473/r14-473_mono.html
2 The whole of France (except Mayotte).
3 Correspondence between families' expectations and take-up of formal childcare (registered childminder or collective establishment).

References

Boyer, D., & Crépin, A. (2018). Baromètre d'accueil du jeune enfant 2017. Stabilité du recours et des souhaits d'accueil. *L'e-ssentiel Bulletin électronique de la Caisse nationale des allocations familiales – Direction des statistiques, des études et de la recherche*, n°179.

Boyer, D. (Ed.), & ONAPE (Observatoire national de la petite enfance). (2018). *L'accueil du jeune enfant en 2017. Données statistiques et recherches qualitatives*. Paris. Caisse nationale des allocations familiales. Issn: 1959 2302. Consulted on December 2019 http://www.caf.fr/sites/default/files/cnaf/Documents/Dser/observatoire_petite_enfance/AJE_2018_bd.pdf

Bressé, S., Le Bihan, B., & Martin, C. (2007, janvier). La garde des enfants en dehors des plages horaires standard. *Etudes et résultats*, n°551.

Brochard, D., & Letablier, M.-T. (2017). Trade union involvement in work–family life balance: Lessons from France. *Work, Employment and Society, 31*(4), 657–674.

Campéon, A., Le Bihan, B., & Martin, C. (2005). Expérimentation d'une offre de garde face aux horaires de travail atypiques et flexibles. *Recherches et prévisions*, n°80, 11–26.

Collet, A., Cartier, M., Czerny, E., Gilbert, P., & Lechien, M.-H. (2016). *Les arrangements conjugaux autour des modes de garde: arbitrages sous contraintes et effets de socialisation.* Rapport de recherche remis à la Direction de la recherche, des études, des évaluations et des statistiques du ministère des Affaires Sociales.

DARES. (2018, juin). Le travail en horaires atypiques: quels salariés pour quelle organisation du temps de travail? *DARES Analyses*, n°30.

Kitzmann, M. (2018). Les grands-parents: un mode de garde régulier ou occasionnel pour deux tiers des jeunes enfants. *Études et Résultats*, DREES, n°107.

Knijn, T., Le Bihan, B., & Martin, C. (Eds.). (2013). *Work and care under pressure: Care arrangements across Europe*. Care and Welfare Series. Chicago, IL and Amsterdam: Amsterdam University Press.

Knijn, T, Martin, C., & Ostner, I. (2018). Triggers and drivers of change in framing parenting support in North-western Europe. In G. B. Eydal and T. Rostgaard (Eds.), *Handbook of child and family policy* (pp. 152–166). Cheltenham: Edward Elgar.

Kröger, T., & Sipilä, J. (Eds.). (2005). *Overstretched: European families up against the demands of work and care*. Oxford: Blackwell.

Le Bihan, B., & Martin, C. (2005). Atypical working hours: Consequences for childcare arrangements. In T. Kröger & J. Sipilä (Eds.), *Overstretched: European families up against the demands of work and care* (pp. 9–33). Oxford: Blackwell.

Le Bihan, B., & Martin, C. (2008a). Public childcare and preschools in France. New policy paradigm and path dependency. In K. Scheiwe and H. Willekens (Eds.), *Childcare and preschool development in Europe: Institutional perspectives* (pp. 57–71). London: Palgrave Macmillan.

Le Bihan, B., & Martin, C. (Eds.). (2008b). *Concilier vie familiale et vie professionnelle en Europe.* Rennes: Presses de l'EHESP.

Martin, C. (2010). The reframing of family policy in France: Actors, ideas and instruments. *Journal of European Social Policy, 20*(5), 410–421.

Martin, C. (2017). Work, family and public policy dynamics in France. *International Review of Sociology, 27*(3), 421–435.

Morgan, K. J. (2006). *Working mothers and the welfare state*. Stanford, CA: Stanford University Press.

Pailhé, A., & Solaz, A. A. (Eds.). (2009). *Entre famille et travail. Des arrangements de couples aux pratiques des employeurs*. Paris: La Découverte.

Sites

www.caf.fr/presse-institutionnel/recherche-et-statistiques/publications/rapport-annuel-de-l-observatoire

www.caf.fr/sites/default/files/cnaf/Documents/Dser/essentiel/179_Barom%C3%A8tre%20petite%20enfance.pdf

https://drees.solidarites-sante.gouv.fr/etudes-et-statistiques/open-data/famille-enfance-jeunesse/article/l-enquete-modes-de-garde-et-d-accueil-des-jeunes-enfants

12 What can employers do? Creating an inclusive workplace that fosters work-family well-being

Hans van Dijk and Loes Meeussen

In this chapter, we first explain the two main components of inclusion at work, *belonging* and *authenticity*, and indicate how these components may be at risk when employees become parents. After that, we discuss how research on diversity climate provides valuable insights into how organisational work-family practices can contribute to parents' feelings of inclusion and subsequently their work-family well-being. Figure 12.1 provides an overview of our framework.

Components of inclusion and shifts therein for new parents

The term *inclusion* refers to the degree to which an employee feels like a valued work group member by being treated in a way that satisfies both the need to belong and the need to be authentic (Jansen, Otten, Van der Zee, & Jans, 2014; Shore et al., 2011). This definition is grounded in the optimal distinctiveness theory (Brewer, 1991), which suggests that people seek a balance between, on the one hand, a need to be accepted and belong, and on the other hand the need for authenticity and to be unique.

The need to *belong* is reflected in people's tendency to form and maintain relationships and identify with social groups. At work, this need to belong is fulfilled when one feels a respected part of the team and organisation, has frequent and pleasant interactions with colleagues, and feels accepted by them. The need to be *authentic* manifests in people's will to retain their individuality and be their distinctive self. In organisations, this need to be authentic is fulfilled when people feel like they can be their true selves at work and feel valued for who they are and what they contribute (Brewer, 1991; Jansen et al., 2014; Shore et al., 2011).

The fulfillment of these two needs enhances well-being in various ways, including by improving high-quality relationships, satisfaction, commitment, and in the workplace also creativity and job performance (Brewer, 1991; Deci & Ryan, 2000; Leary & Baumeister, 2000; Leonardelli, Pickett, & Brewer, 2010; Sheldon, Ryan, Rawsthorne, & Ilardi, 1997; Shore et al., 2011). For employers, it thus is very important to manage and satisfy employees' needs to belong and feel authentic, and hence make them feel included.

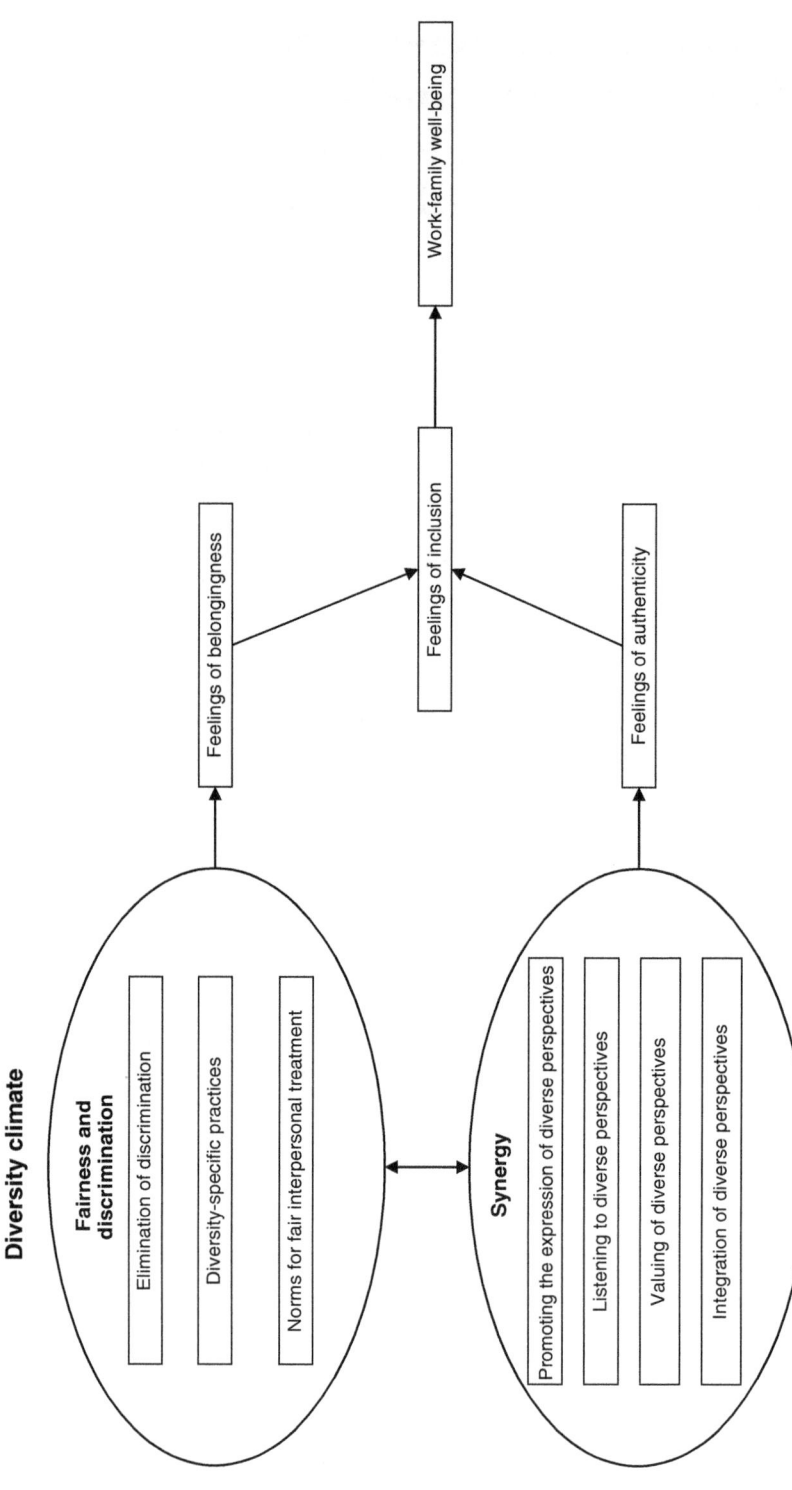

Figure 12.1 A conceptual model linking diversity climate, feelings of inclusion, and work-family well-being

Yet, becoming a parent can challenge employees' belonging and authenticity at work. Firstly, feelings of belonging at work may be at risk as new parents may fear or actually experience devaluation by their colleagues because the new role of being a parent shows a misfit with the ideal worker schema of someone who is fully devoted to work (Blair-Loy, 2001; Williams, Blair-Loy, & Berdahl, 2013). For instance, research has shown that fathers who take up caregiving responsibilities may experience workplace harassment (Berdahl & Moon, 2013), are perceived to be poorer workers and less altruistic at work, and are less likely to be recommended for a promotion or a raise (Rudman & Mescher, 2013; Wayne & Cordeiro, 2003). Similarly, mothers have been shown to be perceived as less competent and receive lower pay compared with women without children. For example, research has shown that mothers face a wage penalty of 5% for every child, and this is independent of years of job experience (Budig & England, 2001; Correll, Benard, & Paik, 2007).

Secondly, employees' feelings of *authenticity* may be challenged when they become parents, because they take on an entirely new role in their lives that comes with novel experiences and perspectives. This new role needs to be incorporated in their sense of self, as it can alter new parents' attitudes and beliefs, and may change how they perform their job and how they combine it with their private life. As a consequence, the ways in which employees are their authentic self at work is likely to change when they become a parent, and their identity may need to be renegotiated with and valued by colleagues and employers (Cha et al., 2019; King & Botsford, 2009).

Thus, although it is very important for employees' well-being and productivity at work to feel included, becoming a parent may jeopardise one's inclusion. We therefore argue that it is pivotal for employers to foster the transition in *belonging* and *authenticity* for employees who become parents, and in the next section discuss more explicitly how they can do that.

What can employers do? Establishing a diversity climate to foster inclusion

Most organisational research on inclusion has been conducted in the areas of diversity and diversity management. Although (new) parents tend to fall outside the scope of research on diversity (cf. van Dijk, van Engen, & van Knippenberg, 2012), its insights in how to foster inclusion for different types of employees are relevant and applicable to organisational practices aimed at protecting or fostering workplace inclusion of new parents.

In the past decade, several studies have shown that, in particular, a diversity climate is important for fostering employees' feelings of inclusion (e.g., McKay & Avery, 2015; Meeussen, Otten, & Phalet, 2014; Nishii, 2013; Shore, Cleveland, & Sanchez, 2018). A diversity climate is defined as "employees' perceptions about the extent to which their organization values diversity as evident in the organization's formal structure, informal values, and social integration of underrepresented employees" (Dwertmann, Nishii, & van Knippenberg, 2016, p. 1137). In their review, Dwertmann et al. (2016) proposed that a diversity climate consists of two components: *fairness and discrimination*, and *synergy*. These components are considered to be complementary, meaning that organisations will only be inclusive when both components are present. In the next section, we explain each component further and outline how the fairness and discrimination component addresses the need to belong and the synergy component addresses the need to be authentic.

Fairness and discrimination

The *fairness and discrimination* component of a diversity climate refers to the "shared perceptions about the extent to which the organization and/or work group successfully promotes fairness and the elimination of discrimination through the fair implementation of personnel practices, the adoption of diversity-specific practices aimed at improving employment outcomes for underrepresented employees, and/or strong norms for fair interpersonal treatment" (Dwertmann et al., 2016, p. 1151). Thus, with its focus on establishing a level playground for all employees, the *fairness and discrimination* component addresses employees' need to belong and has three subcomponents: the elimination of discrimination, the adoption of diversity-specific practices, and norms for fair interpersonal treatment (Dwertmann & van Dijk, forthcoming). Next, we outline how employees can foster each of these subcomponents, with a focus on employees with children.

For new parents, the *elimination of discrimination* would entail that employers eliminate any potential bias against or devaluation of employees with children. For instance, career breaks (e.g., parental leave) and periods of part-time work can be taken into account when comparing different resumes for selection of promotion purposes, such that parents' performance evaluation is based on the actual time they have worked. Also, employers can check for potential bias against parents in their organisation by monitoring data on performance evaluations and promotion and testing for disadvantages of parenthood therein after controlling for other factors such as work hours or potentially available objective indicators of performance.

For the adoption of *diversity-specific practices*, it is important that employers take into account that there is no one-size-fits-all in combining work and family. There are many different types of parents, each of whom may have different needs and wishes: relationship status, the number of children, the health of the child, and the extent to which their partner, family, and friends support in child rearing are but some of the factors that illustrate the potential diversity among (new) parents and family circumstances. This diversity may call for very different preferences in work-family flexibility practices. For instance, divorced parents may especially benefit from a work schedule that allows for working more hours one week and fewer hours the next week, whereas parents of a child with health problems may especially benefit from flexible work hours that allow for doctor visits. Moreover, even within these different groups of parents, individual differences will exist in how to combine work and family: whereas some parents may prefer to put their career on hold, other parents may want to pursue a high managerial position without being seen as 'a parent' at work, and while some parents may want to draw clear boundaries between their work and family life, others may prefer to integrate the two (Rothbard, Phillips, & Dumas, 2005). Thus, to foster organisational belonging and work-family well-being of employees with children, employers can provide a wide range of family-friendly arrangement options to enable employees to seek out their specific strategy to best perform at work in combination with their (new) family. Ideally, such strategies are also renegotiable over time as the situation and hence the needs of parents are likely to change throughout their careers. For instance, employees who work part time may prefer to change to a full-time schedule again as appropriate when their children grow older.

Regarding the *norms for fair interpersonal treatment*, employers should promote these to ensure that employees with children do not experience negative treatment or harassment at work (e.g., Berdahl & Moon, 2013) and feel supported by their team and organisation. Research has shown that support from colleagues and supervisors is a crucial factor in decreasing experiences of conflict between work and family (Byron, 2005; Mesmer-Magnus & Viswesvaran, 2006), as such support is needed for the use and effectiveness of family-friendly arrangements (Allen, 2001; Thompson, Beauvais, & Lyness, 1999). Again drawing from diversity research (Stevens, Plaut, & Sanchez-Burks, 2008), an important factor in creating such support among colleagues is to make sure that employees without children do not feel disadvantaged or left out compared with their colleagues with children who can make use of family-friendly arrangements. Therefore, it is advisable not only to focus on new parents when developing family-friendly arrangement options, but also to broaden the scope to other family responsibilities as well (e.g., employees who care for a sick relative, aging parents, or grandchildren).

Synergy

The *synergy* component of a diversity climate refers to "the extent to which employees jointly perceive their organization and/or workgroup to promote the expression of, listening to, active valuing of, and integration of diverse perspectives for the purpose of enhancing collective learning and performance" (Dwertmann et al., 2016, p. 1151). With its focus on paying attention to the individual employee and valuing her or his role in and contributions to collective learning and performance, the *synergy* component addresses employees' need to be authentic (Dwertmann & van Dijk, forthcoming). Given that the different elements of the *synergy* component (i.e., promoting the expression of, listening to, valuing of, and integration of diverse perspectives) are highly related, in the following we discuss what employers can do to achieve high levels of *synergy*.

Specifically, we argue that it is crucial for employers to endorse the merit of each employee's unique perspective and contributions. Relating this component to employees with children, we argue that, like other life experiences (cf. van Knippenberg & Schippers, 2007), every parenting situation comes with novel experiences and insights. Thus, employees with children may bring new perspectives, methods, skills, and networks in the organisation – and employers can actively stimulate the sharing and integration thereof in the organisation.

Research has shown that while employees with children may experience conflicts between their work and family roles (Carlson, Kacmar, & Williams, 2000; Frone, Russell, & Cooper, 1992), they often also experience these two life domains enriching and facilitating each other (Carlson, Kacmar, Wayne, & Grzywacz, 2006; Greenhaus & Powell, 2006; Hanson, Hammer, & Colton, 2006; van Steenbergen, Ellemers, & Mooijaart, 2007). Such positive experiences of combining work and family have been shown to be bi-directional: on the one hand, parents feel like their work is an enriching part of their life above their family role, and this relates positively to their job satisfaction, commitment, and performance (Kirchmeyer, 1992; van Steenbergen et al., 2007). On the other hand, many parents also feel like their family role enriches or facilitates their work in various ways. For example, research has shown that employees report that their family role provides them with new knowledge, skills, values, and viewpoints that are useful at work, that it makes them happy and energised which makes them a better worker, and that it makes them more efficient and focused during their work time (Carlson et al., 2006; Hanson et al., 2006; van Steenbergen et al., 2007). These novel insights, skills, and positive attitudes can be a strong added value within an organisation – provided that employers listen to and value the input of (new) parents.

Specific practices that increase the level of *synergy* and thereby address new parents' need for *authenticity* include endorsing a work-family enrichment perspective that work and family roles can positively affect each other (van Steenbergen, Ellemers, Haslam, & Urlings, 2008). Employers can also proactively inquire about new parents' ideas, listen to their input, and promote exchanges of thoughts with other employees (van Knippenberg, De Dreu, & Homan, 2004). Moreover, people in higher functions within the organisation can serve as role models to employees with children by openly talking about their role as a parent, how they personally combine work and family, and the ways in which they believe their parental role has provided them with unique experiences, insights, and skills that contributed to organisational learning and performance in their career.

Relationships among components and elements

We argue that the elements of a diversity climate are likely to function based on the principle of the weakest link, such that employees will probably feel included only to the minimum level that each component and element are addressed (Jansen et al., 2014; Shore et al., 2011). For example, regarding elements of *fairness and discrimination*, employers may offer a wide range in family-friendly arrangements, but if new parents feel judged when making use of such arrangements, they are unlikely to feel included and, as a consequence, may refrain from using them. Merely offering a range of family-friendly arrangements thus may not necessarily enhance work-family well-being when parents perceive they will be judged for making use of them. Similarly, regarding *synergy* elements, new parents are unlikely to feel like their *authenticity* is valued when they are stimulated to express their ideas if those ideas are subsequently ignored. If new parents thus have the feeling that they are not listened to, then any practice aimed at stimulating new parents to express their ideas is unlikely to be effective.

The dynamic between the components of a diversity climate is somewhat similar, such that addressing the *fairness and discrimination* component but not the *synergy* component satisfies new parents' need to belong but not their need to be authentic, and is therefore likely to trigger dissatisfaction in employees' need to be authentic. Specifically, in such an organisation, new parents are likely to feel like a burden. Although there are various family-friendly arrangements that help them navigate their family responsibilities, at work they will likely feel that they are expected to conform to the organisational culture and keep their family life private (cf. Shore et al., 2011). In contrast, new parents who work in organisations in which the *synergy* component is addressed but not the *fairness and discrimination* component are likely to experience dissatisfaction in their need to belong. Although such employees may feel like the organisation values their new parental experiences, they will not experience the organisation as helpful in navigating and accommodating their family needs and wishes.

Regardless of which need is unmet, new parents in organisations with low levels of a *fairness and discrimination* or a *synergy* component are likely to feel excluded, which comes at the expense of their work-family well-being. For employers, this means that it is pivotal to pay attention to the requests of new parents, because their requests will be indicative of which components need attention. If new parents feel valued but crave for arrangements to help them navigate their family responsibilities, then employers would do well to pay more attention to the *fairness and discrimination* component. If, however, new parents indicate that they feel like they belong but that their added value is not acknowledged, then employers should pay more attention to practices that strengthen the *synergy* component of a diversity climate.

Conclusions

Taken together, this chapter has outlined how becoming a parent may challenge the *belonging* and *authenticity* components of employees' feelings of inclusion at work. We argued that it is important for employers to create a diversity climate to foster the inclusion of employees with children. Specifically, employers can contribute to employees' feelings of belongingness with *fairness and discrimination* practices such as zero discrimination of parents policies, a range of family-friendly arrangements that corresponds to the broad diversity within employees with family responsibilities, and by fostering a strong family-friendly work norm. Secondly, employers can contribute to employees' feelings of authenticity with *synergy* practices that emphasise the value of new parents' experiences, networks, and perspectives and seek to use them to raise the quality of deliberations and decisions in organisations. In doing so, employers can leverage (new) parents' feelings of inclusion within the organisation and, in turn, enhance their work-family well-being. The main difficulty here is that it is important for employers to address all elements of the two components to foster a diversity climate, because ignoring one may also limit the effectiveness of the other. We therefore recommend employers go over each element of the diversity climate components to assess how well those elements are addressed by organisational work-family practices.

Key learnings from research	*Practical recommendations*
• Work-family practices enhance work-family well-being when they contribute to parents' feelings of inclusion. • To feel included, parents need both to feel like they belong and that their authenticity is valued. • Organisations can foster feelings of belongingness by enhancing (perceptions of) fairness and eliminating discrimination towards parents. • Organisations can foster feelings of authenticity by acknowledging and enabling the added value of parents.	• In designing work-family practices, pay attention to how they shape inclusion. • Work-family practices that only address belonging or authenticity may fail to deliver. • Eliminate discrimination, establish norms for fair interpersonal treatment, and tailor work-family practices to the (changing) needs of individual parents. • Inquire about new parents' ideas, listen to their input, and promote exchanges of thought with other employees.

References

Allen, T. D. (2001). Family-supportive work environments: The role of organizational perceptions. *Journal of Vocational Behavior, 58*(3), 414–435. https://doi.org/10.1006/jvbe.2000.1774

Berdahl, J. L., & Moon, S. H. (2013). Workplace mistreatment of middle class workers based on sex, parenthood, and caregiving. *Journal of Social Issues, 69*(2), 341–636. https://doi.org/10.1111/josi.12018

Blair-Loy, M. (2001). Cultural constructions of family schemas: The case of women finance executives. *Gender & Society, 15*(5), 687–709. https://doi.org/10.1177/089124301015005004

Brewer, M. B. (1991). The social self: On being the same and different at the same time. *Personality and Social Psychology Bulletin, 17*(5), 475–482. https://doi.org/10.1177/0146167291175001

Budig, M., & England, P. (2001). The wage penalty for motherhood. *American Sociological Review, 66*, 204–225. https://doi.org/10.2307/2657415

Byron, K. (2005). A meta-analytic review of work–family conflict and its antecedents. *Journal of Vocational Behavior, 67*, 169–198. https://doi.org/10.1016/j.jvb.2004.08.009

Carlson, D. S., Kacmar, K. M., Wayne, J. H., & Grzywacz, J. G. (2006). Measuring the positive side of the work family interface: Development and validation of a work family enrichment scale. *Journal of Vocational Behavior, 68*, 131–164. https://doi.org/10.1016/j.jvb.2005.02.002

Carlson, D. S., Kacmar, K. M., & Williams, L. J. (2000). Construction and initial validation of a multidimensional measure of work-family conflict. *Journal of Vocational Behavior, 56*, 249–276. https://doi.org/10.1006/jvbe.1999.1713

Cha, S., Hewlin, P. F., Roberts, L. M., Buckman, B., Leroy, H., Steckler, E. . . . Cooper, D. (2019). Being your true self at work: Integrating the fragmented research on authenticity in organizations. *Academy of Management Annals, 13*(2). Advance Online Publication. https://doi.org/10.5465/annals.2016.0108

Correll, S. J., Benard, S., & Paik, I. (2007). Getting a job: Is there a motherhood penalty? *American Journal of Sociology, 112*, 1297–1338. https://doi.org/10.1086/511799

Deci, E. L., & Ryan, R. M. (2000). The "what" and "why" of goal pursuits: Human needs and the self-determination of behavior. *Psychological Inquiry, 11*(4), 227–268. https://doi.org/10.1207/S15327965PLI1104_01

Dwertmann, D. J., Nishii, L. H., & Van Knippenberg, D. (2016). Disentangling the fairness & discrimination and synergy perspectives on diversity climate: Moving the field forward. *Journal of Management, 42*(5), 1136–1168. https://doi.org/10.1177/0149206316630380

Dwertmann, D., & van Dijk, H. (forthcoming). What it takes to foster inclusive norms: A practice guide. In B. Ferdman, J. Prime, & R. Riggio (Eds.), *Inclusive leadership: Transforming diverse lives, workplaces, and societies*.

Frone, M. R., Russell, M., & Cooper, M. L. (1992). Antecedents and outcomes of work-family conflict: Testing a model of the work-family interface. *Journal of Applied Psychology, 77*, 65–78. https://doi.org/10.1037//0021-9010.77.1.65

Greenhaus, J. H., & Powell, G. N. (2006). When work and family are allies: A theory of work-family enrichment. *Academy of Management Review, 31*, 72–92. https://doi.org/10.5465/AMR.2006.19379625

Hammer, L. B., Kossek, E. E., Yragui, N. L., Bodner, T. E., & Hanson, G. C. (2009). Development and validation of a multidimensional measure of family supportive supervisor behaviors (FSSB). *Journal of Management, 35*(4), 837–856. doi:10.1177/0149206308328510

Hanson, G. C., Hammer, L. B., & Colton, C. L. (2006). Development and validation of a multidimensional scale of perceived work-family positive spillover. *Journal of Occupational Health Psychology, 11*, 249–265. https://doi.org/10.1037/1076-8998.11.3.249

Jansen, W. S., Otten, S., Van der Zee, K. I., & Jans, L. (2014). Inclusion: Conceptualization and measurement. *European Journal of Social Psychology, 44*(4), 370–385. https://doi.org/10.1002/ejsp.2011

King, E. B., & Botsford, W. E. (2009). Managing pregnancy disclosures: Understanding and overcoming the challenges of expectant motherhood at work. *Human Resource Management Review, 19*(4), 314–323. https://doi.org/10.1016/j.hrmr.2009.03.003

Kirchmeyer, C. (1992). Non-work participation and work attitudes: A test of scarcity versus expansion models of personal resources. *Human Relations, 45*, 775–795. https://doi.org/10.1177/001872679204500802

Leary, M. R., & Baumeister, R. F. (2000). The nature and function of self-esteem: Sociometer theory. In M. P. Zanna (Ed.), *Advances in experimental social psychology* (Vol. 32, pp. 1–62). San Diego, CA: Academic Press.

Leonardelli, G. J., Pickett, C. L., & Brewer, M. B. (2010). Optimal distinctiveness theory: A framework for social identity, social cognition, and intergroup relations. In *Advances in experimental social psychology* (Vol. 43, pp. 63–113). Academic Press. https://doi.org/10.1016/S0065-2601(10)43002-6

McKay, P. F., & Avery, D. R. (2015). Diversity climate in organizations: Current wisdom and domains of uncertainty. *Research in Personnel and Human Resources Management, 33*, 191–233. https://doi.org/10.1108/S0742-730120150000033008

Meeussen, L., Otten, S., & Phalet, K. (2014). Managing diversity: How leaders' multiculturalism and colorblindness affect work group functioning. *Group Processes & Intergroup Relations, 17*(5), 629–644. https://doi.org/10.1177/1368430214525809

Mesmer-Magnus, J. R., & Viswesvaran, C. (2006). How family-friendly work environments affect work/family conflict: A meta-analytic examination. *Journal of Labor Research, 27*, 555–574. https://doi.org/10.1007/s12122-006-1020-1

Nishii, L. H. (2013). The benefits of climate for inclusion for gender-diverse groups. *Academy of Management Journal, 56*(6), 1754–1774. https://doi.org/10.5465/amj.2009.0823

Rothbard, N., Phillips, K., & Dumas, T. (2005). Managing multiple roles: Work–family policies and individual's desires for segmentation. *Organization Science, 16*, 243–258. https://doi.org/10.1287/orsc.1050.0124

Rudman, L. A., & Mescher, K. (2013). Penalizing men who request a family leave: Is flexibility stigma a femininity stigma? *Journal of Social Issues, 69*(2), 322–340. https://doi.org/10.1111/josi.12017

Sheldon, K. M., Ryan, R. M., Rawsthorne, L. J., & Ilardi, B. (1997). Trait self and true self: Cross-role variation in the big-five personality traits and its relations with psychological authenticity and subjective well-being. *Journal of Personality and Social Psychology, 73*(6), 1380–1393. https://doi.org/10.1037/0022-3514.73.6.1380

Shore, L. M., Cleveland, J. N., & Sanchez, D. (2018). Inclusive workplaces: A review and model. *Human Resource Management Review, 28*(2), 176–189. https://doi.org/10.1016/j.hrmr.2017.07.003

Shore, L. M., Randel, A. E., Chung, B. G., Dean, M. A., Holcombe Ehrhart, K., & Singh, G. (2011). Inclusion and diversity in work groups: A review and model for future research. *Journal of Management, 37*(4), 1262–1289. https://doi.org/10.1177/0149206310385943

Stevens, F. G., Plaut, V. C., & Sanchez-Burks, J. (2008). Unlocking the benefits of diversity. All-inclusive multiculturalism and positive organizational change. *The Journal of Applied Behavioral Science, 44*, 116–133. https://doi.org/10.1177/0021886308314460

Thompson, C. A., Beauvais, L. L., & Lyness, K. S. (1999). When work–family benefits are not enough: The influence of work–family culture on benefit utilization, organizational attachment, and work–family conflict. *Journal of Vocational behavior, 54*, 392–415. https://doi.org/10.1006/jvbe.1998.1681

van Dijk, H., van Engen, M. L., & van Knippenberg, D. (2012). Defying conventional wisdom: A meta-analytical examination of the differences between demographic and job-related diversity relationships with performance. *Organizational Behavior and Human Decision Processes, 119*(1), 38–53. https://doi.org/10.1016/j.obhdp.2012.06.003

van Knippenberg, D., De Dreu, C. K., & Homan, A. C. (2004). Work group diversity and group performance: An integrative model and research agenda. *Journal of Applied Psychology, 89*(6), 1008–1022. https://doi.org/10.1037/0021-9010.89.6.1008

van Knippenberg, D., & Schippers, M. C. (2007). Work group diversity. *Annual Review of Psychology, 58*, 515–541. https://doi.org/10.1146/annurev.psych.58.110405.085546

van Steenbergen, E. F., Ellemers, N., Haslam, S. A., & Urlings, F. (2008). There is nothing either good or bad but thinking makes it so: Informational support and cognitive appraisal of the work-family interface. *Journal of Occupational and Organizational Psychology, 81*, 349–367. https://doi.org/10.1348/096317908X312669

van Steenbergen, E. F., Ellemers, N., & Mooijaart, A. (2007). How work and family can facilitate each other: Distinct types of work–family facilitation and outcomes for women and men. *Journal of Occupational Health Psychology, 12*, 279–300. https://doi.org/10.1037/1076-8998.12.3.279

Wayne, J. H., & Cordeiro, B. L. (2003). Who is a good organizational citizen? Social perception of male and female employees who use family leave. *Sex Roles, 49*(5–6), 233–246. https://doi.org/10.1023/A:1024600323316

Williams, J. C., Blair-Loy, M., & Berdahl, J. L. (2013). Cultural schemas, social class, and the flexibility stigma. *Journal of Social Issues, 69*(2), 209–234. https://doi.org/10.1111/josi.12012

13 Going beyond policies to ease parents back into work and rebalance roles

The importance of idiosyncratic deals

Inés Martínez-Corts and J. Pablo Moreno-Beltrán

Becoming a parent is a personal challenge that implies renegotiating work-family expectations with oneself, with our partners and with our employer. This process may be unfavourable either for the employee or for the person for whom the renegotiation is made. For instance, the employer must invest in newcomers or may feel that the employee is less committed to the organization when he/she asks for family-friendly policies (FFP). Moreover, when re-entering the workforce, parents may feel discrimination because of family responsibilities (e.g., see Chapters 2 and 8) and its negative effects on job satisfaction, organizational attachment, turnover intentions, work-family conflict (WFC) and FFP use (Von Bergen, Von Bergen, & Ballaré, 2008).

In this chapter, we provide insights to avoid/reduce the aforementioned negative view and focus on a win-win process. Despite its difficulties, being a parent is a positive life event which may prompt valuable resources for the parents – for example, emotional stability, relationship skills, patience and time management skills. These resources may spill over into work through a work-family enrichment process (WFE) (Greenhaus & Powell, 2006) and could positively affect work outcomes such as performance, work engagement, job satisfaction, reduced turnover and interpersonal conflicts (e.g., Zhang, Xu, Jin, & Ford, 2018). We emphasize the benefits of idiosyncratic deals (i-deals) to better solve individuals' needs and motivations in accordance with organizational goals.

This positive approach overcomes the traditional way that organizations manage new parents' rebalancing of work-family roles.

Family-friendly policies: required but limited in scope and implementation

Flexible working (flextime and flexplace) and related policies (e.g., job sharing, day-care assistance, paid parental leave, on-site childcare) have widely been demonstrated to reduce WFC and its negative consequences (Allen, Johnson, Kiburz, & Shockley, 2013). However, their use and effectiveness are contingent on employee and organizational characteristics. First, FFP have been demonstrated to be specifically effective for married/co-habiting, parents or female employees compared with other groups such as singles, non-parents, or male employees (Allen et al., 2013; Butts, Casper, & Yang, 2013; Shockley & Allen, 2010). Second, organizational characteristics also have an impact on the use of FFP. For instance, larger organizations, service organizations (as compared with product organizations), private (versus public ownership) organizations, high-tech organizations, organizations with a high proportion of female employees and organizations with a high proportion of unionized employees were positively associated with employee use of FFP (flexitime, teleworking, job sharing, compressed workweek) (Peretz, Fried, & Levi, 2017).

FFP efficacy operates through two different mechanisms as a function of employees' perception of the available policies or their use (Butts et al., 2013). First, FFP availability activates a symbolic mechanism which in turn creates a supportive and caring view of the organization among employees and enhances outcomes such as affective commitment, job satisfaction and intention to stay in a job (Butts et al., 2013). Second, when FFPs are used, an instrumental mechanism is activated, reducing WFC.

Despite the potential benefits of FFP to enhance positive outcomes, when used, they may prevent employees from experiencing negative outcomes such as WFC and its negative consequences (Martínez-Corts & Demerouti, 2017) or from being discriminated against (Dickson, 2008). For instance, although many organizations have a wide range of FFPs available for all employees, in practice, the policies remain out of reach for most workers (Sweet, Catsouphes, Besen, & Golden, 2014). In fact, while FFPs are mostly used by blue-collar workers rewarded for their high performance (den Dulk, Peper, Sadar, & Lewis, 2011), workers in lower levels of the organizations are considered to have lower capacities to negotiate FFPs. Moreover, despite its efficacy for parents – specifically mothers – these groups in organizations are often penalized when re-entering the workplace and need to use FFPs, because they are perceived as prioritizing personal life above work (Leslie, Manchester, Park, & Mehng, 2012).

According to signalling theory (Connelly, Certo, Ireland, & Reutzel, 2011), the quantity of positive signals provided by organizations will result in a more positive work attitude. Moreover, the strategic human resource management theory (Delery, 1998) and the systems theory (Corning, 1998) suggest that these signals should be reinforced by each other. Taking this into account, providing employees with a wide range of FFPs contributes to enhancing a permissible and normative cultural context (Kossek, Lewis, & Hammer, 2010). However, to ensure their efficacy, FFPs should be aligned within and between other organizational policies and strategies (e.g., recruitment, career development, or performance evaluation), creating together a family-friendly culture. In other words, FFPs will be effective in a family-supportive organizational culture (FSOC) where the organization, the supervisors and the co-workers acknowledge, support and value employees' family and personal life. In fact, FSOC and family-supportive supervisors have demonstrated to reduce perceived family responsibilities discrimination over and above the number of policies offered by the organization (Dickson, 2008).

Supervisors deserve a special mention in FSOC. Having training supervisors to provide specific work-family support has been demonstrated to help employees to reduce their WFC (Kossek, Pichler, Bodner, & Hammer, 2011), generating benefits for employees' physical health, job satisfaction, turnover intentions

(Hammer, Kossek, Anger, Bodner, & Zimmerman, 2011), as well as employee's engagement and job performance (Odle-Dusseau, Hammer, Crain, & Bodner, 2016). This is particularly true when employees perceive supervisor behaviour in a creative way to redesign work responsibilities, aimed to improve employees' work and non-work effectiveness (Odle-Dusseau et al., 2016). Therefore, supervisors' work-family support and their creative behaviours may serve as a model for parents to identify individualized and creative ways to rebalance work-family and encourage them to negotiate it.

Since family-supportive supervisors provide parents with instrumental and emotional resources, it has been identified as a powerful antecedent of WFE experiences. Opposite, despite its efficacy to reduce WFC, a recent meta-analysis (Lapierre et al., 2018) demonstrates that FFPs are weak antecedents of WFE. According to Herzberg's (1959) two-factor theory, avoiding WFC as a hygiene factor is necessary but insufficient to promote employees' motivation and positive well-being. Therefore, organizations should focus on interventions to promote WFE (e.g., training supervisors, in addition to reducing WFC experiences) offering FFPs.

Beyond reducing WFC experiences, promoting WFE enhance general well-being and has a positive impact on affective and performance outcomes (Zhang et al., 2018). Specifically, in the family domain, studies have shown that WFE improves family satisfaction (Boyar & Mosley, 2007) and family performance – for example, doing housework, giving social support and advice to family members and keeping family members connected (Carlson, Grzywacz, & Zivnuska, 2009). In addition, the motivation and energy produced improves the employee's overall health as well as generating resources to better cope with stress (Zhang et al., 2018). In the work domain, WFE is positively related to job satisfaction, organizational commitment and turnover intentions (e.g., Chen, Zhang, Sanders, & Xu, 2016), work engagement (Bakker, Schaufeli, Leiter, & Taris, 2008), in-role performance and extra-role behaviours (Zhang et al., 2018).

Because the effect of within domain (i.e. the effect of work-to-family enrichment on work outcomes) is stronger than cross domain (i.e. the effect of work to family enrichment on family outcomes) (Zhang et al., 2018; McNall, Masuda, & Nicklin, 2010), employers would benefit themselves from the resources provided to employees to enhance their enrichment experiences. In other words, as far as organizations promote employees' WFE experiences, they will be investing not only in employees' well-being, but also in organizational outcomes.

Diversity in parents' rebalancing needs

FFPs have usually been designed and negotiated by unions to cover a wide range of employee work-family needs. However, employees' needs to rebalance their roles are diverse, making it difficult to manage effective FFPs for all of them. Next, we explain why not all parents have the same needs when rebalancing their roles. First, employees may hold diverse work-life ideology. Specifically, as Leslie, King, and Clair (2019) suggest, some men and women: a) may believe that work and life compete with or enhance each other; b) may consider work and life as dependent vs interdependent domains; and c) may prioritize family vs work or vice versa. This ideology will determine employees' preferences for specific actions. For instance, mothers may be primarily mothers as a main source or identity; mothers may be primarily workers or may integrate motherhood and work into their identity (Duncan, 2005). Work-life ideology may help managers to understand why employees with the same demands and resources experience different levels of WFC and WFE (Leslie et al., 2019) and use different FFP (e.g., paternity leave, flexplace or flexitime, or just adjust their work responsibilities).

Another source of diverse parental work-family needs is related to social status and sex – that is, being a mother or a father. First, although low-income fathers may be less gender egalitarian than middle-class fathers, they may be more involved in the daily lives of their children because of their partners' non-flexible work hours (Shows & Gerstel, 2009). Second, traditional gender roles and the ideal work culture may make fathers more vulnerable to workplace inflexibility than mothers because they do not feel entitled to ask for flexibility to accommodate their childcare responsibilities (Kelly, Ammons, Chermack, & Moen, 2010). In fact, workplace inflexibility, but not overwork, multiple jobs, odd jobs and non-standard hours, are sources of more stress for fathers than for mothers (Noma-guchi & Johnson, 2016). Therefore, since working-class fathers are still in many families the primary financial providers (McGill, 2014) while also have caregiving responsibilities, they can be more stressed than mothers because of difficulties in keeping a job or negotiating flexible work arrangements.

Finally, work and family cultural meaning and enactment shape the nature and strength of employees' experiences in both domains. For instance, employees in masculine cultures (e.g., the United States) prioritize work; meanwhile in feminine cultures (e.g., Sweden) the priority is the family domain (Leslie et al., 2019). Parents in collectivist cultures (vs individualistic cultures) have a greater sense of connect-edness which makes them more aware of the effect of work on their family lives. Moreover, employees' use of FFPs and the positive response to them is contingent on the national culture. For instance, employees use fewer FFPs in cultural contexts characterized by institutional collectivism, in-group collectivism, high power distance and uncertainty avoidance values (Peretz et al., 2017). On the contrary, employees use more FFPs in cultural contexts characterized by high future orientation, gender egalitarianism, humane orientation, performance orientation and assertiveness val-ues. A misfit between national culture and FFPs may inhibit their use by employees and reduce their positive effect on absenteeism and turnover (Peretz et al., 2017). The aforementioned considerations suggest that employers should allow employees to find the best way to individualize their rebalance of the work-family process. Next, we provide some considerations to individualize the process of negotiating i-deals.

Going beyond policies: negotiating i-deals

When employers allow employees to design their own work-family management strategies, employees have more positive attitudes toward organizations, perform better and are healthier (Kelly, Moen, & Tranby, 2011). Parents are actively sub-ject to (rather than mere spectators of) family and work pressures. Since they play a key role in the process of rebalancing work and family demands (Kreiner, Hollensbe, & Sheep, 2009), employers should ask them and adapt policies to their specific needs.

When negotiating i-deals, parents exhibit proactive behaviours to adjust their work to their new personal needs. I-deals are personalized work arrangements initiated by employees (Rousseau, 2005). Through i-deals, employees seek out resources not available to them otherwise. For instance, it involves individual development opportunities (i.e. challenging tasks, acquisition of skills and career support) and flexibility to customize work scheduling and location (Rousseau, Hornung, & Kim, 2009). I-deals aim to improve the quality of employees´ life by aligning their individual needs with organizational goals. Therefore, negotiating i-deals has several advantages both for employees and employers, allowing for a win-win solution.

Although i-deals help to cope with work demands and contribute to reducing WFC (Liao, Wayne, & Rousseau, 2016), they also enhance WFE experiences dealing with work resources (Tang & Hornung, 2015). For instance, i-deals allow negotiation of developmental experiences or schedule control to enhance self-efficacy experiences. These work resources have been demonstrated to spill over to family, increasing marital satisfaction and family functioning through experiences of WFE (Carlson, Thompson, Crawford, & Kacmar, 2019), the quality of family life (Tang & Hornung, 2015) and family and work performance (Las Heras, Rofcanin, Bal, & Stollberger, 2017). I-deals also have been demonstrated to impact intrinsic and extrinsic work motivation by changing the features of employee jobs and reshaping their work experience. Moreover, the positive spill-over effect may even cross over to the spouse, facilitating spouse marital satisfaction and organizational commitment (Carlson et al., 2019).

I-deals benefit organizations not only indirectly by reducing parents' WFC and enhancing WFE but also directly with a positive impact on organizational commitment, work engagement, performance at work or voice behaviour (Liao et al., 2016). These outcomes imply an active participation of employees in their work environment and therefore improve innovation and competitive advantage (Rank, Pace, & Frese, 2004).

Even though i-deals are individually negotiated, they operate on an organizational level. Therefore, the effectiveness of an i-deal depends not only on its content but also on the interpersonal relations among the parent, the supervisor and the co-workers (Rousseau, 2005). First, an i-deal negotiation would be influenced by the relationship between the employee and the supervisor. Consistent with social exchange theory, a high quality of exchange relations (LMX) is positively related to the successful negotiation of i-deals (Hornung, Rousseau, Weigl, Müller, & Glaser, 2014). Within a same team, high and low LMX among different employees may coexist. These unequal relationships result in negative consequences for job attitudes and co-workers' relations (Henderson, Liden, Glibkowski, & Chaudhry, 2009). However, LMX differentiation won't result in negative employee reactions in organizations with a climate of justice (Erdogan & Bauer, 2010). In other words, when parents negotiate i-deals, it could result in LMX differentiation, but it won't affect co-workers' relation with the parent when there is an appropriate organizational climate (Rousseau, Ho, & Greenberg, 2006).

Second, co-workers' reactions when a parent negotiates i-deals have to be considered for the effectiveness of these i-deals (Lai, Rousseau, & Chang, 2009). Co-workers' acceptance of the negotiated i-deal reduces interpersonal conflicts and contributes to group effectiveness (Liao et al., 2016), may help parents to develop the negotiated i-deal through collaborative adaptive work behaviours (Gascoigne & Kelliher, 2017), or may result in feelings of gratitude or admiration because the acceptance increases opportunity for them to negotiate i-deals in the future (van de Ven, Zeelenberg, & Pieters, 2011). However, co-workers may also feel envy, which promotes a competitive climate and ostracizing (Ng, T.W.H., 2017).

The effectiveness of i-deals in terms of co-workers' reactions is explained by the relationship between co-worker and the organization. Co-worker acceptance of parent i-deals is higher when they have a social exchange relationship with the organization (vs economic exchange relationship) (Lai et al., 2009). In a social exchange relationship (i.e. long-term relationship-based trust and interpersonal attachment), co-workers will look for a broader welfare (Clark & Reis, 1988) and will perceive higher organizational support (Settoon, Bennett, & Liden, 1996). Therefore, they will expect to have equal opportunities to negotiate i-deals as parents do. Opposite, in an economic relationship with the organization (i.e. short-term monetary based; Macneil, 1985) co-workers won't accept parents' i-deals because they will be more sensitive to differential treatment.

As Garg and Fulmer (2017) suggested, the co-workers' affective reactions may be influenced by a primary evaluation. First, co-workers would apprise if it implies for them something positive (e.g., same agreements in the future, a valuable co-worker development), negative (e.g., deprivation of resources or opportunities in the future) or neutral. Second, co-workers would legitimize the negotiation based on the perceived equity and the need for such an i-deal (Marescaux & De Winne, 2016; Rousseau, 2005). Attributions to equity are based on merit (e.g., for obtaining better results or working hard), on the labour market – for example, experience, skill level – and status in the organization – for example, professional vs non-professional. Furthermore, co-workers' attributions to needs are related to "i-dealers'" personal concerns, especially when they are visible (e.g., disability) or generated by factors they do not control (e.g., maternity/paternity) (Rousseau, 2005). Although both attributions generate perceptions of distributive justice, the attributions need to have a greater impact (Marescaux & De Winne, 2016). Thus, parenthood is a key factor in legitimizing i-deals as it relates to personal needs. However, supervisors may be aware of the influence of organizational norms on co-workers' reactions. In organizations in which i-deals are usually based on merit, parent negotiation of i-deals that are primarily based on family needs will be penalized (Garg & Fulmer, 2017).

Conclusions

Traditional FFP are designed to reduce parents' WFC experiences and contribute to an organizational family-friendly culture. However, under certain circumstances, FFP may be harmful for parents because they may feel stigmatized when using the policies and doing so may have a damaging effect on their career development. Another limitation of traditional FFP is to consider that all parents have similar work-family rebalance needs. As was highlighted earlier, a wide range of factors such as work-family identity, cultural values, social status, financial incomes, network support and type of job influence work-family rebalance preferences. When combining all these factors, infinite possibilities emerge.

Negotiating i-deals allows for individualized work-family rebalance management. Because i-deals not only reduce WFC experiences but also enhance WFE experiences, a win-win solution occurs for parents and organizations. Organizations may provide new parents with skills and knowledge to effectively negotiate i-deals to manage their new roles. Initiatives such as workshops, seminars, web-based programs, etc., are valuable resources that organizations could offer to parents when coming back to work to make informed decisions and design their own policies, as well as how to negotiate i-deals and how to implement them (Friedman & Westring, 2015).

Supervisors play a key role in negotiated i-deals. First, they may be a source of inspiration and a model for parents to identify creative work-family management resources. Second, supervisors may promote a trust climate and a quality LMX relationship to facilitate parents' i-deal negotiation and co-worker support. Therefore, organizations should invest in training supervisors to facilitate new parents' return-to-work.

Finally, co-workers also play a key role when parents negotiate i-deals. First, since parents' i-deals are based on a visible need, co-workers will consider it fair (Rousseau, 2005). Second, since employees will share their personal life and work-related needs and expectations with co-workers in a trustful, transparent and open culture, co-workers will help them implement their personal work-family balance strategy (Perlow & Kelly, 2014). Therefore, under certain circumstances, co-workers are a valuable resource for parents to implement their negotiated i-deal.

Key learnings from research	*Practical recommendations*
• Most workers report difficulties and obstacles in negotiating and reaching FFPs.	• Beyond providing employees with a wide range of FFPs, policies should be aligned with a family-friendly culture to ensure their efficacy.
• Parents who can design their own work-family balance strategies have more positive attitudes toward organizations and perform better.	• Employers should adapt policies to employees' specific needs through individualized deals (i-deals).
• Reducing work-family conflict is necessary but insufficient to promote employees' motivation and positive well-being.	• Organizations should focus on interventions to promote work-family enrichment in addition to reducing work-family conflict experiences.
• Co-worker acceptance is a must for i-deals to be effective. It reduces interpersonal conflicts and enhances group performance.	• Developing an appropriate climate in the unit, that is, climate of justice, will lead to fostering the benefits of i-deals.
• Parenthood is a key factor in legitimizing i-deals. However, organizational norms should be considered.	• Supervisors should support work-family initiatives as well as initiate a change in organizational culture and norms.

References

Allen, T. D., Johnson, R. C., Kiburz, K. M., & Shockley, K. M. (2013). Work family conflict and flexible work arrangements: Deconstructing flexibility. *Personnel Psychology*, *66*(2), 345–376. https://doi.org/10.1111/peps.12012

Bakker, A. B., Schaufeli, W. B., Leiter, M. P., & Taris, T. W. (2008). Work engagement: An emerging concept in occupational health psychology. *Work & Stress*, *22*(3), 187–200. https://doi.org/10.1080/02678370802393649

Boyar, S. L., & Mosley, D. C., Jr. (2007). The relationship between core self-evaluations and work and family satisfaction: The mediating role of work family conflict and facilitation. *Journal of Vocational Behavior*, *71*(2), 265–281. https://doi.org/10.1016/j.jvb.2007.06.001

Butts, M. M., Casper, W. J., & Yang, T. S. (2013). How important are work family support policies? A meta analytic investigation of their effects on employee outcomes. *Journal of Applied Psychology*, *98*(1), 1–25. https://doi.org/10.1037/a0030389

Carlson, D. S., Grzywacz, J. G., & Zivnuska, S. (2009). Is work family balance more than conflict and enrichment? *Human Relations*, *62*(10), 1459–1486. https://doi.org/10.1177/0018726709336500

Carlson, D. S., Thompson, M. J., & Kacmar, K. M. (2019). Double crossed: The spillover and crossover effects of work demands on work outcomes through the family. *Journal of Applied Psychology*, *104*(2), 214–228. https://doi.org/10.1037/apl0000348

Chen, W., Zhang, Y., Sanders, K., & Xu, S. (2016). Family-friendly work practices and their outcomes in China: The mediating role of work-to-family enrichment and the moderating role of gender. *The International Journal of Human Resource Management*, *29*(7), 1307–1329. https://doi.org/10.1080/09585192.2016.1195424

Clark, M. S., & Reis, H. T. (1988). Interpersonal processes in close relationships. *Annual Review of Psychology*, *39*, 609–672.

Connelly, B. L., Certo, S. T., Ireland, R. D., & Reutzel, C. R. (2011). Signaling theory: A review and assessment. *Journal of Management*, *37*, 39–67. https://doi.org/10.1177/0149206310388419

Corning, P. A. (1998). The synergism hypothesis: On the concept of synergy and its role in the evolution of complex systems. *Journal of Social and Evolutionary Systems*, *21*, 133–172. https://doi.org/10.1016/S1061-7361(00)80003-X

Delery, J. E. (1998). Issues of fit in strategic human resource management: Implications for research. *Human Resource Management Review*, *8*, 289–309. https://doi.org/10.1016/S1053-4822(98)90006-7

den Dulk, L., Peper, B., Sadar, N. E., & Lewis, S. (2011). Work, family, and managerial attitudes and practices in the European workplace: Comparing Dutch, British, and Slovenian financial sector managers. *Social Politics: International Studies in Gender, State and Society*, *18*, 300–329

Dickson, C. E. (2008). Antecedents and consequences of perceived family responsibilities discrimination in the workplace. *The Psychologist-Manager Journal*, *11*(1), 113–140. https://doi.org/10.1080/10887150801967399

Duncan, S. (2005). Mothering, class and rationality. *The Sociological Review*, *53*(1), 50–76. https://doi.org/10.1111/j.1467-954X.2005.00503.x

Erdogan, B., & Bauer, T. N. (2010). Differentiated leader member exchanges: The buffering role of justice climate. *Journal of Applied Psychology*, *95*(6), 1104–120. https://doi.org/10.1037/a0020578

Friedman, S. D., & Westring, A. (2015). Empowering individuals to integrate work and life: Insights for management development. *Journal of Management Development*, *34*(3), 299–315. https://doi.org/10.1108/JMD-11-2012-0144

Garg, S., & Fulmer, I. (2017). Ideal or an ordeal for organizations? The spectrum of co-worker reactions to idiosyncratic deals. *Organizational Psychology Review*, *7*(4), 281–305. https://doi.org/10.1177/2041386617733136

Gascoigne, C., & Kelliher, C. (2017). The transition to part time: How professionals negotiate "reduced time and workload" i-deals and craft their jobs. *Human Relations*, *71*(1), 103–125. https://doi.org/10.1177/0018726717722394

Greenhaus, J. H., & Powell, G. N. (2006). When work and family are allies: A theory of work family enrichment. *The Academy of Management Review*, *31*(1), 72–92. https://doi.org/10.2307/20159186

Hammer, L. B., Kossek, E. E., Anger, W. K., Bodner, T., & Zimmerman, K. L. (2011). Clarifying work–family intervention processes: The roles of work–family conflict and family-supportive supervisor behaviors. *Journal of Applied Psychology*, *96*(1), 134–150. https://doi.org/10.1037/a0020927

Henderson, D. J., Liden, R. C., Glibkowski, B. C., & Chaudhry, A. (2009). LMX differentiation: A multilevel review and examination of its antecedents and outcomes. *The Leadership Quarterly*, *20*(4), 517–534. https://doi.org/10.1016/j.leaqua.2009.04.003

Herzberg, F. (1959). *The motivation to work*. New York: Wiley.

Hornung, S., Rousseau, D. M., Weigl, M., Müller, A., & Glaser, J. (2014). Redesigning work through idiosyncratic deals. *European Journal of Work and Organizational Psychology*, *23*(4), 608–626. https://doi.org/10.1080/1359432X.2012.740171

Kelly, E. L., Ammons, S. K., Chermack, K., & Moen, P. (2010). Gendered challenge, gendered response: Confronting the ideal worker norm in a white-collar organization. *Gender & Society*, *24*(3), 281–303. doi: 10.1177/0891243210372073

Kelly, E. L., Moen, P., & Tranby, E. (2011). Changing workplaces to reduce work-family conflict: Schedule control in a white-collar organization. *American Sociological Review*, *76*, 265–290.

Kossek, E., Lewis, S., & Hammer, L. B. (2010). Work life initiatives and organizational change: Overcoming mixed messages to move from the margin to the main-stream. *Human Relations*, *63*(1), 3–19. https://doi.org/10.1177/0018726709352385

Kossek, E. E., Pichler, S., Bodner, T., & Hammer, L. B. (2011). Workplace social support and work family conflict: A meta-analysis clarifying the influence of general and wok family specific supervisor and organizational support. *Personnel Psychology*, *64*(2), 289–313.

Kreiner, G. E., Hollensbe, E. C., & Sheep, M. L. (2009). Balancing borders and bridges: Negotiating the work home interface via boundary work tactics. *Academy of Management Journal*, *52*(4), 704–730. https://doi.org/10.5465/AMJ.2009.43669916

Lai, L., Rousseau, D. M., & Chang, K. T. T. (2009). Idiosyncratic deals: Coworkers as interested third parties. *Journal of Applied Psychology*, *94*(2), 547–556. https://doi.org/10.1037/a0013506

Lapierre, L. M., Li, Y., Kwan, H. K., Greenhaus, J. H., DiRenzo, M. S., & Shao, P. (2018). A meta-analysis of the antecedents of work family enrichment. *Journal of Organizational Behavior*, *39*(4), 385–401. https://doi.org/10.1002/job.2234

Las Heras, M., Rofcanin, Y., Bal, P. M., & Stollberger, J. (2017). How do flexibility ideals relate to work performance? exploring the roles of family performance and organizational context. *Journal of Organizational Behavior*, *38*(8), 1280–1294. https://doi.org/10.1002/job.2203

Leslie, L., King, E. B., & Judith, A. C. (2019). Work life ideologies: The contextual basis and consequences of beliefs about work and life. *Academy of Management Review*, *44*(1), 72–98.

Leslie, L. M., Manchester, C. F., Park, T., & Mehng, S. A. (2012). Flexible work practices: A source of career premiums or penalties? *Academy of Management Journal*, *55*(6), 1407–1428. https://doi.org/10.5465/amj.2010.0651

Liao, C., Wayne, S. J., & Rousseau, D. M. (2016). Idiosyncratic deals in contemporary organizations: A qualitative and meta analytical review. *Journal of Organizational Behavior, 37*, S9–S29. https://doi.org/10.1002/job.1959

Macneil, I. R. (1985). Relational contract: What we do and do not know. *Wisconsin Law Review, 5*, 854–905.

Marescaux, E., & De Winne, S. (2016). Equity versus need: How do coworkers judge the distributive fairness of i deals? In M. Bal & D. M. Rousseau (Eds.), *Idiosyncratic deals between employees and organizations* (pp. 107–121, Chapter viii, 132 Pages). New York: Routledge/Taylor & Francis Group. Retrieved from https://search.proquest.com/docview/1767920359?accountid=14744

Martinez Corts, I., & Demerouti, E. (2017). Developing multiple careers: Dealing with work life interaction. In A. Arenas, D. Di Marco, L. Munduate, & M. Euwema (Eds.), *Shaping Inclusive workplaces through social dialogue* (pp. 221–237). Industrial Relations & Conflict Management Series. Cham, Switzerland: Springer.

McGill, B. (2014). Navigating new norms of involved fatherhood: Employment, fathering attitudes, and father involvement. *Journal of Family Issues, 35*, 1089–1106.

McNall, L. A., Masuda, A. D., & Nicklin, J. M. (2010). Flexible work arrangements, job satisfaction, and turnover intentions: The mediating role of work to family enrichment. *The Journal of Psychology, 144*(1), 61–81.

Ng, T. W. H. (2017). Can idiosyncratic deals promote perceptions of competitive climate, felt ostracism, and turnover? *Journal of Vocational Behavior, 99*, 118–131. https://doi.org/10.1016/j.jvb.2017.01.004

Nomaguchi, K., & Johnson, W. (2016). Parenting stress among low income and working-class fathers: The role of employment. *Journal of Family Issues, 37*(11), 1535–1557. https://doi.org/10.1177/0192513X14560642

Odle-Dusseau, H., Hammer, L. B., Crain, T. L., & Bodner, T. E. (2016). The influence of family-supportive supervisor training on employee job performance and attitudes: An organizational work–family intervention. *Journal of Occupational Health Psychology, 21*(3), 296–308. https://doi.org/10.1037/a0039961

Peretz, H., Fried, Y., & Levi, A. (2017). Flexible work arrangements, national culture, organisational characteristics, and organisational outcomes: A study across 21 countries. *Human Resource Management Journal, 28*(1), 182–200.

Perlow, L., & Kelly, L. (2014). Toward a model of work redesign for better work and better life. *Work and Occupations, 41*, 111–134.

Rank, J., Pace, V. L., & Frese, M. (2004). Three avenues for future research on creativity, innovation, and initiative. *Applied Psychology: An International Review, 53*(4), 518–528. https://doi.org/10.1111/j.1464-0597.2004.00185.x

Rousseau, D. M. (2005). *I-deals: Idiosyncratic deals employees bargain for themselves.* New York: M.E. Sharpe.

Rousseau, D. M., Ho, V. T., & Greenberg, J. (2006). I-deals: Idiosyncratic terms in employment relationships. *The Academy of Management Review, 31*(4), 977–994. https://doi.org/10.2307/20159261

Rousseau, D. M., Hornung, S., & Kim, T. G. (2009). Idiosyncratic deals: Testing propositions on timing, content, and the employment relationship. *Journal of Vocational Behavior, 74*(3), 338–348. https://doi.org/10.1016/j.jvb.2009.02.004

Settoon, R. P., Bennett, N., & Liden, R. C. (1996). Social exchange in organizations: Perceived organizational support, leader member exchange, and employee reciprocity. *Journal of Applied Psychology, 81*(3), 219–227.

Shockley, K. M., & Allen, T. D. (2010). Investigating the missing link in flexible work arrangement utilization: An individual difference perspective. *Journal of Vocational Behavior, 76*(1), 131–142. https://doi.org/10.1016/j.jvb.2009.07.002

Shows, C., & Gerstel, N. (2009). Fathering, class, and gender: A comparison of physicians and emergency medical technicians. *Gender & Society, 23,* 161–187.

Sweet, S., Pitt Catsouphes, M., Besen, M., & Golden, L. (2014). Explaining organizational variation in flexible work arrangements: Why the pattern and scale of availability matter. *Community, Work & Family, 17*(2), 115–141. https://doi.org/10.1080/13668803.2014.887553

Tang, Y., & Hornung, S. (2015). Work family enrichment through Ideals: Evidence from Chinese employees. *Journal of Managerial Psychology, 30*(8), 940–954. https://doi.org/10.1108/JMP-02-2013-0064

van, d. V., Zeelenberg, M., & Pieters, R. (2011). Why envy outperforms admiration. *Personality and Social Psychology Bulletin, 37*(6), 784–795. https://doi.org/10.1177/0146167211400421

Von Bergen, A. N., Von Bergen, C. W., & Ballaré, D. A. (2008). Family responsibilities discrimination: What employment counselors need to know. *Journal of Employment Counseling, 45*(3), 115–130. https://doi.org/10.1002/j.2161-1920.2008.tb00051.x

Zhang, Y., Xu, S., Jin, J., & Ford, M. T. (2018). The within and cross domain effects of work-family enrichment: A meta-analysis. *Journal of Vocational Behavior, 104,* 210–227. https://doi.org/10.1016/j.jvb.2017.11.00

14 What we have learned and what we can do to support parents' return-to-work

Cary Cooper and Maria Karanika-Murray

Our contributors have taken us through a journey of understanding the rich and diverse experiences of parents returning to work after having children, exploring the evidence, integrating the learnings, and drawing possible routes to action. A focus on parents is topical, given recent developments worldwide around equality, work, and family. Good practice in supporting parents' return-to-work can only be 'good' if it is founded on an understanding and consideration of the parents' perspectives and experiences. In this final chapter, we integrate lessons for parents, employers, governments, and researchers. We refer the reader to the relevant chapters where the arguments for and value of these lessons are expanded. We conclude by offering our own insights and suggestions for the way forward.

What can parents do?

The answer is: a lot. In this climate of increasing awareness of issues around equality, parenting, and work, parents can work on building their mental/psychological and tangible resources. Positive attitudes and preparedness are a good starting point (Pluut and De Hauw). Being aware of the challenges of returning to work (Martin, Dawkins, Miles, Cotton, and Alter), including negative stereotypes (Junker, Hernandez Bark, and Gloor); reviewing individual needs against the available demands and resources at work and at home (Yarker, Wolfram, and Junker); actively building resources across different life domains (Pluut and De Hauw); and being prepared to negotiate adjustments to work (Lavaysse, Bettac, and Probst) are all important in the family-to-work transition process. Building resilience is essential for parents, which starts by being aware of their rights and entitlements (Martin et al.), remembering their "value as employers and parents" (Junker et al.), and using their new and unique work-relevant parenting skills to their advantage (Junker et al.). When these recommendations are especially important and how to enact them is discussed in the relevant chapters.

What can employers do?

A lot more. For employers, supporting parents entails a focus on understanding the individuals' experiences, providing resources, and supporting change in the workplace culture and upgrading policies. Employers have control over resources in the working environment that impact on all employees' work experience. This responsibility starts with an understanding of individuals' circumstances and changing life events, and an understanding of diversity – specifically, an understanding of parents' needs and open dialogue about what these are (van Dijk and Meeussen), recognizing parents' new, unique transferable parenting skills (Yarker, Wolfram, and Junker), and educating managers on the value of part-time staff and working parents (Yates). In terms of providing resources, employers ought to offer flexibility and support in the transition back into work (Lavaysse, Bettac and Probst; Boyer and Martin), with adjustments tailored to employees' individual needs (Martínez-Corts and Moreno-Beltrán) and investment in cover staff rather than delegation of work to existing staff (Grau-Grau). Coaching for parents in the process of returning to work should be available (Yates), whereas training and development should not only be standard provision for both parents, before and after pregnancy, but should also take a whole-organization approach (Lavaysse, Bettac, and Probst; Pluut and De Hauw; Yarker, Wolfram, and Junker; Martínez-Corts and Moreno-Beltrán), with interventions specifically designed to help build psychological capital and reduce work-family conflict (Martin et al.; Martínez-Corts and Moreno-Beltrán). The employer also has a substantial responsibility to proactively encourage a family-friendly culture, discourage gendered practices and stereotypes, and ensure fairness in policies and practices (Lavaysse, Bettac, and Probst; Pluut and De Hauw; Grau-Grau; Martínez-Corts and Moreno-Beltrán). Through well-designed policies, employers can support inclusion and reduce discrimination (van Dijk and Loes Meeussen). Importantly, a joint focus on developing family-friendly policies *and* promoting a family-friendly workplace culture is more effective (Martínez-Corts and Moreno-Beltrán). The relevant chapters provide more detail on the 'why', 'when', and 'how' of these recommendations for employers implementing change.

What can governments do?

A great deal. Practice goes hand-hand with policy, whilst culture develops in line with the workplace rules, signals, and available resources. Government support is essential for aligning and modernizing policy and infrastructure, including policies, incentives, and fair pay for paternal leave (Lavaysse, Bettac, and Probst; Burgess and Davies). To promote gender equality and support fairness, special attention should be placed on equality-promoting and targeted policies that can enable fathers to be involved from the perinatal period (Grau-Grau; Burgess and Davies). A broader review of parental leave systems and policies, whether they are fit for purpose, and an update of guidance on applying legislation are essential (Burgess and Davies). The availability and affordability of childcare support (or lack of these) is a substantial hurdle for many families and an indirect barrier to equality (Yates; Boyer and Martin) – it is also an area where government support can have an extensive impact.

We have great examples from the Nordic countries on how parental leave can be approached: equal and non-transferable leave, leave being an individual entitlement, fair wages, and job protection for both parents (Kaufman) are among solutions that have been tried and tested successfully. Supporting parents' return-to-work extends to reconsidering early childhood education and care (Kaufman), such that in France, family matters are considered to be "an affair of the state" as illustrated in pro-birth family policies and investment in childcare (Boyer and Martin).

We have seen that some of the underlying problems reside in society and employment. Reshaping some of the ingrained gender norms of working parents (Lavaysse, Bettac, and Probst) and addressing gender stereotyping around fathers (Burgess and Davies) should be a priority. In practice, these can be achieved via measures to incentivize employers to adopt innovative flexible work approaches for parents (Yates); requirements for large companies to report on family-friendly policies as they are required to do on gender pay gaps (Burgess and Davies); and investing in the early childhood education and care workforce (Burgess and Davies).

What can researchers do?

For researchers, the tasks are to continue developing the needed evidence base that can lead to interventions and inform workplace practice and public policy. Research can focus on social support and reciprocity in parenting (Pluut and De Hauw), building domain-specific resilience (Martin et al.), the transferable skills of parenting (Junker et al.; Yarker, Wolfram, and Junker), fathers' experiences (Grau-Grau), and the business case for fair and equitable government and workplace policies (Grau-Grau). Cross-cultural research and research in new contexts are important for understanding the changing nature of fatherhood (Grau-Grau) as well as gender norms and stereotypes more broadly. All the recommendations listed herein, for parents, employers, and governments, require an expanded research evidence. Ultimately, research has an important role not only in translating this knowledge into practice but also in facilitating adoption of new knowledge by those who have the power to make change.

Reflections

To conclude, we distill the insights from these twelve chapters and offer our own insights on supporting parents returning to work.

First, the complexity of the problem is staggering. Correspondingly, there is no one or a simple solution. Our life domains form a complex system. Supporting return-to-work for new parents is thus a complex problem and, as all complex problems, it is composed of many constituent problems, whose parameters can change over time, with ideal solutions that are not immediately obvious or clear, and which can serve multiple goals or functions for multiple actors (Dörner & Funke, 2017). It is not a personal, an organizational, a societal, or a policy problem – it is all of the above. The barriers to achieving work-family well-being are to be found not in the norms, attitudes, culture, structures, policy, or law – they are in all of the above. As a complex problem, it exceeds the resources and capacity of each approach on its own and can therefore only be solved through collective effort (Hung, 2013).

To understand its multiple folds, this complex problem also requires some effort to be put into perspective-taking and going beyond any mental set or "one's inclination to attempt to solve problems in such a way that has proved successful in previous experiences" (Öllinger, Jones, & Knoblich, 2008). The complexity of the issue is undeniable and the need for a multi-actor approach is unavoidable. Our solutions need to be comprehensive across all life domains, empowering for parents and employers, and sustainable in the long term.

Second, we need to work together and learn from one another. Wonderful examples exist of positive action, good practice, and solutions that work in different contexts (by contexts we mean organizations, cultures, countries) which we (governments, employers, and individuals) can learn from and adapt to our own settings and circumstances. To achieve this, we need to consider how we can translate proven solutions to different contexts. Parents, employers, governments, activists, agencies, and influencers share common goals and experiences, but do we have the channels and structures to achieve joint working?

Third, at the heart of practice are attitudes and beliefs. We cannot tackle inequality, unfairness, and low opportunity unless we consider the implications of negative, commonly held, underlying stereotypes and norms and of our role in enacting and reproducing these. For example, we ought to re-evaluate our social norms to accept that mothers, fathers, and workers "can come in all shapes and sizes" (Yates) and that in our diverse society we need solutions that are sensitive to different individuals' and families' needs. We need to identify and, most importantly, reject negative attitudes and counterproductive practices in order to support fairness and equality for people from all stages and walks of life.

Fourth, the importance of government/state support is indisputable. All the great examples from countries that lead the way demonstrate a continuous commitment from the state to support families and promote equality and opportunity. Employers going beyond standard practice is also essential. Both governments and employers are decision-makers on the boundaries, rules, and resources of what families and individuals can achieve.

Fifth, supporting parents' return-to-work has profound benefits for organizations and societies, beyond benefits for individuals and their families. This goes without saying, and we have plentiful concrete evidence to support it. The yields from quick and positive adjustment in the parental return-to-work journey for health and well-being, productivity, and societal prosperity are immense, pervasive, and important building blocks for longer-term welfare.

Sixth, challenging "the way things are done" can help to address the gap between theory and practice. For example, one approach that comes with strong evidence is *gender mainstreaming*, defined as "the (re)organisation, improvement, development and evaluation of policy processes, so that a gender equality perspective is incorporated in all policies at all levels and at all stages, by the actors normally involved in policy-making".[1] A notable example of gender mainstreaming, with potentially transferable lessons and methods, is that of gender mainstreaming for urban planning in the city of Vienna,[2] where gender considerations are a priority for every decision made. As a result, gender mainstreaming has paved the way for taking into account parents' ends and experiences. In the same way, taking a "parenting perspective" can help to achieve personal, social, organizational and economic goals.

Seventh, using a broad brush on the topic was unavoidable, as we mentioned in the Chapter 1. What this book offers is a drop in the ocean, but it is also a force that can guide a needed discussion and potentially kick-start effective action. It is our hope that this discussion will lead to more fine-grained questions, research, interventions, and solutions. Researchers and practitioners need to use a thinner brush to see how this knowledge can be contextualized in different cultures, regions, countries, or types of families, and what each contextual factor means for the additional questions that research and practice should ask.

Finally, we have a substantial volume of research on family and work, but this research lacks unity. We have both focused research and a wealth of knowledge from related fields (e.g., return-to-work from sick leave, gender roles, diversity and inclusion, recovery, work-life balance, etc.) that can enrich our knowledge of parental return-to-work. However, this knowledge has yet to be integrated into a comprehensive body of knowledge that can usefully inform practice. At the same time, this body of knowledge needs to be translated into practice. Starting a conversation among the relevant groups (parents, workers, employers, policy-makers) wth the aim to develop actionable and effective solutions is important but also needs a commitment to constructive dialogue and sustained action from the start.

Notes

1 www.coe.int/en/web/genderequality/what-is-gender-mainstreaming
2 www.wien.gv.at/english/administration/gendermainstreaming/; www.wien.gv.at/stad tentwicklung/studien/pdf/b008358.pdf; www.charter-equality.eu/exemple-de-bonnes-pratiques/a-model-city-for-gender-mainstreaming.html

References

Dörner, D., & Funke, J. (2017). Complex problem solving: What it is and what it is not. *Frontiers in Psychology, 8*, 1153.

Hung, W. (2013, April 24). Team-based complex problem solving: A collective cognition perspective. *Educational Technology Research and Development, 61*(3), 365–384. https://doi.org/10.1007/s11423-013-9296-3

Öllinger, M., Jones, G., & Knoblich, G. (2008). Investigating the effect of mental set on insight problem solving. *Experimental Psychology, 55*(4), 269–270.

Index

Note: Page numbers in *italics* indicate a figure and page numbers in **bold** indicate a table on the corresponding page.